Image and Reality of Changing Pakistan

Dedicated to the

Ideal Pair of

Aditya & Arushi

Image and Reality of Changing Pakistan

Dr. Rajkumar Singh

Ankit Publications
Delhi - 110009

Image and Reality of Changing Pakistan

First Published in 2022

₹ 999

ISBN 978-81-950132-0-3

Published by : **Ankit Publications**

R-69, 3rd Floor,

Model Town-III, Delhi-110009

Tel. : 09891553405

E-Mail: ankitpublications@gmail.com

Laser Typesetting : Aarati Computers, Delhi-110 009

Printed at : Balaji Offset, Delhi

Contents

Preface

The provinces of Pakistan- Sindh, Punjab, Balochistan and Khyber Pakhtunkhwa do not have resemblance roots and cultural background and each province has distinctive language, ethnicity and culture and it cause the cultural diversity in Pakistan. In line the ethnic mobilisation have been a persistent problem in Pakistan's history and considerable angst and blood has been and is being split over this issue. The breakup of the country in 1971 with the emergence of an independent Bangladesh and continuing difficulties in Balochistan are a key reminder of the seriousness of the issue. The present diversities of modern Pakistan have been compounded and become more significant in the era of globalisation. In this new phase the process of social change has initiated processes that unleash ethnic and national movements challenging state systems which were locked in the states during the Cold War. The processes leading to the collapse of nation states, emergence of virulent forms of ethnic movements demanding statehood have been invigorated by the emergence of transnational processes that side-step the nation state, directly intersecting with the locale. It paved the way further for explosion in ethnic and nationalistic conflict. Although Pakistan is a federation, federalism has only been operating partially in its history, which has intensified complaints of majoritarian rule. A highly centralised, top-down style of control associated with authoritarian rule simply exacerbates the difficulty in managing differences as shown in Balochistan's case.

In the circumstances, a fact-finding and analytical book titled, *Image and Reality of Changing Pakistan'*, would help develop a home-grown strategy through a bottom up process of engagement to arrive at a political consensus. There is a need for an open discussion, constitutional convention and public debate so that a consensus might reached incorporating features with which people feel that they have ownership. Even after passing the 18th Amendment, still the relationship between the centre, province and the local level needs to be clarified particularly in the area of fiscal devolution. The revival of local bodies within a federal framework with functioning provincial autonomy is an important question that needs to be dealt with. Multicultural strategies, including 'Positive discrimination, is another approach and need to be considered as a means in removing barriers that limit certain groups entry into key institutions. Both approaches can be combined with a language policy that accurately reflects linguistic diversity in the country.

I wish to thank the institutions and individuals for theirencouragement, cooperation and good wishes that I received and staff of the central libraries at New Delhi and other places where I got a lot of information and analytical/ critical views of different subject experts. They all concerned deserve cordial thanks.

I am deeply grateful to several persons and colleagues. Among teachers late Dr. D.N. Mallik, Dr. Kirtyanand Singh, retired Professors of the University Department of Political Science, BRA Bihar University, Muzaffarpur, have been constant source of guide and encouragement at every stage. Colleagues Dr. Dhirendra Narayan Singh, Department of Political Science MLT College, Saharsa, Dr. (Prof.) Chandra

Prakash Singh, Department of History, Dr. Kumar Jyotivardhan, and Dr. Usha Sinha, Head, University Department of Hindi and Dean, Faculty of Humanities, Dr. Ram Naresh Singh, Department of Maithili, Dr. (Prof.) Pawan Kumar, Dr. Kantesh Kumar and Dr. Kavita Kumari West Campus P.G. Centre, Saharsa and departmental colleagues, Dr. Arjun Kumar Yadav, Dr. Shashank Mishra and Aparna Singh are thankful for their co-operation and goodwishes. Eldest brother the late Suryanath Singh, elder brother Bhuvneshwar Prasad Singh, father-in-law late Shri Ramanand Singh, retired Professor and Head, University Department of Physics, BRA Bihar university, Muzaffarpur, deserve deep sense of gratitude for their sincere goodwishes. I am no less grateful to colleagues and staff of the B.N. Mandal University, North Campus Madhepura and West Campus, P.G. Centre, Saharsa.

I would be failing in my duty if I do not record my honest goodwishes and gratitude to the family members including my wife Dr. Hemlata Singh, son Aditya Priyadarshi, Bahu Arushi and Apurv Adarsh in the completion of the book.

However, for the facts, analysis, views and misjudgements contained in the book I alone am responsible.

25th December 2021 **Rajkumar Singh**

List of Abbreviations

AIML	-	All India Muslim League
AL	–	Awami League
ANA	–	Afghan National Army
ANP	–	Awami National Party
APMO	–	All Pakistan Muhazir Organisation
APMSO	–	All Pakistan Mohajir Student's Organisation
BCE	–	Before Christ Era
BLA	–	Baluchistan Liberation Army
BNP	–	Bangladesh Nationalist Party
BSF	–	Border Security Force
CBM's	–	Confidence Building Measures
CCI	–	Council of Common Interest
CENTO	–	Central Treaty Organisation
CFA	–	Cease Fire Agreement
CIA	–	Central Intelligence Agency
EBDO	–	Elective Bodies Disqualification Order
EU	–	European Union
FATA	–	Federally Administered Tribal Area
FATE	–	Federally Administered Tribal Areas
FBI	–	Federal Bureau of Investigation
FC	–	Frontier Corps
FCR	–	Frontier Crimes Regulation
FCT	–	Federal Capital Territory
FDLs	–	Forward Defence Lines
FP	–	Federal Party

FRD	–	Federal Research Division
GFC	–	Global Financial Crisis
HM	–	Hizb-ul-Mujahideen
HUJI	–	Harkat –ul-Jehad Islami
IB	–	Intelligence Bureau
ICG	–	International Crisis Group
IM	–	Indian Mujahideen
IJI	-	Islamic Jamhoori Ittehad
IOJ	–	Islamiya Okiyya Jote
ISI	–	Inter Services Intelligence & Inter-State Intelligence
JeM	–	Jaish-e-Mohammad
JKLF	–	Jammu and Kashmir Liberation Front
JI	–	Jamaat-i-Islami
JMB	–	Famaatul Mujahideen Bangladesh
JMJB	–	Jagrata Muslim Janata Bangladesh
JSMM	–	Jeay Sindh Muttahida Mahaz
JSQM	–	Jeay Sindh Quami Mahaz
JSTP	–	Jeay Sindh Tarraqi Passand Party
JUI	–	Jamiatul-Ulema –i-Islam
JVP	–	Janatha Vimukthi Peramuna
LeT	–	Lashkar-e-Taiba
LFO	–	Legal Framework Order
LoC	–	Line of Control
MLC	–	Muslim League Council
MQM	–	Muttahida Quami Movement
MUF	–	Muslim United Front
NA	–	Northern Alliance
NAP	–	National Awami Party
NATO	–	North Atlantic Treaty Organisation
NCTC	–	National Counter Terrorism Center
NEC	–	National Economic Council
NFC	–	National Finance Commission

NFZ – No – Fire Zone
NIA – National Investigation Agency
NSA – National Security Act
NSG – National Security Guard
NWFP – North West Frontier Province
OIC – Organization of Islamic Conference
OPEC – Oil Producing European Countries
PDD – Planning Development Department
PML – Pakistan Muslim League
POK – Pak Occupied Kashmir
PPP – Pakistan Peoples'Party
RCO – Revival of Constitutional Order
SAARC – South Asian Association for Regional Cooperation
SCO – Shanghai Cooperation Organisation
SDLA – Sindhudesh Liberation Army
SDGT – Specially Designated Global Terrorist
SEATO – South East Asian Treaty Organisation
SIMI – Students Islamic Movement of India
SNA – Sindh National Alliance
SNMP – Sindh Nationalist Movement Party
TM – Tehreek-ul-Mujahideen
TTP – Tehrik-e-Taliban Pakistan
UAE – United Arab Emirates
UNHCR – United Nation's Human Rights Commission
USD – United States Dollar
USSOCOM – United States Special Operations Command
VoA – Voice of America
WoT – War on Terror
WMD – Weapons of Mass Destruction
WSC – World Sindh Congress
WTC – World Trade Center
WTO – World Trade Organisation

Glossary

Ahmadis	-	*followers of Mirza Ghulam Ahmed Qadiani; a religious minority in Pakistan*
Ahimsa	-	*non-violence*
Alim	-	*religious scholar*
Amir	-	*a person holding authority, a ruler, a head of an organisation*
Arms race nuclear	-	*it refers to the competition to build-up more powerful weaponary*
Atom	-	*the smallest part of an element that can exist*
Balance of combatants	-	*a theory that peace is more likely where potential power are of equal military, political or economic power*
Cold War	-	*the state of extreme hostility between the superpowers*
Containment	-	*a doctrine from 1947on how the US should react to the expansion of international communist influence*
Conventional-war	-	*conventional war is a war waged only with non-nuclear weaponary*
Deobandi	-	*belonging to the Muslim religious seminary of Deoband, India; an orthodox sect which abhors superstition attributed to the Brelavi sect*
Détente	-	*a foreign policy process mainly concerned with an easing of tension between the USSR and the USA*
Deterrance	-	*it refers to the capacity to protect oneself from attack by another nation*

Dharma	-	*appropriate form of moral and religious obligations in Hinduism*
Equilibrium	-	*a state in which a system has its energy distributed in the statistically most probable manner*
Fatwa	-	*a ruling by a jurist on the legality or otherwise of an action*
Fidayeen	-	*suicide-squad tactics*
First strike	-	*the use of strategic nuclear weaponary to attack an enemy without having launched such an attack*
Hindutva	-	*Hindu essence or political identity*
Hudood	-	*a plural of had, punishments under Islamic Law*
Imam	-	*faith*
Islamiat	-	*Islamic religious studies*
Isolationalism	-	*it is a foreign policy strategy in which a nation announces that it has absolutely no interest in international affairs*
Jihad	-	*striving for perfection; spiritual endeavor; holy war*
Kafir	-	*one who refuses to believe in the unity of God, infidel*
Lashkars	-	*armies*
Limited war	-	*the war in question should not spread to involve the superpowers in all-out nuclear confrontation*
Madrassas	-	*religious schools*
Majlis-i-Shoora	-	*consultative council*
Maulana	-	*title given to Muslim religious scholar*
Maulvi	-	*title given to Muslim religious leader*
Muhajir	-	*Muslim migrant*
Mujahid	-	*one who participates in Jehad*
Mujahideen	-	*plural of mujahid*
Nawab	-	*title given to a nobleman or a king*

Neutrality	-	*is often thought of a rather vague state of non-involvement in international conflict*
Nizam	-	*rule or ruler*
Nuclear weapons	-	*weapons in which an explosion is caused by energy nuclear fission,nuclear fusion or a combination of both*
Pakhtun or Pashtun	-	*people of the Afghan race inhabiting mostly in the North-West Frontier Province in Pakistan*
Qazi	-	*a judge or judge of Shariah Court*
Quaid-i-Azam	-	*the great leader, a title used for the founder of Pakistan, Mohammad Ali Jinnah*
Sharia	-	*literally 'a clear path,' a set of moral injunctions constituting Islamic law*
Strategic	-	*it involves longer terms and farther-reaching preparations and planning*
Sufi	-	*Muslim mystic; the word 'sufi' comes from the course Woolen garment, 'suf,' worn by the early mystics of Islam*
Sunnah	-	*tradition of the Prophet*
Tanzeem	-	*organisation*
Terrorist group	-	*political groups which use violence as a matter of policy to pressure a government to support a radical social change*
Ulama	-	*learned authorities on Islam*
Ummah	-	*community*
Wadera	-	*Sindhi landlord*
Warsaw Pact	-	*theoretically initiated as a response to West Germany joining NATO in 1954*
Zamindar	-	*landholder, large or smalls*

1

Introduction

The emergence of a new sovereign nation on 14th August 1947 was a culmination of demand of the Muslims of the subcontinent for their separate homeland and those who participated in the Pakistan movement or sympathized with the idea of distinct Muslim identity realized the need to protect and preserve it. Although the two major communities-Hindus and Muslims lived together for centuries quite peacefully, their different aspects on life and about life had kept them apart. In 1947 the newly independent Pakistan consisted of two distinct parts: the smaller but more densely populated East Pakistan (now Bangladesh), and the much lager West Pakistan, occupying the northwestern portion of the Indian subcontinent. Before making its own constitution in 1956, country's government functioned under a modified 1935 Government of India Act, containing a strong central government as well as governments in several provinces. Particularly after 1971, the country had faced a number of political and economic problems and uncertainties about its future. Throughout in the history, constitutions in Pakistan have been less about limiting the power of authority and more a legal justification for arbitrary action. In the 70 years of independence of Pakistan, the military has been in government for more than half the period, and whenever there have been elections and attempts at democracy, Pakistan's civilian governments have had to struggle to find legitimacy. In recent years Pakistan has been in the news largely for reasons which relate to the rise of fundamentalist Islam across the globe and as a consequence of the war on terrorism. As in many countries and societies various conflicts and contradictions exist in Pakistan, trying to establish their dominance.

Genesis of Pakistan

It was on March 23, 1940 that the Muslim League finally committed itself to the two-nation theory and adopted the Lahore Resolution calling for the establishment of Pakistan as a separate State. The League was now advancing from its previous demands of separate electorates and special weightages to the final full-fledges demand for Pakistan or the splitting up of India into a sovereign Muslim state and a sovereign Hindu state. Its resolution resolved that it is the considered view of this session of the All India Muslim League that no constitutional plan would be workable in this country or acceptable to Muslims unless it is designed on the following basic principle, viz., that geographically contiguous units are demarcated in regions which should be so constituted with such territorial readjustments as may be necessary, that the areas in which the Muslims are numerically in a majority as in the North-Western and Eastern zones of India should be grouped to constitute "Independent States" in which the constituent units shall be autonomous and sovereign. Because the Indian nationalism was dominated by Hindus and had a Hinduised look, a conflict arose in the Muslim mind. Those, among them, accepted that nationalism, were abused by the League leaders and branded as renegades and traitors to Islam and as mercenary paid agents of Hindus and often subjected them to physical violence.(*Chandra,1999*). Many sympathised with it but remained aloof and uncertain while others began to drift in a separatist direction. This led to the cry of division of India of which there were reasons, many contributory causes, errors and mistakes on everyside and especially the deliberate separatist policy of the British Government.(*Nehru, 1946*).

The British policy of divide and rule at the communal level helped them in promoting and propagating the notion that Hindus and Muslims are two separate nations and cannot live together. It was not a new phenomenon. It all began in the 1850s, when on the one hand the nationalist forces were awakening to the growing power of the British colonialists and had started coming together to resist it. On the other hand, the British realised that they would not be to control the 'natives' without creating a schism between them along communal lines. For the British, the mutiny of 1857 was their worst fears come true. It was then onward that they adopted a two-pronged policy in case of India–initiation of constitutional reforms and division of the people on communal feelings. From the record of correspondence at the India office, London, it is clear that the British conjured up, preached and propagated the two-nation theory in a deliberate and consistent manner. In 1859, the colonial administration erected a fence to separate the Babri masjid and Ram chabutra in Ayodhya, allowing the inner court to be used by Muslims andthe outer court by Hindus. (*Akhtar, 2003*).

Events moved fast. The Constitutional advance made in India by the British was not designed to hasten latter's departure from this country but to realign the structure of collaboration and control and thus ensure the flow of advantages(*Gallagher, 1982*). With the introduction of the Mountford Reforms, Muslim identification had acquired a political edge. It became the basis for competition with non-Muslim elites for power and patronage. Friction between the communities increased as some politicians deliberately exacerbated communal tensions to get access to the institutions of power. As a result of this the Muslim identification was inextricably intertwined with the complexities of town politics.

The urban areas were dominated by competing factions led bythe rais who exerted influence on the politics of the mohallahs. The local neighbourhood leadership itself depended on the shifting alliances between the ulama, petty merchants and bazar factions. Now, it reinforced the centrifugal tendency among urban Muslims trying to organise on the basis of religious identification and their aspirations became interlocked with the political rivalry between communities. Appeal to communal identity became the channel to power in the legislative council for urban politicians. The use of religious and cultural emblems had a varying impact, depending on the context. To unify Muslims, schismatic differences had to be temporally relegated to the background by using Islamic idioms and metaphors that only highlighted differences with non-Muslims. The conservatives exploited communalism to break the nationalist hold over Muslims. Thus, the most negative aspect of the Reform was that it conceded for the first time, theseparate electorates to Muslims and later extended to Sikhs and others by the Lord Southborough Committee on franchise. The consequence of recognising separate constituencies for some communities and specific interests was to atomise the political world into smaller particles. The building blocs of constitutional politics provided a number of focifor centrifugal tendencies. The mere fact that Muslims and Sikhs were granted separate electorates, and non- Brahmins and Marathas were conceded reserved seats, encouraged political formations to take place along cleavages based on community at the expense of Indian nationalism.

This initiation of the British was further maintained and enlarged by the Reforms Acts of 1919 and 1935. The new provision had encouraged interest groups to compete for collaboration with the Raj and thus help shield the administration from the onslaught of the nationalist movement. With the 1919 Reforms, the political focus shifted to the Muslims of the rural areas and particularly of Punjab and Bengal who were the dominant in their region. Out of a total of thirty-two seats, twenty-seven were allocated to the, Muslim–majority districts of western- Punjab. Thus, the landlords and agriculturists benefited from the constitutional advance at the expense of the urban interests; and the powerful Muslim Zamindars of the Rawalpindi and Multan areas became dominant in the council. They formed a major centre of centrifugal politics among Muslims. Similarly, in Bengal, thirty-three out of the thirty-nine seats allocated to Muslims were for rural areas, mainly in the eastern districts of Bengal. The most significant impact of the Montagu-Chelmsford Reforms on Muslim politics was the shift of power and influence from the Muslim minority provinces to the Muslim majority provinces (*Samad, 1995*). Before the passing of the Act of 1919, All-India Muslim Organisations were dominated by the Western-educated elite of the United Provinces, Bihar and Bombay. It set in motion the centrifugal forces that were responsible for deflecting Indian politics away from the All-India stage to the provinces.

The India Act of 1935 reconfirmed and consolidated the centrifugal developments initiated explicitly or implicitly by the Reforms of 1919. Itmade provisions for provincial autonomy and an Indian Federation to be composed of the princely states and the provinces of British India, and a legislature in which the representatives of the majority of Indians would be permanently in a minority. The Act also suited the princes who could decide how and when to federate, and they were assured that the centre would remain in British hands. The position of the Muslims was further reinforced by the Communal Award, which gave them separate electorates and weightages. The consequence of the constitutional advance from the Reforms of 1919 to the India Act of 1935 encouraged, in the Muslim majority provinces, powerful centrifugal forces based on community and regional identity. However, the basic parameters of Muslim politics were established by 1937. The Muslims were divided between weak centripetal and strong centrifugal forces. The opposition between the two forces formed the framework for the political developments of the 1940s and ultimately remained the basis of politics in Pakistan. As the independence drew closer, exclusive attention was paid to the politics of the centre and in the process the in consistencies of mass nationalism were often overlooked. By shifting the analysis to an examination of the political developments in the Muslim-majority provinces, it became clear that the rise of mass Muslim nationalism was not a unilinear triumph but a complex process marked by deep inner contradictions.

The British policy of pick and choose among the Muslims, apart from the constitutional causes, was all behind the delay in the development of a Muslim middle class in India. Essentially, the internal conflict in India besides the nationalist struggle against foreign domination, was between the remnants of the feudal order and modernist ideas and institutions. This conflict existed on the national plane as well as within each major group, Hindu, Muslim and others. On the Hindu side an exclusive and rigid social order had come in the way of growth, but it has been undermined and is fast losing its rigidity and, in any event, is not strong enough to obstruct the growth of the national movement in its widest political and social sense. On the Muslim side, feudal elements, as promoted by the British, had continued to be strong and have usually succeeded in imposing their leadership on their masses. There had been a difference of a generation or more in the development of the Hindu and Muslim middle classes, and that difference continues to show itself in many directions, political economic and other. This situation produced a psychology of fear and backwardness among the Muslims and as a solution of the problem they began to strengthen the hold of feudal elements for some time longer and delay the economic progress of the Muslims.

The delay in the development of middle class in the Muslims and the unequal composition of intelligentsia, particularly in comparison to Hindus, had totally changed the class character and nature of leadership in the community. The Muslim intelligentsia, at least, in the initial stage, was composed of thelandlords, whereas the Hindu intelligentsia recruited members from all sections of society. This unequal development of this class also affected differently the growth of nationalism in these two communities. The Hindu intelligentsia, because of its middle-class composition, could seek inspirations from the writings of Bentham, Mill and Comte. They developed a progressive and critical outlook. The Muslim intelligentsia, on the other hand, remained conservative and feared that if such ideas were allowed to spread among the Muslims ,they would havea pernicious effect. They also feared that these ideas would undermine their leadership in the Muslim society. That is why the educationists like Nawab Abdul Latif advised the British to encourage Madarsaeducation instead of English education among the Muslims in Bengal.

Behind the backwardness of the Muslim masses was the policy of the British Government who always ignored all round progress with real and effective planning for the whole of India. The disparate social and economic advancement of thetwo communities intensified this feeling. The rise of a Muslim middle class in the first quarter of this century and its relative backwardness from the Hindu middle class made the Muslims bitter towards the Hindus. In fact, the Pakistan Movement could not have been successful if the upper class of Muslim society which led the movement were not backed by the middle class. Muslims wanted more opportunities of employment in government, commerce, trade and industry. As most of the big landlords were Hindus, the Muslims, in humbler circumstances also felt that their lot would improve if they could form a new State free of Hindu exploitation. The relatively smaller number of Muslim capitalists, bankers and businessmen that emerged by this time mainly in Bombay and Uttar Pradesh saw in the creation of a Muslim State better prospects of profit free of Hindu competition (*Sen, 1983*). Therefore, when Jinnah declared, "We maintain and hold that Hindus and Muslims are two major nations by any definition or test of a nation", almost all Muslims enthusiastically supported this theory. They were waiting economic emancipation, and they felt that they could get it only in a free Muslim State.

Coming of Partition

Nehru's statement that the Congress had agreed only to participate in the Constituent Assembly and regarded itself free to change or modify the Cabinet Mission Plan as it thought best had created a furor in Muslims. Jinnah was also not satisfied with the outcome of the Plan as it was consented by him under "duress". In his speech to the League Council Jinnah argued that he recommended acceptance only because nothing better could be achieved. He was even blamed, by political adversaries for giving up the idea of an independent Islamic State. As Jinnah was in a pensive mood, Nehru's assertion came to him as a bomb-shell. It followed a declaration by Jinnah that the statement of the Congress President demanded a review of the whole situation. It was meant in Muslim circle that the Congress could change the scheme through its majority in the Constituent Assembly, and the minorities would be placed at the mercy of the majority. It affected the thinking of both the, Muslim leadership class and the masses.

Possibility of change in the Cabinet Mission Plan by the majority-owned Congress and the future outcome thereof compelled Jinnah to reiterate his demand for a separate state called Pakistan. At the meeting of Muslim League Council which was held on July 27, 1946 at Bombay, after three day's discussion, authorised Jinnah to take appropriate action. It passed a resolution rejecting the Cabinet Mission Plan and decided to resort to direct action for the achievement of Pakistan. Though, understanding the gravity of the situation drafted a Resolution which made no reference to Nehru's statement and was approved by the All-India Congress Committee on July 7, said, "The Constituent Assembly will naturally function within the internal limitations which are inherent in its task, and will therefore seek the largest measure of cooperation in drawing up a constitution of free India allowing the greatest measure of freedom and protection for all just claims and interests (*Azad, 1988*). With regret to note the decision of the Muslim League Council it hoped that the latter and all others concerned, in the wider interests of the nation as well as their own, would join in this great task. But Jinnah was adamant on Nehru's statement and held that there was no guarantee that the Congress would not change and go back to the approach of Nehru when they had changed so many times while the British were still in the country and power had not come to its hand. Hence, the statement represented the real mind of the Congress.

Jinnah, in the background of being a leader of the Muslim League next to none and authorisation of League Council declared 16 August as the "Direct Action Day". The situation deteriorated further due to improvement of League's position in Bengal and the decision of Bengal Government to declare that day as a public holiday. In the past, political parties had observed special days by organising hartals, taking out processions and holding meetings. As the "Direct Action Day" announcement did not follow any clear and definite programme, for the people of Bengal, and Calcutta in particular, it was a general feeling that on 16 August, the Muslim League would attack Congressmen and loot Congress property. The Muslim League supporters tried to enforce the hartal on Hindu shops in north Calcutta, and in return, Congress and Mahasabha supporters began to interfere with the Muslim processions. After a couple of false starts, the Muslim League's Direct Action took off and became inextricably linked with communal violence. This triggered off a vicious cycle of violent reprisal that left at least 4,000 dead and 10,000 injured. The violence consisted of large crowds battling it out on the streets, and attacks by small hit-squads on isolated families and individuals belonging to the enemy community. Calcutta, being not a city of Bengal but a cosmopolitan one; and consisted of migrants from Bihar, the United Provinces, the Punjab and the Frontier, meant that once the news of the butchery reached their home villages, talk of revenge was on everyone's lips resulting its spread in areas where had, previously, no record of communal riots. The riots brought partition inexorably close at India's doorstep.

Even today, it is true to say that Pakistan was defined by circumstances and not by design. No doubt, the immediate cause of partition was the proliferation to communal riots on larger scale, the policy of the British was not less responsible that forced the pace of events. In fact, a chaotic situation and reign of terror was created by the communal forces. Apart from this, there was every possibility of breaking out of a civil war throughout the country. Separatist forces were active and if partition had been avoided there was every chance of the balkanisation of India through civil wars. It was this situation that prompted Nehru or Patel to agree to partition. "We consented because we thought that thereby we are purchasing peace and goodwill though at a high price .... (*The Hindu, 26 July 1948*)" The "Direct Action" day was a black day not only for Calcutta but for the whole of India. The turn, that events had taken, made it almost impossible to expect a peaceful solution by agreement between the Congress and the Muslim League. The pre-partition violence, high-water-marked by the Great Calcutta Killing of 1946, the unspeakable atrocities during the partition in 1947, the Kashmir war, and the large-scale forcing out of the minorities from the two halves of Bengal, all led to a great vitiation of Hindu-Muslim relations (*Koithara, 1999*). However, Nehru, as a head of the Interim Government, was very anxious to protect the minority community and to maintain the secular character of the country by all means.

The British hastened the division of the country by announcing that the Government had decided to transfer power into Indian hands. It also said that Lord Mountbatten would go to India as viceroy with a mandate to implement the government's decision on the transfer of power. Though the original intention of the Raj was not known at this stage, it was used to boost the moral of the Muslim League which had hardened latter's attitude in its dealings with the Congress. In effect it meant that the British were prepared to divide the country if the rival Indian groups failed to arrive expeditiously at a compromise. In the prevailing situation the British announcement was not seen as a good sign as explained by Nehru in 1956, "The partition of India became inevitable, I should say, less that a year before it occurred. I think now, looking back, that partition could have been avoided if the British Government policy had been different about a year or eighteen months before (*Brecher, 1959*). Partition of the sub- continent, while it in some ways cleared the air, left behind a legacy of communal hatred and unsolved political problems. The final parting occurred under circumstances that neither ruler nor the ruled had anticipated.

Lord Mountbatten replaced Lord Wavell as Viceroy and Governor-General of India and took the oath of office on March 24, 1947. Immediately after the swearing-in-ceremony, he made a short speech in which he stressed the need for reaching a solution within the next few months. With his coming, at the very first meeting, he made it clear that the British Government was fully determined to transfer power. Before this could happen, a settlement of the communal problem was necessary and he desired that a final and decisive attempt be made to solve the problem. The overall situation in the country was deteriorating particularly due to spread of communal riots in different parts of the undivided India and deadlock between the Congress and the Muslim League within the Executive Council. The high-up administrative posts were filled by Europeans who were now convinced that within a short time, power would be transferred to Indian hands and, hence, they were no longer interested in their work thus maintaining law and order situation in the riot-affected areas. On the other hand, the difference between the Congress and the League had reached a stage where agreement could be attained only through the mediation of a third party.

"Not to bend" attitude of the Congress and the League made the stage ready for Mountbatten to arbitrate between. Exhibiting a rare capacity for confounding rival parties to a negotiation and forcing decisions out of them, and possessing incomparable charm. His was a man who was known for his understanding attitude towards the Indian leaders especially with Nehru. He performed the surgical operation of dividing the Indian subcontinent without loss of either time or sentiment. Moving like a dynamo the new comer collapsed every obstacle that brought up before him, succeeded in isolating Mahatma Gandhi from the stream of national decision-making–this being Mountbatten's biggest and most stupefying achievement–and drew together the pragmatic element in the Indian leadership for administering a political operation unparalleled in modern history (*Kothair,1970*).

For a brief moment Jinnah was able to achieve political unity with social hatred in order to extract the maximum benefit from the British and the Congress. The work became easier due to political, rather departmental differences between Sardar Patel and Liaquat Ali who were held the portfolios of Home and Finance respectively in the Interim Government. At the end, after consultations with Hindu and Muslim leaders Mountbatten reported to Attlee in June 1947 that there was no time to loss if Britain was to leave India in an orderly way. It was on his recommendations that the British government decided to advance the date of independence for the subcontinent from June 1948 to August 15, 1947. The decision of the British to withdraw from the Indian subcontinent was appreciated by many for it succeeded in avoiding a bloody struggle as France experienced before it decided to relinquish Indo-China. While there was a section of the people who opposed British decision on the ground that the prevailing situation of the country was not conducive for independence. Keeping the Indian circumstances, in view, at the time Lord Wavell had opposed the decision to set a date for British withdrawal. Maulana Azad, a famous nationalist Muslim of India commented many years later, "Perhaps history will decide that the wiser policy would have been to follow Wavell's advice." The best solution of the problem was replaced by a good solution.

Among the Indian leaders Sardar Patel was first to favour the partition of the country. As he was desirous to retain the portfolio of Home under the arrangement of the Interim government, it was on his initiation that the portfolio of Finance was offered to the Muslim League. Having taken the oath of office Liaquat Ali, the new Finance Minister, started running the department with the advice of some able and senior Muslim officers, resulting in delay and rejection of each and every proposal put up by the Congress members of the Executive Council. It hurt Patel much as he was not in a position to create even the post of a peon without Liaquat Ali concurrence. Till the turn of events in Pakistan's favour at the close of partition, perhaps the very end of Pakistan, for Jinnah, was a bargaining counter, but in fighting for the latter he had overreached himself. His action had so annoyed and irritated Sardar Patel that he was now a believer in partition. He became fifty per cent pro-partition even before Mountbatten appeared on the scene. The new Viceroy, as the perfect planner he was, tipped first Sardar Patel and get him convinced without much effort. Patel began to say openly that he was prepared to have a part of India if only he could get rid of the Muslim League. Sardar Patel, the iron-man of India, was always referred in private talks with Mountbatten, as a walnut – a very hard crust outside but soft pulp once the crust was cracked.

Mountbatten, after winning over Patel, turned his face to Nehru. He was intelligent enough and could read into the minds of all his Indian colleagues. There was no doubt in it that Nehru was a man of principle but he was also impulsive and very amenable to personal influences. It is also said that one factor for the change of Nehru was the personality of lady Mountbatten who possessed an attractive and friendly temperament. At first, Jawaharlal Nehru was not ready for the idea of partition and hence reacted against it, violently. Mountbatten persisted his efforts for a month and at a later stage he also took help from Krishna Menon, an admirer of Nehru since the late twenties, and with him the former succeeded in pursuing Nehru to accept the scheme of partition of India.

Maulana Abul Kalam Azad, the first pro-Congress Muslim leader of national stature and perhaps the closest friend of Nehru was shocked to know that both Nehru and Patel had been won by Mountbatten. He realised that the country was moving towards a great danger. Partition of India would be harmful not only to Muslims but to the whole country. In his view still, the Cabinet Mission Plan was the best solution from points of view, more than one. On the one hand it preserved the unity of India and gave every community an opportunity to function with freedom and honour, on the other. He was convinced that even from the communal point, Muslims could expect nothing better. They would have complete internal autonomy in provinces in which they were in a majority. Also, in the centre they would have more than adequate representation. Despite the best efforts on his part, Azad failed to persuade Nehru and Patel with the difference that the former's mind was working in that direction while the latter spoke openly in favour and was hardly prepared to listen other's point of view.

As was the game plan of Mauntbatten, he was able to

corner Mahatma Gandhi who declared, "If the Congress wishes to accept partition, it will be over my dead body. So long as I am alive I will never agree to the partition of India. Nor will I, if I can help it, allow Congress to accept it." For Azad, Gandhi was the only hope. But after his meeting with Mountbatten Gandhi had change his mind and began to put forward the arguments as presented by Patel. Perhaps he was more influenced by Patel than Nehru while discussing the partition issue. Later it became impossible for Mountbatten to stick to Gandhi's suggestion regarding formation of government by Jinnah as a confidence building measure on the part of Congress and Azad's persuasion to take a firm stand on the Cabinet Mission Plan. Originally, the Cabinet Mission Plan was not the brain child of Mountbatten, he wanted to be remembered in history as the man who had solved the Indian problem. As such, it was not surprising that he was willing to substitute Mission's plan by a plan of partition formulated according to his own ideas. Now, partition of the subcontinent was an accepted fact of national life. The only question to be decided was what the form of partition should be.

With this, the clouds of partition evaporated and now it was an established truth. Though hardly believable at large, more by the common people than by the leaders of the concerned parties. After his return from London on May 30, 1947, Mountbatten issued a White Paper on June 3 which gave all details of the Plan. Among other things, the announcement made partition a definite as the British Government had accepted the scheme proposed by Mountbatten. Congress as well as the Muslim League had accepted partition. Since the Congress represented the entire nation and the Muslim League had large support among the Muslims, normally it was interpreted that the whole country had accepted partition. However, a deep and insight study revealed immediately before and after partition, and to some extent even today, that the acceptance was only in a resolution of the Working Committee of the Congress and on the register of the Muslim League. Maulana Abul Kalam Azad expressed his grief when the All-India Congress Committee met on 14 June 1947 to accept the partition and said;

> Partition was a tragedy for India and the only thing that could be said in its favour was that we had done our best to avoid division but we had failed. Now there was no alternative and if we wanted freedom here and now, we must submit to the demand for dividing India. We must not however forget that the nation is one and its cultural life is and will remain one. Politically we had failed and were therefore dividing the country. We should accept our defeat but we should at the same time try to ensure that our culture was not divided. If we put a stick in the water, it may appear that the water has been divided but the water remains the same and the moment the stick is removed, even the appearance of division disappears.

The scheme of partition as envisaged in Mountbatten's Plan and the announcement that followed the passing of Indian Independence Act, the subcontinent was divided into two parts – India and Pakistan to be freed on 15th and 14th of August 1947, respectively. Now partition was a reality but even today people fail to understand that why the British Government did not accept the advice by a section of intelligentsia including the Congress to extend the date of independence for a year or two. Till now it was the Congress which had been insisting that India should be freed immediately. Now it was the Congress which asked that the solution of the political problem may be deferred and there was none to blame the British if they had conceded the Congress request. It was also made known to the British that if they acted hastily, independent and impartial observers would naturally conclude that the British wanted to give freedom to India in conditions where Indians could not take full advantage of this development. Perhaps, the decision to divide India at an earlier date suited to the larger and long-term British strategic designs.

As a result of the efforts made by Muslim leaders and Jinnah in particular and with the collaboration of feudal and aristocratic elements of Muslim society, Pakistan, as a sovereign and independent nation, came into being on 14th of August 1947. Fourteen August was and is a day of rejoicing for the Muslims of Pakistan, for the Hindus and the Sikhs of the country, it was a day of mourning. The real position is that the people of India had not accepted partition. Their heart and soul rebelled against the very idea. Though the Muslim League enjoyed the support of many Indian Muslims, there are a large section in the community who had always opposed the League. They were naturally deeply cut by the decision to divide the country.

But actually, it was not a division of the subcontinent alone. It divided even the Muslim society into two of the undivided India. Hope and despair were the fate of Muslims – hope for whom who belonged to the newly created country and despair for those who resided in India. It was a peculiar situation that the community was going to face. Jinnah, was largely responsible for creating this abnormal situation who left single message for the Muslims of India while leaving for Karachi that now the country was divided and they should be loyal citizens of India. This parting message created in Muslim community of India a sense of weakness and disillusionment. They kept with themselves only deep regret and anger that Jinnah had deceived them and it left them in dilemma. Though Pakistan is not their country, they hesitate to be with India in all sincerity and goodness.

However, their logic to blame Jinnah, Muslim League and certain elements of undivided Indian Muslim society does not carry arguments, sound and enough. Basically, it was a fault on their part not to realise the real implications of Pakistan. If the Muslim-majority provinces formed a separate state, it was clear that the provinces in which the Muslims were in a minority would form the part of India. Muslims of the Uttar Pradesh and Bihar were a minority and remain so even after Partition. It is a strange but the fact is that these Muslim Leaguers had been foolishly persuaded that once Pakistan was formed, Muslims, whether they came from a majority or a minority province would be regarded as a separate nation and would enjoy the right of determining their own future. It was now clear to them that the only result of partition was that their position as a minority was much weaker than before, in addition, they had through their foolish action created anger and resentment in the minds of the Hindus. Probably everyone thought that all will be well once the British left. Besides, minority rights, human rights, etc. were not very much in the public domain then. The preoccupation of the votaries of the two-nation theory – Jinnah and others – was only with dividing the country based on which community was in the majority in which area. The minorities of those areas were nobody's concern. Psychologically, as it stands today, some Hindus view the Muslims as a potential threat to the country because of their alleged pro-Pakistani feelings and/or their rapid population growth, real or suspected (*Rustamji, 1979*). They suffer, in a sense, from a sort of paranoia. Similarly, the Muslims, to a great extent, do not feel very secure while living amongst a vast Hindu majority. They feel that they are being discriminated against (*Nayar,1980*). In other words, they suffer from a 'minority complex' or worse still, at times from a kind of 'persecution mania, but some observers of contemporary India feel that Indian Muslims now should join the 'mainstream by rejecting the traditional cultural markers which distinguish them from Hindus, and should accept common codes in their social and personal life, so as to enhance the cultural integration between the religious groups.

Social Bases of New Nation

At the cost of country's unity India gained freedom and a new state called Pakistan was came into being on 14 August 1947. Though Pakistan inherited more or less a society that India possessed earlier, the basis for the former's creation, even its fight during national movement, had changed its nature, composition and purpose as well. The new state was a creation of the Muslim League that was founded in 1906 to oppose the Congress. The League therefore had hardly any members who had fought for the independence of the country. They had neither made any sacrifice nor gone through the discipline of a struggle. They were either retired officials or man who had been brought into public life under British patronage. The result was that when the new state was formed, power came into the hands of people who had no record of service or sacrifice. Many of the rulers of the new state were selfish people who had come to public life only for the sake of personal interest. It created a wide gap between the ruler and the ruled. While the public or society that the new state brought with it, was a bewilderingly patchy. There are classes within class, castes within caste, social groups, ethnic groups, linguistic groups, urban modern educated elite, rural, feudal benighted masses, opulent industrialists, rich feudal lords and the seedy hangers– on, the fundamentalists with the arch conservative and orthodox outlook, and the secular, democratic enlightened and liberal section of society with the modernist view of man and society.

When Pakistan emerged as a sovereign and independent nation, its population was not exclusively Muslim but contained several millions of non-Muslim citizens. It was realised at early that the attempt to solve one problem in the wrong way may well create new problems. Any division of the country on religious basis can not separate the followers of these two principal religions of India for they are spread out all over the country. Even if the areas in which each group is in a majority are separated, huge minorities belonging to the other group remain in each area. In giving freedom to separate to one group, other groups, though in a minority, are denied that freedom had compelled to isolate themselves from the rest of India against their emphatic and deeply felt wishes. Thus, despite the favourable circumstances for the creation of Pakistan, geography was against it as Indian Muslims were distributed in a way which made it impossible to form a separate State in a consolidated area. The Muslim-majority areas were in the north-west and north-east. These two regions have no point of physical contact. It can also be imagined simply the status of non-Muslims in a state that had come into being pre-eminently because the Muslims had sought a homeland wherein they could lead a life of their own based on the religion and culture of Islam (*Choudhary,1971*). In other words, Muslim and Hindu, were so intermingled in many parts of the subcontinent that any frontier line was bound to leave millions of Muslim in India and millions of Hindus in Pakistan.

With the creation of Pakistan, it was hoped that once Hindus had India and the Muslims Pakistan, they would live happily ever after. But the reality has been different because of the contrast between India's multicultural democratic polity and Pakistan's theocratic dictatorial one. Even it did not solve the communal problem and made it more intense and harmful. The creation of the new State on the basis of religion and communal hatred gave it a permanent constitutional form and made it much more difficult. The most regrettable feature of this situation was that the subcontinent of India was divided into two States which looked at one another with hatred and fear. Pakistan believed that India would allow her to rest in peace and would destroy her whenever she has an opportunity. Similarly, India was afraid that whenever Pakistan got an opportunity, she would move against India and attack her. Partition, after all, wrote Wilfred Smith, in 1946, "did not solve the communal problem; it simply internationalised it. If Muslims in the present India, constituting a minority of 23.5 per cent, deserve the right to secede, how can one visualise a Pakistan with non-Muslim minorities of 40 per cent and more. If Hindus and Muslims could not live together in India because they were totally antagonistic culture, as Jinnah argued, how could they live together in Pakistan, as he said they would.? (*Ghose, 1987)*

Religion, as a faith, is supreme, but as a basis of nationhood does not carry much weight because it can not unite areas which are different, socially, economically, geographically, linguistically and culturally. History has proved that after the first few decades or at the most after the first century, Islam was not able to unite all the Muslim countries on the basis of Islam. On the basis of it only the Muslims of the subcontinent have three nations: Indian Muslims, Muslims in Pakistan and Muslims in East Pakistan, now Bangladesh. All of them, who happened to be Hindu converts, have the same tradition behind them and culturally, each is full heir to the same heritage that was Indian Islam. It was on this ground that Stanley Wolpert found the doctrine of two nations as an entirely unrealistic attitude and wrote in his *biography of Jinnah*. "What was he talking about? Had he simply forgotten where he was? Had the cyclone of events so disoriented him that he was arguing the opposition's brief? What he pleading for a united India ....". On the other side of the few day's old border, the Congress was saying, "...... the mountains and the seas fashioned India as she is, and no human agency can change that shape or come in the way of her final destiny .... When the present passions have subsided .... The false doctrine of two nations in India will be discredited and discarded (*Ganguli, 2002*). In 1946, Wilfred was surprised to see the making of East and West Pakistan, which should not be logically united in one country. Indeed, the emergence of Bangladesh in 1971 had confirmed the absurdity of the creation of a bisected Pakistan. Even within West Pakistan the three provinces of Sind, Punjab and the Frontier have internal incompatibility and are working for separate aims and interests.

Economically, the undivided India was a strong and more or less self-sufficient economic unit. Later on, when a separate State was created on the basis of majoritarian principle of Hindu and Muslim areas, it became almost sure that the predominantly Hindu regions would comprise the greater part of the mineral resources and industrial areas. While the Muslim areas would be economically backward, and often deficit, areas which cannot exist without a great deal of outside assistance. Hence, at the time of partition Pakistan inherited an economy which was essentially feudal; she gained very few trading firms, very few banks and virtually no industry. In Punjab, sixty per cent of land belonged to the landlords, while in Sind a few hundred big Zamindars owned almost all the arable land. In East Pakistan, however, most of the Zamindars who were Hindus, left for India and their land passed into the hands of the tenants. The economic scene in Pakistan was dominated by the capitalists from Bombay and the Muslim landlords from Northern India who had succeeded in transferring their wealth to Pakistan; they soon found avenues to aggrandise their means manifold. This became possible due to two factors, first, that these landlords and capitalists made the leadership of the Muslim League and secondly that the civil servants who issued licenses for trade and industry were either related or known to them.

In the first quarter of this century, there arose a Muslim middle class which comprised small number of Muslim capitalists, bankers and businessmen that emerged by this time mainly in Bombay and U.P. In the hope of better prospect than in Hindu-dominated India it migrated to West Pakistan. The motive force for Pakistan came largely from this middle-class Muslims of North India, many of whom had been educated at Aligarh. At some level, they identified with the ideas of Syed Ahmad Khan and Mohammad Iqbal.

Pakistan evolved a system which encouraged private enterprise and protected it by high tariffs and other fiscal and monetary measures. In the case of industries in which private capital was inadequate and shy, government stepped in, developed the industries and handed them over to private capitalists. At the time of partition and especially after the outbreak of Korean war, the jute industry of Pakistan became a source of increased earning of foreign exchange. But even this industry of Pakistan was monopolised by a few capitalists from Bombay who has settled in West Pakistan. Cultivators as well as the traders of East Pakistan, now Bangladesh, were deprived from the benefit of this windfall. Thus, a class of vested interests was created in West Pakistan in alliance with civil servants.

From the start Pakistan has developed the type of economy in which economic growth brought affluence to the few at the expense of the many. The feudal families continued to live the life they had been living for centuries. Agrarian laws had not been drastically changed and land ownership remained in the hands of old feudal families. There made a social divide on the basis of economy between the East and West Pakistan on the one hand and among the society of the latter on the other. It forced the economic growth of the country to depend on foreign loan, resulted ultimately in the concentration of economic power in 43 families which owned 76.8% of all manufacturing assets by the end of the sixties. Polarisation of classes in the rural sector and a rapid increase in landlessness were started at an early stage. While the incomes of the rural elite increased sharply following the Green Revolution, the real incomes of the rural poor declined in absolute terms. According to a survey 33% of small farmers operating less than 8 acres suffered a deterioration in their diet. During the 1960s as many as 794,042 small families became landless a labourers (*Rupesinghe and Mumtaz,1996*).

Under a deliberate policy income of the country was transferred into the hands of rich, while they failed to increase their savings significantly – thereby obliging the government to increase its reliance on foreign aid in order to meet its ambitious growth targets. The basic objective of Pakistan's development strategy was to achieve a high growth rate of Gross National Product within the framework of private enterprise supported by government subsidies, tax concessions and import controls. In other words, it was a transfer of income from the poorer sections of society, who were thought to have a low marginal rate of savings, to high–income groups, who were expected to have a high marginal rate of savings. It was thought that by thus concentrating incomes in the hands of the rich, total domestic savings and hence investment could be raised. But the hopes belied before the naked facts that Pakistani entrepreneurs never invested their money only money borrowed from banks or made allegedly from narcotics business. At the dawn of independence, Pakistan's ruling elite consisted of an alliance between landlords and the mascent industrial bourgeoisie, backed by bureaucracy and the military.

The influential position of Pakistani bureaucracy can be traced back to the national movement. During the last days of British rule, the Muslim League was also assisted by a few ambitious Muslim bureaucrats, who rightly thought that their promotion in Pakistan would be easier. Since the freedom struggle was essentially a constitutional one, the state apparatus of the colonial regime remained in tact, albeit in a weakened condition. The bureaucracy, which constituted the steel frame of the Raj and the army, continued after the emergence of Pakistan to determine the parameters within which political and economic changes were to occur. In the period of its struggle for Pakistan, Muslim League was a movement rather than a party. It was therefore unable to establish an organisational structure or develop a political culture on the basis of which people's power of the people could be institutionalised and used to subordinate the army and the bureaucracy to a political system. In the League there also remained a contradiction between its leadership and the followers. While the nationalist movement was headed by modern intelligentsia, most of the League leaders were zamindars or ex-bureaucrats. In the post-partition phase this organisation was taken over by landlords whose political interest lay in constraining the process of political development and, when ruling in the name of the people, in confining politics to a struggle for sharing the economic spoils amongst various factions of the political elite. The power of the bureaucracy also increased in Pakistan due to the fact that its leaders like Jinnah, Liaquat Ali Khan and other Muslim League leaders had no knowledge of running the day-to-day administration of the government and so they largely depended on bureaucrats. Another factor which further consolidated the power of the bureaucrats was that Jinnah instead of becoming the Prime Minister chose the mantle of Governor-General. As Jinnah was a virtual dictator, this action of Jinnah weakened the tradition of Parliamentary democracy in Pakistan, made the post of Governor-General more important than that of Prime Minister and ultimately encouraged the bureaucrats to by-pass the Ministers in making decisions and formulating policies for the state. They began to derive their power directly from the Governor-General. Soon the bureaucracy in Pakistan, as in other authoritarian countries, became Janus-faced. They look both ways, before and after, ahead and backwards and shift their loyalty as the situation warranted without much effort. When corrupt politician rules the country, bureaucracy had its heyday. When generals became rulers, bureaucrats effortlessly began to help the chair with their expertise and experience of managing the country (*Mathur,2001*).

Thus, from the early fifties, in the background of this social and political weaknesses, the nexus between the bureaucrats and the army began to take a definite shape in

Pakistan. During 1951-1958 there was an alliance between the bureaucracy and the army through the 'gang of four' consisting of Ghulam Muhammad, Chaudhry Muhammad Ali, Iskandar Mirza and General Ayub Khan. The dominance of the bureaucracy supported by the army vis-à-vis the political system can be judged from the fact that in April 1953 the then Governor-General Ghulam Muhammad, who was an old bureaucrat dismissed the Khawaja Nazimuddin government even though the Constituent Assembly had given it a vote of confidence. Nazimuddin was the first Prime Minister of East Bengal and his feudal background had made him unresponsive towards middle class aspirations. His eagerness to hold on to power forced him to be a puppet in the hands of the ruling clique of West Pakistan. He was so loyal to the central authority that on the request of the latter, he sacrificed six seats of East Bengal to West Pakistan and thus, reduced her representation in the Constituent Assembly. Because at the time of independence the East Bengal had fifty-six per cent of the population of Pakistan it was given forty-four seats in the Constituent Assembly out of seventy-nine and the majority belonged to East. Despite the loyalty of such an extent Nazimuddin was dismissed by a bureaucrat-turned Governor-General and the Constituent Assembly met again to vote in favour of Muhammad Ali Bogra, who had been nominated to this office. Apart from this the Governor-General also began to nominate other ministers of the cabinet and assign their respective portfolios. Thus, it was on the connivance of bureaucracy and the army that the state power effectively passed into the hands of the Governor-General and the bureaucracy and military. The function of the Constituent Assembly was reduced merely to rubber-stamping their actions.

Administrative Set-up of Pakistan

As administrative divisions formed an integral tier of the government at independence in 1947, the new nation of Pakistan was comprised by two wings-the eastern and western, separated by India. At the time three of the provinces of Pakistan were subdivided into ten administrative divisions. The single province in eastern wing called East Bengal, had four divisions-Chittagong, Dacca, Khulna and Rajshahi. The province of West Punjab had four divisions – Lahore, Multan, Rawalpindi and Sargodha. The North-West Frontier Province had two divisions-Dera Ismail Khan and Peshawar. The hasty partition of the Indian subcontinent in August 1947 not only intensified the existing mutual suspicions and fears but also gave birth to many new complex problems. Compared to India, these problems were for more numerous and onerous for Pakistan as India was not only an 'ongoing concern' but also inherited a well-developed administrative setup (*Cheema,1990*). In the circumstances, Pakistan, the new state, was not only confronted with the important task of setting up an administrative structure but also faced almost chaotic conditions in those areas that formed Pakistan. In addition, the August and September of 1947 had given the worst possible start to these two Dominions who faced the massive problem of resettling the refugees and resolving the question of migrants' property.

After independence between August 1947 and March 1948, the rulers of princely states such as Bahawalpur, Khairpur, Kalat, Las Bela, Kharan, Makran, Phulra, Amb, Swat, Dir, Chitral, Hunza and Nagar acceded their states to Pakistan, giving up control of their external affairs, while all retaining internal self-government, at least to begin with. This was lost by stages until and by 1974 all of these states had been fully integrated into Pakistan. In 1948, the area around Karachi was separated from Sind Province to form the Federal Capital Territory. In 1950 the North-West Frontier Province was expanded to include the small states of Amb and Phulra and the name of West Punjab province was changed to Punjab. The Baluchistan States Union was formed in 1952 by the four princely states of Southwest Pakistan. Thus, between 1947 and 1955, Pakistan comprised five provinces East Bengal, West Punjab, Sind, North-West Frontier Province (NWFP) and Baluchistan with one territory called Federal Capital Territory. The Baluchistan States Union formed in 1952 was made combining Kalat, Kharan, Las Bela and Makran and used the flag of Kalat.

Originally in 1930 Sir Mohammad Iqbal conceived the idea of Pakistan by uniting the four states of the northwestern British Empire, the partition of subcontinent was the result of Pakistan movement led by Muhammad Ali Jinnah and came into existence on 14 August 1947. Since then, the country had been without a consolidated written constitution, and all Pakistani state affairs had been run under constitutional acts of British Indian empire enacted in 1935 and 1947. The Government had prolonged difficulty in administrating East Bengal, with its border with Eastern India, and the four provinces, which border Western India, Iran, China and Afghanistan. Thus, keeping in view, the administrative difficulties, the idea of 'One Unit System' was conceived by Malik Ghulam, the then Governor General of Pakistan, whose drafting was completed by Prime Minister Mohammad Ali Bogra who had made the first official announcement on 22 November 1954. The National Assembly of Pakistan passed a bill merging of all West Pakistan into a single province on 30 September 1955 and finally it was implemented on 14 October 1955. Earlier in 1954, Prime Minister Mohammad Ali Bogra praised the idea and said,'There will be no Bengalis, no Punjabis, no Sindhis, no Pathan, no Balochis, no Bahawalpuris, no Khairpuris. The disappearance of these groups will strengthen the integrity of Pakistan. Iskander Mirza who put forward the bill in the Assembly also gave following reasons;

i. It would end the curse of provincial prejudices.

ii. It would allow the development of backward areas.

iii. It would reduce administrative expenses.

iv. It would make it easier to draw up a new constitution.

v. It would give East and West Pakistan maximum autonomy.

As a follow up of the plan after the general election of 1954, the four provinces and Tribal areas were merged in the western wing. The province was composed of twelve divisions and the provincial capital was established at Lahore. The province of East Bengal, now Bengladesh, was renamed as East Pakistan with the provincial capital at Dacca. The federal government moved the country's capital in 1958 from Karachi to Rawalpindi while the federal legislature moved to Dacca. West Pakistan formed a single and united political entity but with marked linguistic and ethnic distinctions. The One Unit policy was regarded as an administrative reform that would reduce expenditure and help eliminate ethnic and parochial prejudices. However, with the military coup of 1958, trouble loomed for the province when the office of Chief Minister was abolished and the President claimed executive power over West Pakistan.

Overall, 'One Unit' created more problems internally in West Pakistan, even the disparity between West and the East was neither removed nor was any other issue was resolved. At the time of division of land between the two Dominions in 1947, it was crystal clear that East Pakistan was 1000s kilo meter far from West Pakistan. West Pakistan was itself divided into four provinces while West Pakistan was considered one province. It was difficult for east Pakistani to be prosperous with privileges which it had. There were a lot of hurdles between the two includinglanguage and sharing of power. This apart, West was more developed and it had a strong military and bureaucracy. Despite goodwill regarding 'One Unit' on the part of Government, the fact can not be denied that merging of the provinces created further troubles and tribulations. The circumstances of one unit could not bring prosperity and development in the country.

Even recently in October 2011. *The Dawn,* in a Flashback:

'One Unit' termed the period 'a dark chapter' in the history of Pakistan. It viewed the system especially in context of Sindh province which had already suffered the effects of a similar system during its 89-year annexation (1847-1936) by the Bombay Presidency. It wrote, after independence, a group of politicians backed by vested interests were determined to exploit the resources of Sindh on one pretext or the other. The scheme of One Unit was not a new one. Right from the inception of Pakistan, vested interests had their eyes set on Sindh's natural resources but they could not put their plans in action as longas Quaid-i-Azam was alive. Right after his death, plans were set afoot' (*The Dawn,16 October2011*). The idea of implementing it was raised time and again including one in 1949 on the floor of the first Constituent Assembly. Later it got favour of General Ayub Khan, who in one of the cabinet meetings in the capacity of commander-in-chief and defence minister, expressed his opinion on One Unit plan by saying that it was his plan to make West Pakistan one province. General Iskander Mirza who finally piloted the 'One Unit' bill too said that it was a road roller and any small stone coming in the way would be crushed. At the time and in afterwards, in the absence of a Constituent Assembly, provincial assemblies were the only forums to pave way for the One Unite Scheme and the only weighty opposition it would invite from the Sindh province. As expected, agitation against the scheme was begun by lawyers, students, writers and peasants but it was crushed by brute force and ultimately the federal government of the time succeeded in managing the bill passed by the provincial assemblies of all provinces including the Sindh.

The evaluation and analysis of 'One Unit System' that worked in Pakistan from 1955 to 1970 is still active and Naazir Mahmood in an article in *The News* on 26 July 2015 reminded in context of presentday democracy in Pakistan that from 1947 to 1955, in all 22 provincial cabinets were dismissed or forced to resign-five in East Bengal, four in

Punjab, four in NWFP, and eight in Sindh.

No government was changed through a no-confidence vote in the provincial legislatures. Most governments were removed while they commanded the majority support in house and were forced out at the behest of the central powers that be (*The News, 26 July 2015*). Even before the civil military became unbalanced in the nascent Pakistan, the centre province antagonism had started shattering the dream of a decent democracy. At the juncture it was wrong to suggest that the entire Muslim League was in favour of a strong centre, but actually the gang of four comprising Ghulam Mohammad, Major General Iskander Mirza, General Ayub Khan and Chaudhary Mohammad Ali was adament to have a strong centre in Pakistan. Those who tried to stand firm for the protection of provincial rights were shown the door and declared as traitors working against the national interest. In nutshell, the scheme was a campaign of a few against the will and interest of general public which cast a dark shadow over the administrative setup of the then infant nation called Pakistan.

In addition, one potential factor of this growing tendency was the landslide victory of the United Front. As a result, there emerged a possibility that the desire of the civil and military bureaucracy to keep a strong centre within their fold might be thwarted should the smaller provinces side with Bengal. The formation of a 'One Unit' would give the centre a greater chance of arm twisting to get favourable decisions from one provincial assembly rather than dealing with three provinces (Punjab, Sindh and NWFP), one chief commissioner's provinces (Baluchistan) and numerous princely states. Overall impacts of the 'One Unit System' were;

1. Although political benefits were going in favour of West Pakistan yet the people of different provinces of West Pakistan protested against this new scheme and insisted on the separate distinct identities of regional

cultures of the provinces.

2. The objectives mentioned as a cause of the "One Unit" were not met.
3. Expenditures were not controlled and limited, additionally some related issues were aroused. Remote areas of the country were totally ignored and some local problems emerged with high intensity.
4. Actually, the objectives of One Unit could not be achieved, rather the power concentrated in few hands; hence the demand of the restoration of small provinces came up through various movements.
5. In East Pakistan, many political parties and groups questioned the principle of parity between the two wings and perceived that the whole of the West Pakistan is together against the East Pakistan. These facts increased sense of alienation among them.
6. Ironically, after the East broke away to form Bangladesh, the Punjab province insisted that politics in the rump West Pakistan now be decided on the basis of a straightforward vote, since Punjabis were more numerous than the other groups, such as Sindhis, Pathans or Baloch.
7. The 'One Unit Scheme' sustained the highly centralized and bureaucratic political order that suffered from a legitimacy crisis in the NWFP and Sindh. Some leaders of Baluchistan, too, opposed the 'One Unit Scheme'.
8. Since our leaders failed to apprehend the plural nature of the culture of our country and since they did not identify themselves with the true national identity, so the consequent identity crises at last resulted in the separation of East Pakistan in 1971.

After all the one-unit system remained enforce from 1955 to 1970. Although it was brought to reduce expenditure and to eliminate provincial prejudices, the military coup of 1958 signalled difficulties when the first military President,

Ayub Khan, abolished the office of Chief Minister of West Pakistan in favour of Governor's rule. In 1960 the federal capital moved from Karachi to Rawalpindi and later to Islamabad when Constitution finished in 1966.Eventually, in 1970, the one-unit system of West Pakistan was abolished by President Yahya Khan and four new provinces were created along with some changes in Pakistani Kashmir.

References

Akhtar, Javed (2003). 'Beyond Real Estate'. *The Hindustan Times*, 15 July.

Azad, Maulana Abdul Kalam (1988). *India Wins Freedom*. New Delhi, Orient Blackswan, p. 167.

Brecher, Michael (1959). *Nehru: A Political Biography*. London, Oxford University Press, p. 174.

Chandra, Bipin (1999). 'Tryst with Tyranny'. *The Hindustan Times*, 22 December.

Cheema, Pervaiz Iqbal (1990). *Paksitan's Defence Policy, 1947-58*. NewYork, Palgrave Macmillan, pp. 23-24.

Choudhary, G.W. (1971). *Pakistan's Relations with India 1947-1966*, Meerut, Meenakshi Prakashan, p. 146.

Gallagher, John (1982). *The Decline, Revival and Fall of the British Empire: The Ford Lectures and Other Essays*.Cambridge, Cambridge University Press, p. 155.

Ghose, S.K. (1987). *Muslim Politics in India*. New Delhi, Ashish Publishing House, pp. 127-28.

Koithara, Verghese (1999). *Society, State & Security, The Indian Experience*, New Delhi, Sage Publications, p. 114.

Kothari, Rajni (1970). 'Why Jamshedpurs? Basic Factors Behind Communal Riots', *Mainstream*, 9 June.

Mathur, A.B. (2001). 'Nehru: The Man and Statesman'. *Administrative Change*, Vol. XXVIII, No. 2 and Vol XIX, No. 1,

January-December, (Jaipur), p. 108.

Nayar, K. (1980). 'Between the Lines:Communalism: Old Fears and New Danger'. *The Indian Express,* 10 December.

Nehru, Jawaharlal (1941). *The Discovery of India,* United Kingdom, Meridian Books, p.351.

Rupesinghe, Kumar and Khawar Mumtaz (eds.) (1996). *Internal Conflicts in South Asia.* New Delhi, Sage Publications, p. 40.

Samad, Yunus (1995). *A Nation in Turmoil-Nationalism and Ethnicity in Pakistan, 1937-58.* New Delhi, Sage Publications, p. 15.

Sen, Anupam (1983). 'The Political Elites of Pakistan: Their Role in Pakistan's Disintegration'. *The Political Elites of Pakistan and Other Sociological Essays.* New Delhi: Amar Prakashan, pp. 78-80

2

Constitutional Developments of Pakistan

Constitutional Background

Under the Indian Independence Act, 1947, the British Crown relinquished its sovereign power over India and transferred those powers to the newly established dominions of India and Pakistan on 14 August 1947. The Government of India Act 1935 was amended to bring it in consonance with the aims and objectives of independence as laid down in the 1947 Act. The combination of these two constitutional instruments served as an interim constitutional order for both countries until their respective constituent assemblies adopted their own constitutions. Following independence, Pakistan took three Governor Generals, four Prime Ministers, two constituent assemblies (1947-1954 and 1955-56), and nine years of protracted constitution making process to produce the first constitution of Pakistan in 1956. However, it was rejected on the final day of its adoption (29 February 1956) by all Hindu minority parties and the largest Muslim political party (the Awami League) from East Pakistan, now Bangladesh. The military dictator General Ayub Khan who took over the country on 7 October 1958, abrogated the

1956 constitution and imposed the first martial law in the country. The new ruler, Ayub Khan enacted the 1962 constitution through an executive order. The current constitution, enacted by the third constituent assembly in 1973, was twice suspended by military coups of General Zia-ul-Haq (1977-1985) and General Musharraf (1999-2002), and at the times of its restoration, both in 1985 and 2002, the military regimes amended it in ways that fundamentally changed its Islamic and federal character. From the beginning the Islamic character of state and federalism were the two vexatious questions that prevented the forging of consensus among ethno national groups on constitutional design of the instruments that have governed the polity.

The federal discourse in Pakistan has been and continues to be structured by two antithetical visions of identity, both articulated by two competing forces. The centripetal forces, representing the state elites, have aimed at creating a homogenous society and a monolithic national identity, employing Islam as a unifying force in the service of building a centralized Muslim Nation State, despite the multiethnic and deeply divided character of the society. The centrifugal forces, representing the diverse ethnic, linguistic, cultural and regional groups on the other hand have been pushing back against the officially sponsored nation-and state building project and making counter- demands for constitutional recognition of the multiethnic character of the polity and their accommodation in a multinational framework within a decentralized federal order.

In nutshell, the political and constitutional history of Pakistan over the years has been quite enigmatic. The unprecedented political crises, security threats, failure of domestic and external policies impaired the political development of the country considerably. In the country the political system was dominated by bureaucratic military elites. They developed symbiotic relationship along with feudal lords who readily accepted the policy of second fiddle. Military along with bureaucracy collaborated to re-structure the political system and brought constitutional changes to consolidate power (*Ahmed and Begam,2015*). On the other hand, the political parties were unable to capitalize upon political power. They remained averse to solving political issues, invariably contributed in strengthening the hands of extra constitutional forces. The ineffective system of accountability. weak organization of judiciary and social backwardness were among other factors which hampered political development to a large extent.

Making of 1956 Constitution

The first Constituent Assembly of Pakistan was preceded by the Constituent Assembly of India, which first met in the Indian Parliament on December 9, 1946 in Delhi, while India was under British rule. It originally included the provinces that now compose Pakistan and Bangladesh and the representation of the princely states of India. In June 1947 the representatives of the Constituent Assembly of India from Sindh, East Bengal, Baluchistan, West Punjab and the North West Frontier Province withdrew to form the Constituent Assembly of Pakistan, meeting in Karachi. On the eve of independence and the end of British rule, Pakistan's first Constituent Assembly was convened on August 11, 1947 and Muhammad Ali Jinnah remained its President until his death on September 11, 1948. Subsequently, Liaquat Ali Khan headed the chair for three years and produced the Objective Resolution. Liaquat Ali Khan, the President of Pakistan's Constituent Assembly, presented it in the assembly on March 7, 1949 and out of 69 only 21 members voted for it. All the amendment proposed by minority members were rejected and consequently, all of them voted against it. The resolution proclaimed that the future constitution of Pakistan would not be modelled entirely on a European pattern, but on the ideology and democratic faith of Islam. The key features of the Objective Resolution were as follows:

- Islamic State
- Federal Structure
- Distribution of Powers
- Equality before Law
- Independence of Judiciary
- Urdu and English be the National Languages.

After assuming charge as Prime Minister, Chaudhary Muhammad Ali and his team worked hard to formulate a constitution. The committee, which was assigned the task to frame the constitution, presented the draft Bill in the Constituent Assembly of Pakistan on January 9, 1956 and despite opposition by the Bengali autonomists and several other sections of society, it was adopted and was enforced on March 23, 1956. With this Pakistan's dominion status ended and the country was declared as Islamic Republic of Pakistan. The first constitution of Pakistan consisted of 234 articles, divided into 13 parts and 6 schedules along with following features:

1. Pakistan was declared as an Islamic Republic.
2. The constitution provided for the federal form of government with three lists of subjects: federal, provincial and concurrent. The federal list consisted 33 items, provincial of 94 items and concurrent list of 19 items.
3. Though the constitution provided for the Parliamentary form of Government, yet it declared that the executive authority of the federation would be in the President.

   Any Muslim citizen of Pakistan, who was at least forty years old, could be elected as the President of Pakistan.
4. President could appoint from among the Members of National Assembly a Prime Minister who had to take the vote of confidence from the house in two months.

5. Ministers could be taken from outside the National Assembly but they were to get themselves elected within six months.

6. President had the power to summon, prorogue, and dissolve the Assembly on the advice of the cabinet.

7. Prime Minister and his cabinet were to aid and advise the President. The President was required to follow the advise of the cabinet except where he was empowered to act in his own discretion.

8. The constitution entitled for a Unicameral Legislature. National Assembly was to consist of 300 members. Age limit of a candidate for a seat in National Assembly was 25 Years.

9. Principle of parity was accommodated in the constitution. West Pakistan was treated as one unit and seats were divided equally between the two wings of the country.

10. Members of the Assembly were to be elected on the basis of Direct Elections conducted on the basis of Adult Franchise.

11. The Provincial structure was similar to that of the centre. There were 300 members in both provincial assemblies. Ten additional seats were reserved for women. Punjab was given 40% seats in the West Pakistan Assembly.

12. It was a written constitution.

13. It was a flexible constitution and two third members of the Assembly could bring amendment in the constitution.

14. Fundamental Rights were made justiciable. However, the President had power to suspend the fundamental rights in case of emergency.

15. Elaborate provisions were made for the higher judiciary to ensure its independence.

16. Urdu and Bengali were declared as the state languages. However, for the first twenty years English was to continue as an official language.

In addition to these, the Constitution of 1956 provided for a provincial structure, each province had a provincial legislature elected directly by the people and even in the provinces parliamentary system was introduced that meant that Chief Minister would be the head of the government. He is to be responsible to the provincial assembly. The governor would be appointed by the President in consultation with the Prime Minister. The governors' functions were ceremonial; the provincial executive power was exercised by the Chief Minister and not by the governor. In this federal set-up that Pakistan adopted centre was strong although provincial autonomy was given to the provinces but centre was strong. Traditionally centre in Pakistan has been strong going back to the British period. So, the tradition of the strong centre was existed because there were certain powers with the centre that enabled it to step in the provincial domain. For example, in case of any exigencies the federal government could exercise emergency powers. It means that if federal government exercises emergency powers the domain and the autonomy of the provinces could be restricted. Besides, if for some reason there is a constitutional breakdown in a province that the provincial government cannot function or central government has concluded that provincial government and Chief Minister cannot function in accordance with the constitution then president could ask the governor to take over the administration. Thus, although provincial autonomy was there but centre was strong under the 1956 constitution.

Earlier to the adoption of 1956 constitution the Objective Resolution invited plethora of problems. The language issue, distribution of seats in the Legislative Assembly and the division of powers between the federation and the federating units germinated agitational politics in East Pakistan. At the time, the arbitrary use of powers by the governor generals seriously jeopardized the working of political system. The growing influence of army and bureaucracy in the politics also rang alarming bells for the politicians who looked incapacitated to counter such preponderance. These developments negatively carved the process of political development. In the circumstances the failure of 1956 constitution also intensified political crisis. The appalling economic conditions were creating more uncertainties among the masses. In amid environment of political and economic chaos, military had to capture the reins of the government in 1958. Ayub Khan emerged as a saviour of a frustrated nation. He abrogated the Constitution of 1956 and attempted to re-structure political order. He blamed politicians for creating political turmoil. The activities of the politicians were brought under heavy restraint by the Elective Bodies Disqualification Order (EBDO) in 1959. The new ruler, to give country a type of democracy which the people could understand. He introduced the system of Basic Democracies in 1959 (*Yousuf, 1999*). These steps and overall environment of the country paved the way for passing a new constitution for the nation in 1962.

Making of 1962 Constitution

The Constitution of 1962 was the fundamental law of Pakistan from June 1962 until martial law was declared in March 1969. The short-lived Constitution of 1956 was abrogated in October 1958 by President Iskander Mirza, but shortly afterwards General Ayub Khan deposed Iskander Mirza and declared himself president. Having assumed presidential authority on 17 February 1960 Ayub Khan appointed a commission to report on the future political framework for the country. The commission was headed by the former Chief Justice of Pakistan, Muhammad Shahabuddin, and had ten other members, five each from East Pakistan and West Pakistan composed of retired judges, lawyers, industrialists and landlords. The report of the Constitution Commission was presented to President Ayub on 6 May 1961 and thoroughly examined by the President and his cabinet. In January 1962, the cabinet finally approved the text of the new Constitution. It was promulgated by President Ayub on 1 March 1962 and finally came into effect on 8 June 1962. The second constitution of Pakistan contained 250 articles divided into twelve parts and three schedules. Salient features of the Constitution of 1962;

1. The Constitution of 1962 was a written document.
2. It was a rigid constitution. If an amendment to the constitution is passed by at least two-thirds majority of the parliament then it becomes a part of law after authentication by the President.
3. It introduced a federal system in the country. It consisted of a central government and two provincial government comprising East and West Pakistan.
4. It adopted Presidential form of Government in which President was the head Executive of the nation. He was empowered to nominate the ministers of his cabinet.
5. It provided for a Unicameral Legislature.
6. The indirect method for the presidential election had been adopted under which the President was elected by an Electoral College, comprising 80,000 Basic Democrats, equally distributed between the two provinces.
7. In it, there were two provincial governments. Each of them was headed by a governor. He enjoyed powers in the province which the President enjoyed in the centre. The Governor was empowered to appoint provincial ministers with the sanction of the President of Pakistan.
8. Each province was provided with a legislature. It originally consisted of 150 members. However, later this number was increased to 218.
9. According to the 1962 Constitution the President should be a Muslim with the term of 5 years. He was able to

promulgate Ordinances and veto against legislated laws only override-able by two-thirds of the National Assembly.

10. Under the provisions the President was not allowed to hold any office of profit in the service of Pakistan but was not prevented from holding a managing private property.
11. In the 1962 Constitution no law would be passed against the teaching of Quran and Sunnah and the existing laws would be made Islamic in Character.
12. The Constitution of 1962 laid down fundamental rights of speech and expression, freedom to choose profession and freedom to profess religion. With regards to civil rights, familiar right such as the rights of life, livery and property were granted.
13. The judiciary was responsible for the interpretation of laws and executive orders in the light of the principles embodied in a written constitution.
14. A Supreme Judicial council was to be established, consisting of two judges of Supreme Court, chief justice of Supreme Court and two judges of high courts.

The 1962 Constitution established a federal system of government which meant two types of government at the centre and government at the provincial level. At the time there were two provinces and so there were two governments functioning within the limits defined by the constitution. It provided one list of subjects, one set of powers were clearly laid down in the constitution and those were the powers of the central government. So, the one list of subjects pertains to the powers of the central government and the rest of the powers were given to the provincial governments. However, like the constitution of 1956, the federation under 1962 Constitution had a strong centre, because there was a powerful president. A president had enough powers to manage the central as well as provincial affairs. In the context if we look at the emergency powers then there is greater freedom to intervene in the provincial affairs. So, it was a strong centre under the 1962 constitution, although provincial autonomy was there, a provincial setup a governor with his cabinet and governor was appointed by the President and each province had its legislature for law-making purposes. Here the authority of the governor was strong; he was the head of the government at the provincial level. So, we can say that there was provincial autonomy administration but centre was strong under the 1962 Constitution.

Making of 1973 Constitution

The 1973 constitution was the first in Pakistan to be framed by elected representatives. Unlike the 1962 constitution it gave Pakistan a Parliamentary democracy with executive power concentrated in the office of the Prime Minister and the formal head of the state-the President-limiting to acting on the advice of the Prime Minister. In contrast the 1962 constitution granted executive power to the President and abolished the office of the Prime Minister. It also institutionalized the intervention of military in politics by providing that for twenty years, the President or the defence minister must be a person who had held a rank not lower than that of lieutenant general in the army (*Marinos and Adam, 2011*). The 1962 constitution was suspended in 1969 and abrogated in 1972. In the seven years period between 1962-69, numerous political and economic upheavals, protests and a war with India in 1965 Ayub Khan left the scene and took his constitution with him after imposing martial law on March 25, 1969. The first ever general elections were held under the new Chief Martial Law Administrator General Yahya Khan according to the Legal Framework Order (LFO) he introduced abolishing One-Unit, ending East West parity and utilizing adult franchise. Due to lack of effective conflict resolution skills, East Pakistan separated on December 16th, 1971 becoming independent Bangladesh.

After the dismemberment of Pakistan in 1971, the Pakistan People's Party (PPP) formed the government and partially enacted the 1962 constitution. President Zulfikar Ali Bhutto called for a constitutional convention and invited the leaders of all political parties to meet him on 17 April 1972 that include the leaders and constitutional experts of the Islamic political parties, conservative parties, socialists and communist parties. The law experts, constitutional analysts, and country's reputed clergyman worked on formulating the constitution that represents the will and desire of people. Unlike earlier attempts, the convention was not meant for new laws or piecemeal alterations, but for the sole and express purpose of revising the 1956 articles. On 20 October 1972, the draft was revived by all leaders of the political parties and signed the declaration of adopting the constitution in the National Assembly on 2 February 1973. Ratified unanimously on 19 April 1973, the constitution came full effect on 14 August 1973. On the same day the successful vote of confidence movement in the Parliament endorsed Zulfikar Ali Bhutto as the elected Prime Minister.

In contrast to the constitutions of India and Bangladesh, the constitution reflected a heavy compromise over several issues to maintain a delicate balance of power among the country's institutions. The constitution defined the role of Islam. Pakistan was to be a Federation of Four Provinces and shall be known as the Islamic Republic of Pakistan, introduction of checks and balances, separation of powers, and provided the federal system under which the government should governed. The constitution established a "Bicameral Parliament" as a legislative authority that consists of the Senate as Upper house and National Assembly as Lower house. Another major innovative introduction in the Constitution is the establishment of the National Finance Commission (NFC) consisting of the Provincial and Finance Minister and other members to advice on distribution of revenues between the federation and the provinces. The constitution's first parts introduce the Islamic way of life, promotion of local government, full participation of women in national life, protection of minorities, promotion of social and economic well being of the people, and strengthening the bonds with the Muslim world and to work for international peace.

Unlike the previous documents the constitution cannot be changed, instead constitutional amendments are passed; altering its effects (*Khan, 2012*). Amendments to the constitution are made through the Parliament, where a two-thirds majority and voting is required in both houses for a constitutional amendment to take its effect, in accordance to the Constitution. In addition to this, certain amendments which pertain to the federal nature of the constitution must be ratified by a majority of state legislatures. As of 2015, 21 amendments have been introduced to the constitution. Among the most important of these are the Eighth (1985) and seventeenth (2004) which changed the government from a parliamentary system to a semi Presidential system. However, in 2010 the Eighteenth Amendment reversed these expansions of presidential powers, returning the government to a parliamentary republic and also defined any attempt to subvert, abrogate, or suspend the constitution as an act of high treason.

However, from the start of the framing of constitution in Pakistan, the most contentious issue has been and continues to be relationship between the centre and the provincial units. No state can truly be a federation if it is centralized to the extent that Pakistan is. Case in point is the delay in the National Finance Commission (NFC) award that has caused unnecessary harm to the provincial governments. Secondly, there needs to be explicit mention of the items in the provincial list-which also needs expansion-and these items should be under the sole jurisdiction of the province. In other words the current list needs to be replaced by a provincial list. The centre should retain authority on matters of Foreign Relations, Money, Defence and Communication but Education needs to be dealt with by provinces. Provisions can be taken by the government to ensure quality education by taking nation wide tests for higher education and the provinces need to work together so that an individual getting a degree in one province is eligible for a post in another province as well.

Federalism in Constitutions of Pakistan

In general, there are two major modes of federalism in which the concept is put into practice. The first mode is called dual federalism. Under this modality the constitution is designed to create two separate and independent tiers of government. The relationships are mediated and spheres are defined by clearly demarcated areas of responsibility. The second is the cooperative federalism. This modality takes various parts of the government as part of single government system. It works through cooperation between various levels of government. The various levels of governments are characterized more by cooperation and shared functions than by conflict and competition. In the case of federalism in Pakistan, it had denied the views expressed by Muhammad Ali Jinnah in November 1945, "The theory of Pakistan guarantees that federal units of the National Government would have all the autonomy that you will find in the constitution of the United States of America, Canada and Australia. But certain vital powers will remain vested in the Central Government such as monetary system, national defence and federal responsibilities".

Despite all the politics of representation and language, the constitution which emerged in 1956 was federal in character but centralized (*Adeney, 2009*) in spirit which deliberately undermined the ethnic cleavages' and the one-unit formula. As one scholar has rightly put it, 'This created two provinces, one linguistically homogeneous (East Pakistan spoke Bengali) and the other linguistically heterogeneous (Western wing spoke Punjabi) but there were other significant linguistic groups who spoke Pashtu, Sindhi, Urdu or Balochi. Although the constitution tried to soften the centralizing impact of the Government of India Act 1935 since under the article 106(i), the federal list was shortened with thirty items which were sixty-one earlier and provincial list had 94 items. While the concurrent list was also reduced to 19 items there are views that it was still enough to centralize the administrative and economic development system by the central government. The central government had overriding powers in the matters of economic development, national security, and coordination amongst the provinces (*Choudhury, 2005*). Unfortunately, in a sudden development the Legislative Assembly was dissolved in 1958 ahead of anticipated national elections and the reins of power later went in the hands of the military, with Commander-in-Chief Ayub Khan who ruled the country under marital law between 1958-1962 without any constitutional apparatus. The dissolution of assembly created serious difficulties in relationships between the Eastern and Western parts of Pakistan and had long term impact on the performance of its federal system.

In 1962 a new constitution based on "Basic Democracies" while retaining the One Unit was created (*Kundi and Jahangir,2002*). At the time Ayub Khan was able to get support for continuation of his rule from the military and civil bureaucracy. Being over-developed federal institutional designs (*Alavi,1972*) under the imperialist British Raj, these two institutions provided the strength of execution. In other words, the system was called close to the British vice regal system of 1940s (*Sayeed,1967*). In fact, as to the One Unit and Basic Democracies Ayub Khan ignored the recommendations of the Committee which was formed for the constitution of 1956. Both of these arrangements had recommended for federal form of government with maximum autonomy given to the federating units. Ayub Khan was more interested in having a strong central government with appeal to Pakistani nationalism. Nevertheless, the constitution retained the federal structure of 1956 constitution and had three lists – Centre, Provincial and Concurrent. Going tangent to the federal system of governance, 49 items were listed as federal while residual powers were given to the federating units but no items were specified. Emerging from the support of military and civil bureaucracy, the constitution tilted the balance of power towards the central government and federal legislature with provincial legislature having virtually nothing to legislate about. After seven years in a significant development Yahya Khan succeeded Ayub khan by imposing martial law in 1969, abrogated the One Unit, and conducted free and fair elections. The results of the elections were both surprising and devastating that ultimately led to dismemberment of East Pakistan to become Bangladesh in December 1971.

After the creation of Bangladesh in 1971, a new constitution was drafted in 1973 which replaced the interim constitution of 1971. It retained a federal system, but unlike the previous constitution created a bicameral legislature. It had a upper house called Senate having 60 seats and a lower house called National Assembly which had 200 seats. The four units of the federation equally represented in the Senate while the National Assembly seats were divided on population basis. It is also distinguishable from the previous ones because it created the Senate having equal representation of all federating units so that similar provinces like Balochistan are represented and the Senate plays a role in the system of checks and balances. The 1973 constitution created the form of federal structure of the state and had two lists: one federal and the other concurrent. In the upper house of Senate, each federating unit contributed 14 members for four years term while half of them retired after two years. The federal list having 67 subjects was for the federal government while the concurrent list provided opportunity for the provincial legislature to draft laws on the subjects However, in case of a dispute, according to Article 143, the rights of the central government must be supreme and prevail.

In addition to these, in order to strengthen the spirit of federation, a Council of Common Interest (CCI) was created. It was to be appointed by the President and must have Chief Ministers of provinces with equal members from the Federal Government. The Council had exclusive jurisdiction over hearing of complaints regarding water supplies from the natural resources such as supply of waters from rivers. The Council was also supposed to formulate policies related to railways, electricity, oil and gas and industrial development. But surprisingly, in terms of functioning of the constitution, the Bhutto regime which drafted this document showed inkling for a stronger role of the Central Government which created disgruntlement amongst the Baloch and Pashton parts of the federating units. The federal government also tried to silence the opposition parties within the National Assembly and behaved like a Bonapartist State. The state of affairs gave a serious blow to federalism and what was left was crowded out by the martial law regime of Zia-Ul-Haq who put the constitution in abeyance for eight years.

Status of Provinces and Constitutional Amendments

The Eighth Amendment is considered as a landmark in the constitutional history of Pakistan. It not only altered the very form of the constitution from purely parliamentary to semi-presidential, but also changed the constitutional and political history of the country. The 1973 Constitution of Pakistan envisaged a Parliamentary System of government with the balance of power tilted towards the Prime Minister. The President could not exercise his powers without the concurrence of the Prime Minister. While the constitution was held in abeyance with the coming of Zia-ul-Haq the country was run in a unitary fashion. During this period a number of presidential orders were issued. These orders took the form of the 8th amendment when the constitution was restored through a Presidential order. This order was known as Revival of the Constitution of 1973 Order (RCO) on March 2, 1985. In this order sixty-five Articles were amended, substituted, added, modified, deleted and omitted. After this amendment office of the President was made more powerful than it was under the original constitution of 1973. Now President was given the right to nominate the Prime Minister, Governors of the Provinces and Judges of High Court and Supreme Court, including the Chief Justice. Democratically elected Prime Minister thus became subservient to the President.

However, the most controversial power awarded to the office of the President was under the Article 58 (2) b, which was the power of dissolution of the National Assembly at his own discretion. The said Article changed the entire complexion of the constitution. After the passing of Article 58(2), b the National Assemblies were dissolved on four occasions using its powers. The dissolution of the Assembly by President Zia-ul-Haq in 1988, President Ghulam Ishaq Khan in 1990 and in 1993 and President Farooq Leghari in 1996 are subject to a lot of speculation. In the amendment the federal structure of the constitution was not changed. It rather increased the legislative powers, tenure of members and provincial representation in the Senate – the upper house of Parliament. The Senate has equal representation of all provinces and representation from Federally Administered Tribal Area (FATA). The number of members of the Senate were also increased from sixty-three to eighty-seven with five seats from each province reserved for technocrats, ulema, or professionals. Seats for women were also increased in the National Assembly from ten to twenty and this increase continued till the third general elections. In addition, the Senate was enabled to initiate legislation as needed with two third majority rather than simple majority to legislate. These amendments in the Constitution gave greater powers to the smaller provinces in the matters of decision making.

Seventeenth Amendment is basically the Legal Framework Order that has been accepted as part of the constitution with minor modifications and may be therefore, termed as an LFO amended Constitution. Unfortunately, On October 12, 1999 Pakistan again lapsed into a military regime when General Pervez Musharraf staged a coup d'état against the elected government of Nawaz Sharif. Day after the take over, on 13 October General Pervez Musharraf, in his speech announced a seven-point agenda which included a clause about strengthening of the federation by removal of inter provincial disharmony and restoration of national cohesion. To continue to holding power beyond three years, as mandated by the Supreme Court General Pervez Musharraf held a referendum on April 30, 2002 and whose result went in his favour. Following the result in his favour the second LFO was promulgated on August 21, 2002 which tried to centralise the system of government though it paradoxically professed to have established a reformed local government system. The LFO of 2002 has been described as against the spirit of the constitution- parliamentary form of government and provincial autonomy.

The general elections were held in February 2002 and having alliance with religious parties, the 17th amendment was passed in December 2003. This amendment again increased the powers of the President who could now dissolve the legislative assembly however, a clause was added that the Supreme Court will have the jurisdiction for a review of the decision. Besides, the amendment did not alter the federal character of the state in any fundamental way despite having introduced a new shape of local government system.

However, the 18th Amendment is the latest amendment to the Constitution of 1973. It was passed by the National Assembly on April 8, 2010, the Senate passed it on April 15, 2010 and the President signed it on April 19, 2010. The amendment removed the power of the President to dissolve Parliament. Presidential assent turned Pakistan from a semi Presidential to a parliamentary republic, and renaming North-West Frontier Province to Khyber Pakhtunkhwa. In addition, the amendment has increased the judicial independence by which appointment of judges in Supreme Court will be done through a judicial Commission. The President will not unilaterally impose emergency in the provinces and the President will also not appoint the Chief Election Commission. Under the 18th Amendment of the Constitution, a serious attempt has been made to revive the following principles of the 1973 Constitution:

1. Federal Parliamentary System of government.
2. Prime Minister as Chief Executive.
3. President to be a symbolic head – bound by the advice of the Prime Ministers in all matters.

The package is expected to counter the sweeping powers amassed by the Presidency under former Presidents General Zia-Ul-Haq and General Pervez Musharraf and to ease political instability in Pakistan. In line the 18th amendment that has been passed by the parliament, gives the provincial governments greater autonomy under the constitution by abolishing the concurrent list and other related provisions. In addition, the laws governing marriage, contracts, firearms possession, labour, educational curriculums, environmental pollution, bankruptcy and in 40 other diverse areas the provinces would have exclusive jurisdiction and each provincial assembly will be responsible for drafting its own laws on the issues. It also potentially impacts the mandate of several federal ministers and by implication increases the roles and responsibilities or the related institutions and administrative structures at the provincial level.

However, if after the passing of 18th constitutional amendment, the people of small provinces were once again cheated away and the promise of provincial autonomy was largely limited to cosmetic changes and use of buzz words. Indeed, it was the long-standing demand of provinces to do away with concurrent list and restore sole provincial jurisdiction as provinces had enjoyed under British before

Pakistan was created. What actually has happened under the 18th amendment that the central government has assumed the jurisdiction over most important subjects and let provinces have jurisdiction over less important subjects? On several counts the 18th amendment failed to meet expectations of small provinces:

1. Failed to reaffirm the principles of 1940 Resolution principles namely the promises of provincial autonomy and sovereignty.
2. Failed to include Baluchi, Pashto, Punjabi, and Sindhi as national languages of Pakistan.
3. In reference to Article 39 it failed to include a provision that the military will strive to build a truly national organization that is ethnically-balanced and representative of all minorities of Pakistan. A provision should have been made to achieve this balance within five to ten years.
4. Likewise, in reference to Articles 59 and 73 it failed to change the composition of Senate as the exactly 25 members from each province will be elected to Senate in a national vote and would hold a veto over any law passed by the National Assembly.
5. There is also inconsistency between Federal and Provincial laws as per Article 143.
6. In addition, a disturbing change has been made in Article 63 which would enable every convicted criminal to be part of the Parliament after five years of his release from jail irrespective of the fact why that person was convicted.
7. The amendment made in Article 156 reversed the earlier provision and now the Prime Minister can appoint four members of the National Economic Council (NEC), thereby further diminishing the participation of provincial governments in how national economy is handled. This is another serious attack against provincial autonomy.

References

Ahmed, Sheikh Nadeem, Begum Sajida (2015). Historical Perspective of Political and Constitutional Development in Pakistan, *Journal of Humanities and Social Science,* Vol. 20, Issue 2, pp. 77-89.

Yousuf, Hamid (1999). *Pakistan: A Study of Political Development 1947-97*. Lahore: Sang-e-Meel Publications, p. 72.

Marinos, Diamantides and Adam Gearey (2011). *Islam Law and Identity*. Routledge, p. 198.

Khan, Iftikhar A. (2012). 'Parliament can't make laws repugnant to Constitution: Chief Justice. *Dawn News,* 24 June.

Adeney, K. (2009). 'The Limitations of Non-consociational Federalism: The Example of Pakistan'. *Ethnopolitics,* Vol. 8, No. 1, pp. 87-106.

Ariyo, A. (2003). Theories of Federalism, Fiscal Policy and Growth in Africa: Fiscal Federalism, Decentralisation and the Incidence of Taxation. *Economic Commission for Africa,* Addis Ababa, 7-9 October.

Alavi, H. (1972). 'The State in Post-colonial Societies: Pakistan and Bangladesh'. *New Left Review,* Vol. 74, pp. 59-81.

Choudhury, G.W.) 2005). *Constitutional Development in Pakistan*. Lahore: Law Inn Publishers.

Kundi, M.A. and Jahangir, A.M. (2002). Federalism in Pakistan: Issues and Adjustment. *Asian Affairs* (online) pp. 23-36.

Sayeed, K.B. (1967). *The Political System of Pakistan*. Boston, Houghton Mifflin Co. p. 101.

3

Province: Punjab, Sindh and Khyber Pakhtunkhwa

Today, the nation Pakistan is composed of its four provinces- Punjab, Sindh, Khyber Pakhtunkhwa and Balochistan along with several territories. In the context several findings show an existence of diversities among different provinces which spread to their culture, language, economic status, political influence and even to historical background. As a result, the nature of subcultures within provinces and the level of their impact in socio-political milieu remain a significant consideration in national polities. During the 1960s the economic disparity between East and West Pakistan fuelled the movement and subsequently Bangladesh emerged in 1971. Also, in late 1970s and 1980s the issue of regional disparity between the provinces acquired explosive potential. Among provinces not only overall income inequality is prevalent but also a vast gap is existent in rural and urban areas, labour income and non-labour income. Identification of inequality in different spheres is important if policies aiming at reducing inequalities are considered seriously as different cause require different policies. The structures of inequalities in the provinces are required to reduce urgently in view of emerging disappointments which pose a direct threat to national unity and integrity.

Province Punjab

The name 'Punjab' is compound of two Persian words Panj (five) and ab (water) and was introduced to the region by the Turko-Persian conquerers of India and more formally popularised during the Mughal Empire. Punjab literally means "The Land of Five Rivers" referring to the rivers: Jhelum, Chenab, Ravi, Sutlej, and Beas. It is the second largest province of the country spread over 205,344 kilometer after Balochistan and is located in the northwestern edge of the geologic Indian plate in South Central Asia. The capital and largest city is Lahore which was the historical capital of the wider Punjab region. Other important district cities include Multan, Faisalabad, Sheikhpura, Sialkot, Gujranwala, Jhelum and Rawalpindi. Nearly 60% of Pakistan's population lives in Punjab. The geographical position and a large multi-ethnic population strongly influence Punjab's outlook on national affair and induces in Panjab a keen awareness of the problems of the Pakistan's other important provinces and territories. With an estimated population of 110,012,442 as of 2017, it is bordered by the Pakistan provinces of Sindh, Balochistan, and Khyber Pakhtunkhwa. It also shares borders with the Indian states of Punjab, Rajasthan and Jammu and Kashmir.

Punjab has been inhabited since ancient times and Indus Valley Civilization, dating to 2600 BCE was first discovered at Harappa. In 326 BCE, Alexander the Great defeated king Porus at the battle of the Hydaspes near Mong, Punjab. It was later invaded by Tamerlane, Babur, and Nader Shah. But Punjab reached the height of its splendour during the reign of the Mughal Empire, which for a time ruled from Lahore. Following a successful rebellion, Sikh-led armies claimed Lahore in 1759. Punjab also remained central to the independence movements of both India and Pakistan, with Lahore being site of both declaration of Indian

Independence and the resolution calling for the establishment of Pakistan. The province was formed when the Punjab province of British India was divided along religious boundaries in 1947 by the Radcliff Line after partition (*Dalrymple, 2015*). Now it became West Punjab and East Punjab. Western Punjab was assimilated into the new country of Pakistan, while East Punjab became part of modern-day India. The part of the Punjab now in Pakistan was a major region of British Punjab, and was home to a large minority Hindus and Sikh migrated to India while Muslim refugees from India settled in the Western Punjab and across Pakistan.

Economy

Today, Punjab has the largest economy which contributes 57.5% to Pakistan's Gross Domestic Product, followed by Sindh 27%, Khyber Pakhtunkhwa 8%, Balochistan 3%, Azad Kashmir 2.3% and Gilgit-Baltistan 1.5% respectively. In fact, its economy has diversified base spanning from agriculture to telecommunication, information technology manufacturing industry, engineering, steel, chemicals and construction materials. Over the last 65 years, Punjab's economy has done better than the average for Pakistan. For the final quarter of the 20th century the provincial product grow at a rate 0.1 per cent more than the national average; 5.1 per cent a year compared to five per cent for Pakistan as a whole. According to the annual report published by the Lahore-based Institute of Public Policy an interesting finding was observed about the relative rates of economic growth for Pakistan taken as a whole for the province of Punjab. The province does much better than the country when the economy is moving at a sluggish pace. For instance, in the relatively sluggish 1990s, when the national product increased at a rate of 4.4 per cent a year, Punjab's gross income increased at a rate of 4.8 per cent (*Burki, 2012*). Likewise, its share in agriculture is larger than the national average.

The economy of Punjab is mainly agriculture based,

although industry makes a substantial contribution. Despite its dry climate, extensive irrigation makes it a rich agricultural region. The province is playing a leading role in agricultural production. It contributes about 63740.4 thousand tonnes which is about 59.85 per cent towards total agricultural production in the country. Commodity wise Punjab is contributing 74.12 per cent cereals, 81.75 per cent pulses, 55.45 per cent cash crops, 9.39 per cent edible oil, 59.95 per cent fruits and 77.54 per cent vegetables of the total production ofthese commodities at national level (*Badar, 2007*). Total agricultural production of Punjab over the years has also increased considerably. Majority of farmers in the Punjab are small with land holdings up to 5 hectares and owners of such farms are practicing subsistence farming under deficit as theiryield of major crops is far less than the progressive farms. However, the agricultural sector in recent past has initiated its journey towards commercialisation but this sector has not yet become fully self supportive. Farming community lacks proper knowledge and is not properly equipped to meet the challenges of modern agriculture and the World Trade Organization (WTO). Majority of farmers are illiterate and are unable to make rational decisions on their own and need institutional support.

Table-01

Historical Population Figures

Year	Population	Urban	Rural
1951	20,540,762	3,568,076	16,972,686
1961	25,463,974	5,475,922	19,988,052
1972	37,607,423	9,182,695	28,424,728
1981	47,292,441	13,051,646	34,240,795
1998	73,621,290	23,019,025	50,602,265
2017	110,012,615	70,008,451	40,401,164

Since independence, Punjab also industrialised rapidly and in later years new factories were established in Lahore,

Sargodha, Multan, Gujarat, Gujranwala, Sialkot and Wah. Now it is Pakistan's most industrialised province with the industrial sector making up to 24% of the province's gross domestic product (*Planning Development Department 2015*). Punjab is known in Pakistan for its relative prosperity and has the lowest rate of poverty amongst all Pakistani provinces. A clear divide is present between the northern and southern portions of the province with poverty rates in prosperous northern Punjab amongst the lowest in Pakistan, while some in south Punjab are among the most impoverished. Punjab is also one of South Asia's most urbanised regions with approximately 40% of people living in urban areas. Its human development index rankings are high relative to the rest of Pakistan.

The major ethnic groups of Pakistan in numerical size include: Punjabis, Pashtuns, Sindhis, Siddis, Saraikis, Muhajirs, Baloch, Hindkowans, Chitralis Gujarati and other smaller groups such as Kashmiris, Kalash, Burusho, Khowar, Hazara, Shina, Kalyu and Balti are found in the northern parts of the country. Among them Punjabis in Pakistan are an Indo-Aryan group of people and can be divided into sub-clans. Although the Nuristanis constitute another sub grouping amongst the Indo-Iranian peoples but are not indigenous to Pakistan. Punjabis speak the language called Punjabi, a northwestern Indo-Aryan Language. They have many different dialects and that depends in what region of Punjab they are from. They make up 78.7 million (45%) of Pakistan's total population and are divided into several tribes such as Arain, Awan, Rajput, Gujar, Jat (*Nazir,1993*). In addition, Punjabi Muslims are a linguistic, geographic and religious ethnic group living in the region of Punjab, found between eastern Pakistan and northern India. Forming the majority of Punjabi ethnicity at large Punjabi Muslims are those who profess Islam and speak the Punjabi language. With a population of more than 90 million, they are the largest ethnic group in Pakistan and the third largest Muslim ethnicity after the Arabs and Bengalis. The majority of Punjabi Muslims are adherents of the Sunni branch of Islam. The homelands of Punjabi Muslims are mainly concentrated in the Pakistani province of Punjab.

Table-2

Languages Spoken in Punjab

Name of Language	Spoken in %
Punjabi	75.2%
Saraiki	17.4%
Urdu	4.5%
Pashto	1.2%
Balochi	0.7%
Sindhi	0.1%
Others	0.9%

Table-3

Religions in Punjab

Religions	Followers in %
Islam	97.21%
Christianity	2.31%
Others (Sikhs, Parsis and Hindus)	0.48%

The Punjabis found in Pakistan belong to groups known as biradaris. In addition, Punjabi society is divided into two divisions, the Zamindar groups or qoums, traditionally associated with farming and moeens, who are traditionally artisans. Some Zamindars are further divided into groups such as the Rajputs, Jats, Shaikhs, or Muslim Khatris, Gujjars, Awans, Arains and Syeds. People from neighbouring regions, such as Kashmiris, Pashtuns and Baluch, also form sizeable portion of the Punjabi population. A large number of Punjabis descend from the groups historically associated with skilled profession and crafts such as Sunar, Lohar, Kumhar, Tarkhan, Julaha, Mochi, Hajjam, Chhimba Darzi, Teli, Lalari, Mallaah, Dhobi and Mirasi. Punjabi people have traditionally and historically been farmers and soldiers which has transferred into modern times with their dominance of agriculture and military fields in Pakistan. Also, they have been quite prominent politically, having had many elected members of Parliament.

Until 1947, the province of united Punjab was ruled by a coalition comprising the Indian National Congress, the Sikh-led Shiromani Akali Dal and the Unionist Muslim League. However, the growth of Muslim nationalism led to the All India Muslim League becoming the dominant party in the 1946 elections. As Muslim separatism increased, the opposition from Punjabis Hindus and Sikhs increased substantially. Communal violence on the eve of Indian independence led to the dismissal of the coalition government, although the succeeding League ministry was unable to form the government and secure majority. Along with the province of Bengal, Punjab was partitioned on religious lines-the Muslim-majority West becoming part of the new Muslim state of Pakistan, and the Hindu and Sikh East remaining in India. West Punjab was virtually cleansed of its Hindu and Sikh populations, who were forced to leave for India, while East Punjab and Delhi were virtually cleansed of their Muslim population.

Political Status of Punjab After 1947

In fact, the absence of central-state apparatus in the territories constituting Pakistan gave it a different turn not only in initial years but also thereafter. As a consequence, provinces continued to be the main arena of politics. Those engaged in constructing and managing the new central government apparatus were politicians with the weakest or no social bases of support in the province and they were not able to stand their ground against civil servants trained in the true tradition of colonial bureaucratic authoritarianism (*Jalal, 1995*). This tilting in the balance of power from the political to the administrative arms of the state bent relations between the centre and the provinces out of shape and also provided a pretext for incessant bickerings between Punjabis and the non-Punjabis (*Bose and Jalal, 2004*). The ensuing tussle between the centre and the provinces augured poorly for the political process.

Earlier too, during the British administration Punjabis showed the most promise in the region and they were considered by them as the most quickly adaptive of British military operations and practices and therefore best serve their interests (*Hurst, 1996*). As a result, the British most often chose Punjabis for recruitment in the British colonial armies-shortly after partition, Punjabis constituted 66 per cent of Pakistan's army. Their predominance in the military, in turn, led to the formation of a Punjabi elite class, whose greater access to education and influential positions in the government paved the way for later Punjabi control of the bureaucracies and government departments. An example of the clout that the Punjabis have wielded to Pakistani politics is evident in the decision to move Pakistan's capital from Karachi to Sindh to Islamabad in the Punjab during Ayub Khan's regime. As the most powerful and highly compensated ethnicity in Pakistan's government, the Punjabis are often the targets of the other ethnicities of Pakistan. Many of the disenfranchised view the Punjabis as having received a greater share of Pakistan's wealth than is their due. In line initially, the idea of One Unit System was floated and later piloted by the Punjabi clout.

As a result of the 'One Unit Scheme' all the provinces of West Pakistan were treated as single province from 14 October 1955 to 30 June 1970 and the province of Punjab took birth, in its present form on 1 July 1970. Earlier in case of Punjab, there was direct governor rule in 1949-1951, when the provincial chief minister of that time was removed and assemblies dissolved. The Governor of Punjab is appointed head of state of the provincial government. The governor is designated by the Prime Minister and is normally regarded a ceremonial post. However, throughout the history of Pakistan, the powers of provincial governors were vastly increased, when the provincial assemblies were dissolved and the administrative role came under direct control of the governors, as in the cases of martial laws of 1958-1972 and 1977-1985, and governor rules of 1999-2002. The first governor of Punjab was Sir Francis Mudie when it was first formed on 15 August 1947, while the present incumbent is Malik Muhammad Rafique Rajwana continuing since 7 May 2015.

The Provincial Assembly of Punjab is a unicameral legislature of elected representatives of the province of Punjab. In government, unicameral legislature is the practice of having one legislative or parliamentary chamber. The unicameral legislature, called Assembly is located in Lahore. It was established under Article 106 of the Constitution of Pakistan as having a total of 371 seats with 66 seats reserved for women and eight reserved for non-Muslims. Further, according to clause 2-A of Article 130, the Governor of a province invites the member of the Provincial Assembly to be the Chief Minister who commands the confidence of the majority of the members of the Provincial Assembly as ascertained in the session of the Assembly summoned for the purpose in accordance with the provisions of the constitution. As per constitutional provision the last election held in province Punjab in May 2013 and Mian Muhammad Shehbaz Sharif of Pakistan Muslim League is the Chief Minister of Punjab since 8 June 2013.

It is commonly said that Punjab is synonymous with Pakistan, and vice versa, which seems to relegate the other provinces and autonomous regions to the status of outliers.

From the start in politics, Pakistan's elites, political, bureaucratic and military have long hailed from Punjab and shaped the country's policies to the Province's advantage. Till recently (2009), Punjab received the lion's share of nation revenues simply by virtue of having the largest population, never mind its actual needs or contributions to the national budget. Also, the government and military have long allotted prime agricultural land and urban real estate in other parts of Pakistan to Punjabi officers and senior bureaucrats (*Yusuf, 2014*). But on the other, Punjab itself is not a monolith. Some of the Province's southern districts are among the country's poorest, and their inhabitants have grudges of their own against Lahore-based politicians. Water and energy shortages kept Punjab's economic growth rate at 2.5 per cent between 2007 and 2011, compared with 3.4 percent for the country overall.

In addition, these resentments animate the politics of Pakistan's other provinces and threaten national unity. A separatist movement in Baluchistan tapped grievances against Punjabis and they say that Punjabis are exploiting Baluch gas and mineral resources to spur industrial growth in the province. Concerns about Punjabi domination have soared since the spring of 2013, when Prime Minister Nawaz Sharif of the Pakistan Muslim League was returned to power for the third time. He belongs to a Lahore-based industrial family with close ties to Punjab's business elite and a can-do-attitude to governance that features flashy development schemes. This apart, Punjab has been able to progress because it has been relatively unimpeded by terrorism. Earlier in 2008, Shabaz Sharif, Nawaz's brother and Punjab's Chief Minister appealed to the Pakistani Taliban not to attack the province and the request was largely heeded. Likewise, the PMLN government at the centre started pushing for peace talks with the Taliban. In line, the central government is considering concessions, including swamping prisoners, granting and amnesty to Taliban fighters and even giving the group a political role in the Federally Administered Tribal Area (FATA) along the border with Afghanistan. Many Pakistanis describe the policies as a ploy to sacrifice the tribal areas in order to save Lahore. Such perceptions only heighten inter-provincial tensions, just at a time when the county needs to be more united than ever.

Sindh Province of Pakistan

Sindh is one of the four main provinces of modern Pakistan having an area of 140,914 km and 47,886,051 population according to census held in 2017. Others alike it is a state of federal parliamentary republic, more or less at similar system of government with a directly elected Provincial Assembly in which the leader of the largest party or coalition is elected Chief Minister. In the country provincial governors are appointed by the Federal Government of Pakistan whose tenure lasts for five years. It is comprised of a former Sindh Province, State of Khairpur and former Federal Capital territory. After conquest by the British in 1843 Sindh had been part of the Bombay Presidency but on 1 April 1936 Sindh Division was separated from the Bombay Presidency and made into a province of British India. On the eve of independence and partition of the subcontinent Sindh Assembly passed resolution of joining the newly State Pakistan and became a province on 14 August 1947. Again, the province was merged into the province of West Pakistan in October 1955 under the One Unit Policy but regained its status of province after dissolution of the policy on 1 July 1970. Its status as province is continuing as provided in Pakistan's constitution of 1973.

Historical Background

The word 'Sindh' is derived from the Sanskrit term Sindhu which is a reference to Indus River. The Greek who conquered Sindh in 325 BC under the command of Alexander the Great rendered it as Indos, hence the modern Indus. Sindh's first known village settlements date as far back as

7000 BCE. Permanent settlements at Mehrgarh, currently in Balochistan, to the west expanded into Sindh. This culture blossomed over several millennia and gave rise to the Indus valley Civilization around 3000 BCE. It was a Bronze Age civilization (3300-1300 BCE; mature period 2600-1900 BCE) mainly in the northwestern regions of South Asia, extending from what today is northeast Afghanistan to Pakistan and northwest India (Singh, 2008). This indigenous civilization collapsed around 1700 BCE perhaps due to a massive earthquake. It was conquered by the Persian Achaemenid Empire in the 6th century BC. Later in the late 4th century it was conquered by a mixed army led by Macedonian Greeks under Alexander the Great. In 711 AD, Muhammad bin Qasim conquered the Sindh and Indus Valley, bringing South Asian societies into contact with Islam. Most probably, the Balochi people migrated form Baluchistan during the Little Ice Age and settled in Sindh and Punjab. The Little Ice Age is conventionally defined as a period extending from the sixteenth to the nineteenth centuries or alternatively, from about 1300 to about 1850 (*Matthews and Briffa, 2005*). In the year 1524 Sindhi Amirs welcomed Mughal Empire and in the coming centuries Sindh became a region loyal to the Mughals. When the British East India Company forces led by General Charles James Napier came, he conquered Sindh in February 1843 defeating the Talpur Balochs at the Battle of Miani. After 1853 the British divided Sindh into districts and later made it part of British India's Bombay Presidency.

From the earlier, although Sindh had a culture of religious syncretism, communal harmony and tolerance due to Sindh's strong Sufi culture in both Sindhi Muslims and Sindhi Hindus partook, the mostly Muslim peasantry was oppressed by the Hindu moneylending class and also by the landed Muslim elite (*Kumar and Kothari, 2016*). Sindhi Muslims eventually demanded the separation of Sindh from Bombay Presidency, a move opposed by Sindhi Hindus. Another campaign in the early 20th century which attracted Sindhi

Muslims was the Khilafat Movement for which support had been generated by the Sufi pirs of Sindh. The Khilafat Movement (1919-22) was a Pan Islamic, political protest campaign launched by Muslims of India to influence the British government not to abolish the Ottoman Caliphate. In that time period Sindh emerged at the forefront of the Khilafat cause. By the time Sindhi nationalist movement had begun in favour of Pakistan movement, mainly out of a desire of the Sindhi Muslim business classes to drive out their Hindu competitors. By 1936 Sindh was separated from the Bombay Presidency. Elections in 1937 resulted in local Sindhi parties winning the bulk of seats. Although Sindhis had expressed civil support initially for partition, several events changed their enthusiasm for the creation of Pakistan (*Kukreja, 2003*). By the mid-1940s the Muslim League gained a foothold in the province and after winning over the support of local Sufi pirs (*Ansari, 1992*) came to have the support of the overwhelming majority of Sindhi Muslims for its campaign to create Pakistan.

In fact, Sindh had never submitted to British subjugation and always played an important role in the struggle for Pakistan. The Muslims of Sindh supported the 'Jihad Movement' under the leadership of Syed Ahmed Shaheed Barelvi and also fought the British in the first war of independence of 1857. In line the separation of Sindh from the Bombay Presidency was the first step towards the foundation of Pakistan. When Muslims of Sindh realised the importance of separation of Sindh, the All India Muslim League passed a resolution in 1925 urging separation. Subsequently, under the Government of India Act 1935, Sindh was made a province with its own Legislative Assembly on April 1, 1936. It followed the Sindh Provincial Muslim League Conference held its first session at Karachi in October 1938 under the presidentship of Quaid-i-Azam. Again, it was the province of Sindh which first adopted the resolution for an independent Muslim state. As the movement for Pakistan moved forward it was the only Sindh Assembly of undivided India which passed a resolution on March 23, 1943, presented by G.M. Syed, a Sindhi leader, on the lines of the Lahore Resolution in support of Pakistan (*Eijazuddin, 2010*). And lastly on June 26, 1947 the Sindh Assembly, at a special session, decided to join the new Pakistan Constituent Assembly and became the first province to opt for Pakistan. This dominating role of Sindh suddenly changed in Pakistan's Post-independence era.

Sindh After 1947

The cultural homogeneity of Sindh that embraced both Hindu and Muslim speakers of Sindhi in the colonial period was severely disrupted by the partition of India and Pakistan in 1947. Most Hindu Sindhi speakers migrated to India, where they form a minority scattered among speakers of other languages. Their leading position in the urban society of Sindh in Pakistan was assumed by the immigrants known as Muhajirs, the Urdu-speaking Muslims who came from the town of India. Initially till January 1948, the Province Sindh unlike the experiences of Punjab or Bihar or, to a lesser extent, Bengal violence was not constitutive. There were remarkably few episodes of physical violence in Sindh. For example, three months after partition, when Acharya Kripalani visited Sindh as President of the Indian National Congress, noted, 'There was only a slight exodus of the Hindus and Sikhs from Sindh. It did not suffer from any virulent fanaticism. To whatever faith the Sindhis belonged, they were powerfully influenced by Sufi and Vedanta thoughts. This made for tolerance (*Kripalani, 2004*).

Unlike the provinces of Bengal and Punjab, Sindh was not partitioned; it went in its entirety to Pakistan, thus avoiding the complete separation of religious communities and the tearing apart of families, homes, and linguistic and cultural communities that were the hallmarks of partition. Although the Karachi riot of 6 January 1948 was local and directed mostly at Sikhs from Punjab seeking refuge in Karachi, Sindh was engulfed by fear. As a result, the rich and prosperous Hindus of Sindh began to flee, more out of fear of persecution and violence rather than its actual experience (*Hiranandani, 1981*). Not only that the Hindu Sindhis who migrated to India came with misfortune. In India the government policy regarding refugees was largely driven by the Punjab experience. This meant that refugees from other areas, such as Sindh and Bengal, where there had been relatively less violence as compared to Punjab, were viewed, both by the government and the general public, as cowards who had migrated unnecessarily (*Bhavnani, 2016*). Refugees from Punjab were privileged over other refugees, in terms of both popular attitude and the government's willingness to accommodate them and to allocate resources for their rehabilitation.

The province of Sindh was not divided between India and Pakistan but the existing proportions between different religious and linguistic groups was changed by the arrival of hundreds of thousands of Muslims from India and the eventual departure of large numbers of Hindus and Sikh to India. The vast majority of refugees who arrived in Pakistan were from East Punjab. Those who arrived in Sindh headed for Karachi, which was now the capital of Pakistan, and the country's foremost port and financial and industrial centre (*Ansari, 1995*). As a result of the influx of Muslim refugees from India and the concomitant exodus of Hindus and Jains, Karachi went through a dramatic demographic and social change. Within a few years of partition, Karachi had gone from having a predominantly caste Hindu population to having majority Muhajir population, while Sindhis became a minority both in the city and in the province. (*Gayer, 2014*). It increased the city's population by extraordinary proportions.

In the context both-the responses of local Sindhi Muslim politicians to the inflow of refugees and meaning as well as the theme of the word "Muhajir underwent a change. After the outbreak of communal violence in early September

1947, followed by another in January 1948, Hindus and Sikhs started leaving Karachi in huge numbers. The Hindu exodus was viewed with increasing anxiety on the part of Sindhi Muslim politicians because Hindus were seen as vital contributors to the economic and professional life of the city. And so initially the Sindhi authorities went to great lengths to slow their departure urging them to stay, but on the other occasions, especially after the episode of January 1948, they facilitated their departure. In case of Muslim refugees from India too, at first, Sindhi authorities welcomed them but later attempted to check the entry of more refugees in opposition to the wishes of the Pakistani government. Local Sindhi politicians saw the newcomers not only as a huge economic drain on the province, but also as catalysts for the Hindu exodus. Further in the 1950s, there was anther wave of migration to Sindh in response to the heightened communal violence in India. The Sindh government's responses to refugees-including asking them to return to India and the imposition of a permit system led many Muhajirs to believe that they were not very welcomed after all in the Pakistani homeland of their dreams.

In Pakistan Muhajirs are the Urdu speaking emigrants from India's Muslim provinces who settled in the towns and cities. Originally, the word Muhajir was the part of Pakistan's political vocabulary from the outset as a means of encouraging Muslim solidarity between newcomers and those who already lived within the territory of the newly-carved Pakistani nation state (*Verkaalk, 2008*). The term Muhajir alludes to the migration of the first Muslims from Mecca to Medina-a migration initiated by the Prophet himself. Simultaneously, the use to the term allowed the state to constitute those who are already living within Pakistan, making the task of welcoming the arrivals a quasi-religious duty. For instance, Liaquat Ali Khan, the Prime Minister of Pakistan said in August 1948, 'The Government of Pakistan is fully aware of the difficulties of the Muhajireen and all over efforts are directed towards an end' that is to improve their lot. So long as each and every refugee is not suitably resettled the Pakistani government would not relax its efforts (*Frotscher, 2008*). Clearly, the term Muhajir was initially deployed in a capacious and positive sense to evoke sympathy for the migrants from India; more over, it included all migrants from India to Pakistan irrespective of where they came from and what language they spoke-it did not have an ethnic connotation.

However, the meaning of the term "Muhajir" changed after these post partition years. It came to be used as a synonymous for 'refugee' in the negative sense as someone who is a passive object of charity-which is why it did not become the principle term of self-identification for the displaced Muslims from India. They saw it as a label imposed by others. But in contrast, the migrants from India perceived themselves to be by their right and not by invitation as saw themselves as founders of the nation. Over the years, the term Muhajir gradually shifted from being on all embracing term for migrants to a pejorative word that referred to the migrants, Indian past. Noting its shifting meaning one analyst aptly added: Once it had meant welcome". Now it meant: "You are not from here" (*Verkaaik, 1994*). The term was therefore a constant reminder of their outsider/foreigner origins and of their belated arrival into the Pakistani nation-space.

Economy

Province Sindh of Pakistan is its second largest state and plays a pivotal role in the national economic and development agenda. The country's largest port city, Karachi, is the financial capital of Pakistan. The province comprises of 23% country's population and 18% of its land area. It has the highest concentration of urban population at 49% as compared to an overall country average 32.5%, making it the most urbanised province of the country. Its contribution to the national Gross Domestic Product (GDP) is around 33%. Sindh collects 70% of Pakistan's Income Tax and 62% of Sales Tax. In addition, it has 54% of country's textile units, 45% of its sugar mills, 20% of pulp and paper mills and 35% of edible oil processed locally. It accounts for 34% of total industrial capacity in large scale manufacturing and 25% of small-scale manufacturing. Not only that its diversified economy also comprises of a well-developed agricultural base supported by an effective irrigation network on the Indus. Around 14% wheat, 30% rice, 30% sugar cane, 25% cotton and 30% vegetable crops grown in Pakistan are from Sindh (*Sindh Board of Investment, 2017*). This provides immense opportunity for setting up export based agriprocessing industry in the province.

Agriculture, despite its declining share, is the largest employer in the province. The total cultivated area is 4.9 million hectares of which cropped area is 3.9 million hectares. Fifty percent of the cultivated land is used for foods crops and 25 percent for cash crop. In the national context, 16 percent of Pakistan's wheat, 42 percent of rice, 23 percent of cotton and 31 percent of sugarcane are produced in the province. Fisheries exports outside and within the country also originate mainly from the coastal areas of Sindh. The quantum index of crop production has doubled since 1985-86 (*Husain, 2014*). Gradually, the agriculture sector has undergone expansion at 3.5 percent annually while the manufacturing sector by 6.4 percent. A major structural transformation has taken place within the agriculture sector. Livestock's share of sectoral value added has risen from 31 percent in 1972 to 65 percent in 2008. The estimated labour force in Sindh is about 20.4 million. An unemployment rate of about 8 percent implies that 1.6 million people do not have productive jobs. Seventy percent of rural inhabitants earn their livelihood from livestock, dairy, fisheries, and forestry.

Next to agriculture is industry which has a share of 38 percent in the Gross Provincial Product and the growth rate has been quite impressive except for the late 1980s and the early 1990s when the deterioration of law and order in Karachi slowed down industrial growth. The same phenomenon has also been observed in the past five years when energy shortages and worsening security situation and ethnic, sectarian violence have once again led to a declining growth rate in the industrial sector. Within the industry large seal manufacturing dominates the sector with a share of 62 percent followed by small scale manufacturing with 8 percent. The quantum index manufacturing with the base year of 1980-81 has risen three times in the last three decades. However, despite phenomenal growth in this sector, direct employment has not expanded proportionately. Most of the jobs have been created by informal supplier of goods and services such as contractual employees and also by small and medium enterprises.

In the context it is also to mention that Sindh's natural resources such as oil, gas and coal have not yet been fully exploited. In a country facing acute energy shortages the substitution of country's own natural resources over imported fuel oil would have taken priority. But this has not happened so far and the level of economic activity is being suppressed because of this policy and implementation failure but recently Sindh's public finances have improved considerably since the 2009. The Gross Provincial Receipts in financial year 2013 were Rs. 426 billion of which more than three fourth were transfers from the Federal Divisible pool and straight grants and less than one fourth were collected as provincial taxes and non-taxes revenues. Total expenditure was Rs. 505 billion divided between current and Development Expenditure in the ratio of 72.28 in view of the large infrastructure and social sector needs this ratio has to shift in favour of larger allocations towards development expenditure.

Religion

Sindhis are a Sindhi speaking socio-ethnic group of people originating from Sindh now a province of Pakistan. Today Sindhis that live in Pakistan are predominantly Muslim but there are also smaller minorities of Hindus and Christians.

After the partition of India in 1947, a large number of Indian Muslims (Muhajirs) flocked into Pakistan and settled in the prosperous Sindh region. At the same time Sindhi Hindus migrated to India in large numbers, while many of those who remained converted to Islam. Sindh's population is mainly Muslim (91.32%), and Sindh is also home to nearly all (93%) of Pakistan's Hindus, who form 8.5% of the province's population. The majority of Muslims are Sunni Hanafi followed by Shia Ithna ashariyyah. The non-Muslim communities include Hindus, Christians, and Zorastrians. Sindhis as a whole are composed of original descondants of an ancient population known as Sammaat, sub-group related to the Baloch origin are found in interior Sindh and to a lesser extent Sindhis of Pashtuns origin. Sindhis of Balochi origins make up about 30% of the total Sindhi population, while Urdu-speaking Muhajirs make up over 19% of the total population of the province while Punjabi are 10% and Pasthuns represent 7%.

Islam in Sindh has a strong Sufi ethos with numerous Muslim saints and mystics, such as the Sufi poet Shah Abdul Latif Bhittai, having lived in Sindh historically. One popular legend which highlights the strong Sufi presence in Sindh is that 125, 000 Sufi saints and mystics are buried on Makli Hill near Thatta (*Schimmel, 1986*). The development of Sufism in Sindh was similar to the development of Sufism in other parts of the Muslim world. In the 16th century two Sufi tareeqat (orders)-Qadria and Naqshbandia were introduced in Sindh. Sufism continues to play an important role in the daily lives of Sindhis. It is also Pakistan's highest percentage of Hindu residents, with 8% of Sindh's population overall and 11.6% of Sindh's rural population, classifying itself as Hindu and over 40% of regiments in Tharparkar District identifying themselves as Hindu communal harmony between Sindhi Muslims and Hindus is an example of Sindhi's pluralistic and tolerant Sufi culture.

Hinduism, as in other areas of the Indian Subcontinent,

was the earliest religion predominantly practiced in the Sindh region in modern-day Pakistan. The region of Sindh has historically been, and still is, home to the largest community of Hindus in Pakistan. Following the Arab Muslim conquest in the 8th century, Islam spread throughout the region and over the period of time Islam became the faith practiced by majority of Sindhi people. The Islamic religion, coupled with traditional influences and exposure to and interaction with Hinduism, has shaped the diverse Sindhi culture (*Wakabayashi and Kothari, 2009*). Starting with Muhammad bin Qasim and Habbari dynasty, the Delhi Sultanate and later the Mughal Empire ruled the region.

In comparison to Islam and Hinduism Sikkism is a religion that originated in the Punjab region of the Indian subcontinent about the end of 15th century. It is one of the youngest of the major world religions. The fundamental beliefs of Sikhism, articulated in the sacred scripture Guru Granth Sahib, include constant spiritual meditation of God's name, being guided by the Guru instead of yielding to capriciousness of mind or psyche, living a householder's life instead of monasticism, throughout action to dharma, being of selfless service to others, equality of all human beings, and believing in God's grace (Cole and Singh 1995). In the early 21st century there were nearly 25 million Sikhs worldwide, the great majority of them living in the Indian State of Punjab.

Language

The original inhabitants of ancient Sindh were believed to be aboriginal tribes speaking languages of the Indus Valley Civilization around 3300 Before Christ (B.C). Later the Indo-Aryans are believed to have founded the Vedic civilization that existed between the Sarasvati River and Ganges River around 1500 BC. Sindhi is an Indo-Aryan language of the historical Sindh region, spoken by the Sindhi people. It is the official language of the Pakistani province of Sindh.

Most Sindhi speakers are concentrated in Pakistan in the Sindh province and in India, the Kutch region of the Sate of Gujarat and in the Ulhasnagar region of the state of Maharashtra. The remaining speakers in India are composed of the Sindhi Hindus who migrated from Sindh, which became a part of Pakistan and settled in India after the independence of Pakistan. Sindhi language is spoken in Sindh, Balochistan and Punjab provinces of Pakistan as well as the states of Rajasthan, Punjab and Gujarat in India and immigrant communities in Hong Kong, Oman, Indonesia, Singapore, UAE, UK and the United States.

The Sindhi language and other native languages of Pakistan are struggling to be officially given the status of national language in Pakistan. Before the inception of Pakistan, Sindh was the national language of Sindh. There are many Sindhi language television channels broadcasting in Pakistan such as KTN Sindh, TV, Awaz Television Network, Mehran TV and Dharti TV. The Sindhi language has also moved in the sphere of software. Sindhi Computing is the term used for the software developed for the Sindhi language. In line it has developed Sindhi language keyboards for the Windows OS and Android smart phones. The Sindhi Language Authority has developed a software which will end the barrier between the Arabic Sindhi script and Devanagari Sindhi script.

Table-4 : First language of Sindh (census, 1998)

Languages	Speaker in %
Sindhi	59.7%
Urdu	21.1%
Punjabi	7%
Pashto	4.2%
Saraiki	1%
Others	4.9%

According to an estimate (2016) 27 million people speak Sindhi language in the province. Today, Sindhi in Pakistan is heavily influenced by Urdu with more borrowed Perso-Arabic elements, while Sindhi in India is influenced by Hindi and borrowed more elements in Sanskrit. Other languages in the province include Gujarati and Parari Koli, a language spoken by only 2,50,000 natives of Sindh (1995). Only 7.3% of people Karachi's residents are Sindhi-speaking. Karachi is populated by Muhajirs who speak Urdu. In addition, other immigrants' communities in Karachi are Pashtuns from Khyber Pakhtunkhawa, Punjabis from Punjab and other linguistic groups from various regions of Pakistan.

Nationalist Movements and Alienation

In today's Pakistan Sindh is known for its distinct culture which is strongly influenced by Sufism, an important marker of Sindhi identity for both Hindus and Muslims in the province. It is famous for the enormous number of saints and mystics who lived there and preached peace and brotherhood. Several important Sufi shrines are located throughout the province which attract millions of annual devotees. Karachi, the capital of Sindh, is Pakistan's most ethnically diverse, with Muhajirs, or descendants of those who migrated to Pakistan from India after 1947 and throughout the 1950s and 1960s, making up the majority of the population (*Khalidi, 1998*). As a result, Karachi and other urban centers of Sindh have seen ethnic tensions between the native Sindhis and the Muhajirs boil over into violence on several occasions. In the context Sindhi nationalist movement asserts that Sindhis, an ethno-linguistic group mainly found in Pakistan and India are a nation. The Sindhi nationalist movement's demands have ranged from greater cultural, economic and political rights, to political autonomy, to outright secession from Pakistan and the creation of an independent state referred to as Sindhudesh.

After partition the majority of refugees who left India

by force or by choice from areas other than Punjab came to Sindh and settled principally in the cities, such as Karachi, Hyderabad and Sukkur. The Muhajirs became such a large percentage of urban Sindhi population that they gained a great measure of control over the region's cities. The Muhajirs, who were economically and educationally better off than Sindhis, pushed the Sindhis out of competition. They captured government jobs and business. Further, although the Indian Punjabis had been able to assimilate quickly into the population of Pakistan's Punjab, the Muhajir failed to do so to any significant degree in Sindh creating sharp divisions in the Sindhi society. Moreover, as time progressed, the Punjabi dominated government in Islamabad came to join in an alliance with the Muhajir middle classes for mutual political support. This led to preferential treatment' of the urban centered Muhajirs by Islamabad at the expense of more rural Sindhis (*Hurst, 1996*). At the time, Liaquat Ali Khan, the first Prime Minister of Pakistan, a Muhajir, was the principal leader of the Muhajirs. In the beginning many of Pakistan's top bureaucrats were Urdu-speaking and exercised a high degree of influence over country in the early formative years. This civil military nexus brought Punjabis and Urdu speaker close to each other. One additional contradiction appeared in the ethnicity of Sindh since the Baluchs and Gujaratis emigrated in Sindh in early years and were accepted as Sindhis. In the changed circumstances the Sindhis realised that they are not only to deal with Punjabi domination of the state but also to compete with the relatively advanced Muhajirs. During the first decade after partition, the Urdu-speaking Muhajir along with the Punjabis, had come to occupy a dominant position in Pakistan's political and bureaucratic arena (*Wright, 1974*).

The liberal or leftist approach to the ethnic problem in Sindh considers the economic contradictions within the Pakistan, especially Sindh, socio-economic structure, responsible for creating class conflicts along the lines of rural versus urban, feudal versus middle class and ruling elites versus have nots. It also looks at the question of nationalities in a deterministic way, tracing its origin in the Pakistani capitalist order which it considers to be a derivative of the neo-colonial world order, carried on by the privileged classes in Pakistan (*Malik,1997*). Combined with the demographic and economic statistics, linguistic controversy played a crucial role in ethnic mobilisation. The imposition of Urdu as the national language by the ruling class on other linguistic groups alienated the Sindhis. The Sindhi language and culture were overshadowed by the Urdu language and Hindustani culture of the Urdu speaking people, which politicized the Sindhis (*Ahmed, 1992*). Feroz Ahmed, a leading Sindhi intellectual, pinpointed the causes for the resurgence of nationality sentiments in Sindh and recounted, 'Along with immigration the ideological orientation of the power elite as the main reason for Sindhi alienation. Islam, integrity of Pakistan and the Urdu language became the code words for national domination. In the name of Pakistan's unity and integrity, the very foundation of unity was eroded' (*Ahmed, 1985*). In addition, he blamed the exploitation of Sindhi resources by the Punjabis and felt that Sindh has always suffered because of conspiracies against it. The refugees replaced the Hindu exploitative class and even Karachi was initially taken away from Sindh.

In the circumstances, the first Sindhi supported political movement for the creation of a Sindhi state called Sindhudesh was floated by some Sindhi nationalist parties. The movement is based in the Sindh region of Pakistan and was conceived by the Sindhi political leader G.M. Syed. It emerged in 1967 under the leadership of Syed and Pir Ali Mohammed Rashdi in opposition to the One Unit Policy, the imposition of Urdu by the central government and to the presence of a large number of Muhajir settled in the province (*Hanif, 2012*). Later in mid-1980s, Sindhi disenchantment with the Pakistani government erupted into open warfare. During Zia's regime, guerrilla units raised in the Sindh confronted the Punjabi federal troops from Islamabad. However, poorly organised and ill-prepared insurgency was eventually crashed by the use of coercive power of the state (*Harrison, 1981*). However, Sindhi ethno-nationalism, based on a separate Sindhi identity, had made inroads among young intellectuals largely due to the efforts of G.M. Syed who had been a one-time supporter of the demand for Pakistan. He was a charismatic leader with articulate ideas and sufficient economic resourcefulness to support his espousal of what was later known as Sindhi nationalism. He began his own political movement known as the Jeeye Sindh Movement. In the late 1980s he became the unchallenged leader of Sindh National Alliance (SNA), which brought together various ideological groups but failed to win any seat in the 1988, 1990 and 1993 elections.

In post-independence Pakistan, the machinations of the Pakistani state convinced Syed, that Sindhis would be marginalized in set up and later in 1972 he proposed the formation of an independent nation under the name 'Sindhudesh'. It was a call for the liberation and freedom of Sindhis from Punjabi Muhajir-imperialism. Sindhi separatists totally reject the Parliamentary way of struggle for getting freedom and rights. The concept of Sindhudesh is also supported by the Sindhi Diaspora including Sindhis in India, most of whom had to be relocated out of Sindh after Partition, leaving behind their property as evacuee trust under reciprocal government supervision. However, with the continuous defeat in elections held in the 1980s and 1990s it was largely weakened, although Syed later advanced his position towards openly demanding separation from Pakistan and the build –up of an independent Sindhudesh in his book, 'Heenyar Pakistan khey tuttan Khappey and Sindhudesh – A Nation in Chains' (*Jalal, 1995*).

Recently the movement for Sindhudesh re-emerged after the death of Benazir Bhutto, the former Prime Minister of Pakistan (2008) and also gained popularity, Sindhi nationalists judge that Sindh has been used to the advantage of people from non-Sindhi ethnic groups citing the dominance of Muhajir people in key areas of Sindh including Karachi, large scale migration to Sindh from other regions of Pakistan, including Khyber Pakhtunkhwa, alleged Punjabi dominance in defence sector, an increase in Taliban migrants moving to Sindh; as well as terrorist related attacks on the region and believe this to be the cause of recent troubles in Sindh. In the province, now there are many pro-Sindhudesh organisations such as the Jeay Sindh Quami Mahaz (JSQM), World Sindhi Congress (WSC), Sindhudesh Liberation Army (SDLA), Jeay Sindh Tarraqi Passand Party, Jeay Sindh Muttahida Mahaz (JSMM), Sindh Nationalist Movement Party (SNMP), and Jeay Sindh Students' Federation, as student wing of various separatist organisations struggling for the freedom of Sindhudesh following the ideology of G.M.Syed, founded in 1969.

Bashir Khan Qureshi, is the chairman of Jeay Sindh Quami Mahaz, who expressed his desire for the Urdu speaking community to integrate with Sindh, calling them 'brethren and part of Sindhi nation (*Daily Times 2012*). 'The Sindhi nation has been waiting for the last 64 years to secure independence since Punjab has assumed all the powers of the federation, including civil bureaucracy, military and judiciary, while all the resources of Sindh have been placed at the disposal of Islamabad'. Jeay Sindh Quam is the main guardian of Jeay Sindh theory, a legacy inherited from the G.M. Syed and it believes in peaceful independence based on non-violence. This apart, Jeay Sindh Muttahida Mahaz is one of the major separatist political party in Sindh, Pakistan, that believes in the separation of Sindhudesh from Pakistan.

In contrast to the above, is the Sindhu Desh Liberation Army, a terrorist organization based in Sindh province. A series of minor blasts took place on railway lines, the attacks carried out between November 2010, and February 2011 were claimed by the SDLA, who left pamphlets on the scene that mentioned 'atrocities' being carried out against Sindh and promising to continue their struggle till Sindh was granted "freedom". The SDLA claims moral inspiration from Baluchistan Liberation Army (BLA), which they term as a response to "Punjabi domination" of the Pakistani State. Recently a new left-wing party, Sindh National Movement Party, for a politically, culturally, economically and geographically independent Sindh was formed in December 2011. It wants to see Sindh as it was in 1843 before the British conquered it.

Despite all these, till date no Sindhi nationalist party has been ever voted into power in Sindh at any level of government. Even some nationalist parties and associations are banned for terrorist, anti-state and sabotage activities by the Pakistani government. In March 2012 a Sindhudesh rally was organized which had a notably low turnout, followed by a freedom march by the pro-separatist Jeay Sindh Qaumi Mahaz (JSQM) which, according to sources, gathered hundreds of thousands of people to demand independence for Sindhudesh (*Express Tribune, 2012*). Further, a strike called by the pro-separatist Jeay Sindh Muttahida Mahaz (JSMM) on 25 January 2014, resulted in a complete strike in the province, excluding some areas of Hyderabad, Tando, Allahyar, Matiari and Ghotki. In nutshell, Sindhis feel that they are a separate and full-fledged nation, so they have been struggling for self-determination of Sindh.

In the country Muhajirs are the Urdu-speaking Muslims who migrated to Pakistan when the country emerged independent from the British Raj in 1947. Karachi was then home to a very diverse set of ethnicities including Urdu and Gujarati speaking immigrants, Punjabis, Pasthuns, Baluch and foreigners from several South Asian countries. Muhajirs advanced in commerce and the bureaucracy, but many resented the quota system which facilitated Sindhis in gaining university slots and civil service jobs. It was this very ethnic rivalry that led Muhajir political mobilization, which was further provoked by the stagnant economy and the conditions of Biharis in Bangladesh concentration camps (*Cohen, 2004*). On the other systematic discrimination of Muhajirs continued and they were aggrieved by Z.A. Bhutto's policies in the 1970s which were perceived as anti-Muhajir and Pro-Sindhi (*Ahmar,1996*). The language controversy in 1972 further alienated the Muhajirs from Bhutto's government when the Sindh Assembly dominated by the Sindhi-speaking members of Pakistan People's Party (PPP), passed a language bill declaring Sindh to be a provincial language along with Urdu. Besides, the government decision to introduce an urban-rural quota in Sindh aroused the Muhajir's fear of loosing jobs and socio-economic status. These steps of the government dropped Muhajir's share of jobs and admission in reference to that of Punjabis, Pathans and Sindhis. After Bhutto, the military regime of Zia-ul-Haq also disappointed Muhajirs, although they supported the regime initially.

Thus, the frustration and grievances of Muhajirs against the Pakistani establishments since its inception gave birth to a systematic secular and pro-Muhajir political organisation. First it was founded as a student organisation All Pakistan Muhazir Organisation (APMSO), in 1978 by Altaf Hussain which further became the Muhajir Qaumi Movement (MQM) in 1984. In 1997, the MQM removed the term Muhajir from its name and replaced it with "Muttahida" meaning "United" thus welcoming all ethnic groups of Pakistan into its fold. Supporters of Muhajir nationalism and the MQM point out that the search for identity among Muhajir is logical and that many common factors can legitimize the feeling of a 'Muhajir nation', common language, similar culture, common history of migration from India, and hostile and discriminatory attitude of ruling elites, collective sufferings at the hands of various regimes. Muhajirs accept the ideology of Muhajir nationalism based on equal rights and social justice. Their feelings of relative deprivation and loss of hope in the prevailing political order galvanized their sense of identity vis-à-vis Sindhi and other ethnic communities, setting the stage for confrontation with the state establishment.

At the same time critics of the MQM argue that Muhajirs do not have any basis for claiming discrimination or oppression since they continue to be over represented in key sectors of Pakistani society the bureaucracy, management positions in the private sector, print and electronic media, the medical and legal professions and educational institutions. Some critics also consider Muhajir nationalism a myth on account of two reasons; (i) the term Muhajir is a temporary mark of identification for people who migrated from India to Pakistan at the time of partition, and (ii) Muhajirs do not belong to a single ethnic community but comprise various ethnic and racial groups having roots from the several provinces of India. But perhaps the single most important factor in the emergence of the MQM and Muhajir ethnicity was the secession of East Pakistan and the emergence of Bangladesh. It was a defining moment for the Muhajirs in two specific ways; (i) Bangladesh demonstrated the hollowness of the two-nation theory, and (ii) the important outcome for Muhajir identity was the Bihari refugee question. The MQM with its broad support base in Karachi and its surrounding, politically became a potent force against the Pakistan People's Party who tried to symbolise it as anti-state and pro-Indian group, converting the region in most troubled areas of Pakistan.

Provincial Politics

Unlike the movement for separate state Sindhudesh, the Muhajir backed political organization, MQM, known as a party that holds strong mobilising potential in Karachi, having traditionally been the dominant political force in the city (*Mitra, 2004*). Presently, it is the second largest party in Sindh and overall the fourth largest party in Sindh in the National Assembly of Pakistan after the Pakistan Muslim League, Pakistan people's party, and Pakistan Tahreek-e-Insaaf (*Election Commission of Pakistan 2013*). In its early years

MQM drew enormous crowds, the epitome of which was the rally of August 8, 1986 at Nishtar Park, Karachi. Three years into its existence, MQM won the November 1987 local body elections in Karachi and Hyderabad and had several mayors win unopposed. The result of general elections of 1988 went in favour of PPP and an alliance with the MQM Pakistan Peoples Party formed a coalition government in Sindh province on the basis of a 59-point agreement called Karachi Accord. The MQM then had a larger mandate in urban Sindh in comparison to PPP whose majority of support came from rural areas of Sindh. However, within a few months of the agreement, differences surfaced and MQM ministers in the Sindh Cabinet resigned because the agreement was not implemented (*Haq,1999*). Their alliance broke up in October 1989 and MQM joined hands with PPP's opponents and became engaged in public benefit initiatives.

In the elections of 1990, MQM emerged as the third strongest party in the country and this time, it formed alliance with Pakistan Muslim League to establish a provincial government in Sindh whereas PML formed a federal government. During these times small factions of MQM separated themselves from the main body of the party. The largest among these is MQM Haqiqi which was formed by Ataq Ahmad and Amir Khan. It is generally believed that MQM Haqiqi was formed by the collusion of Pakistani government in power and the Establishment/Inter-Services Intelligence (ISI) to weaken MQM and was supported by successive governments and the military. As a result, from 1992 to 1994, the MQM was the target of the Pakistan's Army's 'Operation Clean-up'. The period is regarded as the bloodiest period in Karachi's history, with thousands MQM workers and supporters killed or gone missing. It drove many MQM leaders and workers underground and allowed a splinter group, the MQM (Haqiqi), to claim to be the real MQM. The army tried to get rid of Altaf Hussain by patronising the Haqiqi faction and enabled MQM to start a turf battle against

MQM of Altaf group, forcing most top leaders and activists into hiding. However, the federal government gave the reasoning behind this operation, known as the 'Operation Clean-up" as the government's attempt to end terrorism in Karachi and to seize unauthorized arms (*Gibran, 2009*). In protest the MQM boycotted the subsequent 1993 general elections but participated in provincial elections and secured 27 seats in assembly while its political rival PPP won 56 seats.

After the general elections of 1993 the Pakistan Peoples Party formed the government in Sindh and at federal level. Whereas MQM Haqiqi failed to gain any seats at federal or provincial level. It followed a political violence in 1993 and 1994. During the 1994 violence, heavy political killings were reported between MQM, MQM factions and Sindhi nationalist groups. At the moment the ongoing militancy operation failed to stamp out violence and, despite massive cost and publicity, could not restore order in the city. In the mid-1990s, MQM created widespread political violence that affected Pakistan's southern Sindh province, particularly Karachi, the port city that is the country's commercial capital. In the mid-1990s, the US State Department, Amnesty International, and others accused the MQM and a rival faction, MQM Haqiqi, of summary killings, torture, and other abuses. Such polarisation presented the most serious threat to the Pakistani state and civil society (*Malik, 1996*). The party's use of extra-legal activities in conflicts with political opponents has earned it the accusation of terrorism (*Ahmed, 1991*). The party's strong hierarchical order and personalist leadership style led to some critics labelling the MQM as fascist.

As a result of activities related to different types of violence state operations against the MQM continued in coming years and decades. Since May 1990 when for the first time an operation was launched by the Sindh police to target MQM workers in Pakka Qilla Hyderabad, it moved further, operation clean-up (1992-94), during Benazir Bhutto's tenure (1994-96), after the assassination of Hakeem Said (1998-2000) and presently the Karachi Targeted Action (2013). Due to rise in target killing and organised crimes of extortion, kidnapping for ransom and increased time rate of the city, Karachi operation began by the Nawaz Sharif government in 2013 with the intention of creating a peace in the city. In line, in 2015 MQM's Headquarter Nine Zero was raided twice by the paramilitary rangers leading to the event of 22 August 2016 in which the Headquarter was sealed and hundreds of MQM offices were bulldozed.

Other provinces alike, Sindh is governed as its powers and structure provisioned in 1973 Constitution in which 29 districts come under its authority and jurisdiction. The government includes the cabinet, a unicameral legislature with head of government known as the Chief Minister. The Chief Minister is invariably the leader of the party represented in the Assembly, selects members of the Cabinet. The Chief Minister and Cabinet are thus responsible for the functioning of the government and are entitled to remain in office so long as it maintains the confidence of the elected Assembly. The head of state of the province is known as the Governor. The Provincial Assembly of the Sindh has 168 members, 29 seats are reserved for women and 9 seats for non-Muslims. Syed Murad Ali Shah of Pakistan Peoples Party is presently the Chief Minister of Sindh since 29 July 2016 and having 94 members in the Assembly. The main opposition party in Sindh is MQM which has won 50 seats in the general elections held in 2013.

Province Khyber Pakhtunkhwa

United 2010 the North-West Frontier Province (NWFP), and now Khyber Pakhtunkhwa, is one of the four administrative provinces of Pakistan with Peshawar as is capital. Located in the northwestern region of the country along the international border with Afghanistan, Khyber Pakhtunkhwa is the third largest province of Pakistan by the size of both population and economy though it is geographically the smallest of four. It comprises 10.5 of Pakistan's economy, and is home to 11.9 of Pakistan's total population with the majority of the province's inhabitants being Pashtuns, Hazarewal, Chitrali, and Kohistanis. Its territorial area is 74,521 km (28,773 mile) and population as per 2017 record 30,523,371 with density of 410 per kilometer. Pashto and English are official language of the province. It is the site of the ancient kingdom Gandhara, including the ruins of its capital Pushkalavati near modern day charsadda. Originally a stronghold of Hinduism and Buddhism, the history of the region was characterized by frequent invasions under various Empires due to its geographical proximity to the Khyber Pass. The present name Khyber Pakhtunkhwa means the "Khyber part of the land of the Pashtuns or Pakhtuns, while only the word Pakhtunkhwa means Land of Pashtuns".

Brief History

In the peak times of Indus Valley Civilization (3300 BCE- 1300 BCE) the Aryan began their migration into India around 2000 BCE. Coming from the west, these semi nomadic conquerors entered through the present-day Khyber Pakhtunkhwa and initially settled along the Swat, Gomal, Kurram and Kabul Rivers. Over the course of several hundred years more and more Aryans entered the subcontinent and migrated eastwards into modern day India. The Persians conquered Gandhara in the 6th century B.C. and made it one of the provinces of the Achaemenid Empire. In 327 BC Alexander's army invaded and advanced to Nicaea, where the king of Taxila and other chiefs joined him. Though Alexander did not stay long in the subcontinent but his reign had a significant impact. Greek culture influenced the culture of the region for a thousand year after. A prominent example of this is the fusion of Indian and Greek art elements that became known as Gandharan art style. After Alexander his general Seleneus claimed the Indian territories, but in

305 BC, Chandragupta Maurya fought Selucus and emerged triumphant from the power struggle. In the Maurya Dynasty'. Ashoka the Great, the third Mauryan Emperor, after fighting the Kalinga War and seeing the destruction he had caused, embraced Buddhism and tried to be a good ruler to his people. The Kushans succeeded Mauryan Empire who also contributed to the growth of Buddhism in the subcontinent. The decline of the Kushan Dynasty and other brief conquests of the region paved the way for Shahi Dynasty. Hinduism began to take root in the region since most of the later Shahi Kings were Hindus. The Gandharan Civilization was uprooted as Hinduism gradually replaced Buddhism. Even though the Arabs had been in contact with the Pathans since the middle of the 7th century, it was in 1001 AD when Mahmud of Ghazni defeated Jayapala, the last Hindu Shahi King of Gandhara. The local Pathans of the area, after initial oppose, eventually embraced Islam and later helped Ghazni in a number of wars. The Ghaznavid Empire marked the beginning of a long Muslim rule in the region.

Babar, the founder of Mughal Empire first entered the subcontinent via the Khyber Pass in 1505 but his fifth and final march into the continent began in 1525 and a year later in 1526 when he defeated the last Lodhi King and paved the way for Mughal rule over this area till the 18th century. Babar united many tribes in the area including the Yusufzais, under his banner and led them to many regions in India. He won the hearts of Pathans over a short span of time. After Babar's death, Humayun succeeded him. But a Pathan named Sher Shah Suri took control of the region, although Humayun regained the throne fifteen years later and his son Akbar succeeded him but could not conquer all parts of Khyber Pakhtunkhwa. In the wake of Aurangzeb's death in 1707, the empire split into competing kingdoms and Nadir Shah, a Persian ruler, gained control over the province with support from the Pathans. One of his renowned successors, Ahmad Shah Abdali (1747-1772), except

Marathas invasion in the early 1750s, launched several campaigns from the Peshawar Valley into many places across India. The province remained a part of Afghanistan, which had been established as the first Pathan State by Ahmad Shah Abdali, till its conquest by the Sikhs in 1818.

The Sikhs invaded Khyber Pakhtuankhwa in 1818 under the command of Maharaja Ranjit Singh and first annexed Dera Ismail Khan and then went on to become masters of the entire province. In 1823 the Sikhs took hold of Peshawar, plundered the city and burned the Bala Hissar Fortress. They razed down numerous architectural monuments, including the Mahabat Khan Mosque. However, the Sikhs did make some contributions such as building Khyber Pakhtunkhwa's first palnned city known as Haripur. Following Maharaja Ranjit Singh's death in 1839, the Sikhs fought amongst themselves and ultimately, the East India Company took hold of the province. In 1849, Khyber Pakhtunkhawa came under the British rule.

Following the treaties of Lahore and Amritsar, the British amnexed the frontier territory after the proclamation of 29 March 1849. for a short time, the Districts of Peshawar, Kohat, and Hazara came under the direct control of the Board of Administration at Lahore but about 1850 they were formed into a regular Division under a Commissioner. Dera Ismail Khan and Bannu, under one Deputy Commissioner, formed part of the Leiah Division till 1861, when two Deputy Commissioners were appointed and both districts were included in the Derajat Division, an arrangement maintained until the formation of the North – West Frontier Province (NWFP). The province was created during the colonial rule of the British Empire and was a province of British India. As a province of British India, it had area of 38, 665 square miles, of which only 13,193 was under direct control of the British, the remainder occupied by the tribes under the political control of the Agent to the Governor-General. However, the British East India Company led many campaigns into areas controlled by the Pathan tribes and secured their confidence. The early British officers played a pivotal role in winning the hearts of Pathans. So strong was the relationship between the British and the Pathans that during the rebellion of 1857 many people in Peshawar and surrounding areas supported the British, while the rest of India was mutinous. When the muting was finally suppressed, it was clear that the frontier districts had proved to the British government a source of strength rather than of danger (*Imperial Gazetteer 2 of India, 2013*). In a further development to have a formal boundary between Afghanistan and Khyber Pakhtunkhwa, in the year 1893, Sir Mortimer Durand and Abdur Rahman Khan, the amir of Afghanistan agreed upon an international border that came to be known as the Durand Line. It now separates the Pakistani regions of Baluchistan, Khyber Pakhtunkhwa and FATA from Afghanistan.

For the first time under the British Empire Khyber Pakhtunkhwa, was inaugurated as province at Shahi Bagh in 1902 by Lord Curzon and in 1931 it was elevated to the status of a governor-ruled province. At the same time the province was also a hotbed centre of the Indian independence movement. Mirza Ali Khan, a wazir from Waziristan, spearheaded a civil disobedience movement against the British in 1936. The Khilafat and Hijrat movements also took place in the region but were not successful. Another popular freedom movement was launched by Abdul Ghaffar Khan, also known as Bacha Khan, and his brother Dr. Khan Sahib. It was a nonviolent movement and their followers were known as Khudai Khidmatgar or Servants of God. Khyber Pakhtunkhwa was granted self-government status in 1937. After Independence in 1947 the province decided to join Pakistan in a referendum conducted in July 1947. According to the official results 99.02% votes were cast in favour of Pakistan while only 0.98% were cast in favour of India.

Khyber Pakhtunkhwa After 1947

Even before the merger of Khyber Pakhtunkhwa into the present Pakistan, the Durand Line drawn marking the boundary between India and Afghanistan, which also separated Pashtun inhabited area in two parts gave birth and rise to Pakhtun nationalism (*Bahadur, 1994*). On the eve of independence in June 1947, Mirzali Khan, Bacha Khan and other Khudai Khidmatgars declared the Bannu Resolution, demanding that the Pashtuns be given a choice to have an independent state of Pashtunistan composing all Pasthun majority territories of British India, instead of being made to join the new state of Pakistan. The British Raj refused to comply with the demand of this resolution (*Shah and Vaqar, 1993*) and instead the British held a referendum to choose joining between Pakistan or India which went in favour of Pakistan. As the Pasthunis were forced to join Pakistan against their will its leaders and the Red Shirts were throughout treated as traitors in Pakistan. However, after partition, its leadership recognised the emergence of Pakistan as a settled fact and espoused the reorganisation of provincial boundaries under which all Pashtu speaking areas would be united as a single province and to be named Pakhtunistan and operating under the federal set up of Pakistan. Abdul Wali Khan, who formed the Awami National Party, confined himself to demanding for regional autonomy (*Chakravarty, 1976*).

In modern Pakistan the movement for Pakhtunistan gained ground on two emotive issues- transborder linkage with the Pakhtuns in Afghanistan and the fear of cultural, social and economic submergence at the hands of the dominant Punjabi-Muhajir elite in the state structure. As compared to Baluchi consciousness, the Pakhtuns of NWFP could claim that their ethnicity is backed by greater historic depth as well as a greater sense of cohesion. But it never expressed itself as violently as its Baluch variation. The reasons for its might have been that although they have been discriminated against to some degree by Islamabad, in general, the Pashtuns have met with better treatment from Pakistan's regimes than have the Baluch, Sindhis, or Muhajirs. In comparison, the Pashtuns have a significant presence in the professional organisations and leadership of Pakistan, especially in its military. Emphasising the strategic significance of the province, the government had established the key military establishments in the frontier. Even in the regime of General Mohammad Ayub Khan, who was himself a Pashtun from Hazara district, did not help the cause of Pakhtunistan.

Since independence, the process of democratisation, institutional strengthening and national integration had but marginally succeeded in Pakistan. It was mainly due to the two conflicting goals, a strong centralised government and the demand for provincial autonomy. To consolidate their own power, any criticism on the policies of the federal government by the nationalists and smaller provinces was treated as a gesture of treason by the incumbent regime. In line, Bhutto's programme of socialism coupled with his skill of making powerful and effective speeches radicalised the urban sectors in the second half of the 1960s. In fact after the decade of military rule in the country he was able to boots the hopes of the public for restoration of democratic rule. But in contrast, when transfer of power took place ot Bhutto, the PPP dealt with the opposition very brutally to the extent that their role in democracy was not to tolerated (*Khan and Rehman, 2017*). The case of provincial governments of National Awami Party (NAP) and Jamiat-e-Ulama-i-Islam (JUI) is Balochistan and Khyber Pakhtunkhwa is evident. The dictatorial style of Bhutto was mainly because he was a product of Ayub Khan's Martial Law. On the other hand, the opposition to pressurise him politically, opted with more preference to the politics of agitation rather to participatory politics. Although after Bhutto assumed power there was a significant change in the policies towards the NWFP as emphasis was laid more on economic integration, his handling of political affairs in the province by appointing a non-representative person as the Governor without consulting the democratically elected party, brought him in confrontation with the Awami National Party. He imposed central rule in 1973 in the Khyber Pakhtunkhwa on the pretext of a threat to the national security and in 1975 installed a puppet government and banned the ANP. This further multiplied the grievances of the Pashtuns as they felt they would never get a fair deal from the government.

After Bhutto, General Zia-ul-Haq came to power and initially, to strengthen his support base, sympathised with the Pashtun leaders who were anti-Bhutto elements. But after the execution of Z.A. Bhutto, apparently there was no threat to his rule and thereafter, he hardened his stand towards the Pakhtun issue. On the other hand, an additional factor was added to the NWFP which paved the way for further crises in ways more than one. The influx of around three million Afghan refugees fleeing from the Soviet invasion in December 1979, and Afghanistan's subsequent civil war had provided a greater push for the re-establishment of Pakhtunistan, as the stress of the refugee problem strained the nerve of NWFP. During the 1980s Soviet war in Afghanistan, many Afghans left their country (*Lorch, 2001*). As a result of political unrest, mass arrests, executions and other human rights violations and civil war millions of refugees escaped to Pakistan and Iran. The migration began in December 1979, and continued through the 1980s. In late 1988, about 3.3 million Afghan refugees were housed in 340 refugee's camps along the Afghan-Pakistan border in Khyber Pakhtunkhwa. Among them 60 percent constituted ordinary Afghans who arrived with nothing and are largely dependent on Pakistan and international efforts for sustenance. According to census of Afghans in Pakistan, a 2005 Pakistani Ministry of States and Frontier Regions report, the ethnic breakdown of Afghans in Pakistan was Pashtuns (81.5%), Tajiks (7.3%), Uzbeks (2.3%), Hazara (1.3%), Turkmen (2.0%), Balochi (1.7%) and others (3.9%). The government of Pakistan receives $ 133 million per year ($ 78 per person) from the UNHCR for hosting Afghans.

However, as with the other ethnic nationalists, the Pashtun movement is itself divided between the different options for the future. These differing views include the strengthening of the NWFP and its membership in a new Pakistan redesigned along confederation lines, the creation of a greater Afghanistan, which would incorporate the existing Pashtun regions of Pakistan, the outright secession of the province to truly return to a fully autonomous Pasthtunistan (*Selig,1986*). In the context, the restoration of democracy in 1988 has not brought any significant change in the outlook of the leaders towards provincial autonomy. In 1997, the issue of renaming the NWFP as Pakhtunkhwa, associated with the ethnic aspiration and identity of the Pashtuns came to the forefront. Although the name was first used in the National Assembly in November 1990, in the year 1997 it was approved by the democratically elected constitutional assembly of the province. Now in the 21st century, in May 2008, to accommodate a demand by the people of NWFP who voted for the ANP, the PPP proposed that the name of the North-West Frontier Province to be changed to Pakhtunkhwa, but at time the Muslim League Nawaz opposed the name change, it however, occurred in early 2010 when Pakistani Senate confirmed the name change to Khyber Pakhtunkhwa in the 18th amendment to the Constitution of Pakistan with a unanimous 90 votes on 15 April 2010.

Society of Khyber Pakhtunkhwa

Since the 2nd millennium BC, the region now inhabited by the native Pashtun people had been conquered by Ancient Iranian peoples, the Medes, Achaemenids, Greeks, Mauryas, Kushans, Hephthalites, Sassanid's Arab Muslims, Turks, Mughals, and others, Arab Muslims arrived in the 7th century and began introducing Islam to the native Pashtun people, some of the Arabs settled in the Sulaiman Mountain and slowly became Pashtunised over time. Later the area fell to the Turkish Ghazuavids whose capital was at Ghazni, with Lahore serving as the second power house. Further the army of Genghis Khan arrived in the 13th century and began destroying Persian-speaking cities in the north while the Pashtun territory was defended by the khilji dynasty of Delhi. In the 14th and 15th century, the Timurid dynasty was in control of the nearby cities and towns, until Babar captured it in 1504. However, despite sharing a common language and believing in a common ancestry, the Pashtuns first achieved unity in the 18th century after being under foreign rule for many centuries. The eastern part of it was ruled by the Mughal Empire, while the Western parts were ruled by the Persian Safavids as their easternmost provinces. By 1738 the Mughal Empire was overtaken by Nader Shah after whose death in 1747, Ahmad Shah Durrani created his own large and powerful Durrani Empire. The new Empire united all the different Pashtun tribes as well as many ethinc groups. Parts of the region around Pashawar was invaded by Ranjit Singh and his Sikh army, but a few years later they were defeated by the British Raj who reached the region from the east.

Following the decline of the Durrani dynasty and the establishment of the new Barakzai dynasty in Afghanistan, the Pashtun domains began to shrink as they lost control over parts of South Asia to the British, such as the Punjab region and the Balochistan region. In the further imperialistic Great Game between the British and the Russian Empire, in 1893, as part of a way for fixing the limit of their respective sphere of influence, the Durand Line Agreement was signed. In 1905 the North-West Frontier Province (today's Khyber Pakhtunkhwa) was created and roughly corresponded to Pashtun majority regions within the British domain. The FATA area was created to further placate the Pashtun tribesmen who never fully accepted British rule and were prone to rebellious. Since the late 1940s with the dissolution of British India and independence of Pakistan, some righd

Pashtun nationaliste proposed merging with Afghanistan or creating Pashtunistan as a future sovereign state for the local Pashtun inhabitants of the area. However, both of their proposals were turned down by the British (*Roberts, 2003*), and finally they decided to merge with the Pakistani federation. Further during the 1950s to late 1960s Pashtuns were promoted to higher positions within the Pakistani government and military, thereby integrating Pashtuns into the Pakistani state and severely weakening secessionist sentiments to the point that by the mid 1960s popular support for an independent Pashtunistan had all but disappeared.

The Pashtuns are the second largest ethnic group of Pakistan and mainly concentrated in the west and northwest, inhabiting mainly Khyber Pakhtunkhwa, the Federally Administered Tribal Area (FATA) and northern Baluchistan. It borders Afghanistan to the north-west, Gilgit Baltistan to the north east, Azad Kashmir to the east, the federally Administered Area to the west and south, Balochistan to the south and Punjab and the Islamabad capital territory to the south-east. The main ethnic group in this region is the Pashtuns; other smaller ethnic groups include most notably the Hazarewals and Chitralis. However, as a result of the Sovit invasion of Afghanistan in 1979, over five million Afghan refugees poured into Pakistan, mostly choosing to reside in the NWFP, nearly 3 million. The event changed the social composition / status of society and became a base for the Afghan resistance fighters and the Deobandi ulama of the province played a significant role in the Afghan jihad with Madrasa haqqaniyya becoming a prominent organisational and networking base for the anti-Soviet Afghan fighters (*Sana, 2008*). The province remained heavily influenced by events in Afghanistan thereafter.

As a result of the Soviet invasion of Afghanistan and the subsequent jihad and civil war, 3.7 million Afghan refugees came to Pakistan the majority of whom settled in refugee camps in the peri-urban areas of the NWFP and

Balochistan. Most of the Afghan refugees, like the majority of the population of NWFP are Pashto-speaking Pakhtuns and so the Afghan migration considerably increased the number of Pashto-speakers in Pakistan. The Afghan migration also led to the strengthening of the religious establishment in Pakistan. Especially Khyber Pakhtunkhwa has been a site of militancy and terrorism that started after the attacks of September 11, 2001, and intensified when the Pakistani Taliban began an attempt to seize power in Pakistan starting in 2004. Armed conflict began in 2004, when tensions, rooted in the Pakistan Army's search for al qaeda fighters in Pakistan's mountainous Waziristan area in FATA escalated into armed resistance. Khyber Pakhtunkhwa is also the main theatre for Pakistan's Zarb-e-Azb operation- a broad military campaign against militants located in the province, and neighbouring FATA. According to the latest census of Pakistan conducted in 2017, the population detail of the province is as below.

Table-5

Population of Khyber Pakhtunkhwa (census 2017)

	Urban	Rural	Total
Population	5729634	24793737	30523371
Male	2972367	12495278	15467645
Female	2756577	12298236	15054813
Transgender	690	223	913
Household	741074	3104154	3845168

Economy

From beginning the Pakhtuns accompanied the grievance that the NWFP had been kept in a state of underdevelopment largely because of the dominance of the central government by non-Pakhtuns and particularly by the Punjabis. Ever since the creation of Pakistan, the underdevelopment of the frontier was the central theme of campaigns launched by Khan Abdul Ghaffar Khan and his son, Wali Khan. The NWFP, now Khyber Pakhtunkhwa since 2010, lagged behind every other province, in both gross and per capita regional product. It also lagged behind Sindh and Punjab in the number of large-scale industrial units. Moreover, Punjab was the main beneficiary of the Green Revolution with 91.2 per cent of the tube wells located in that province, whereas in the Pashawar division, with its fertile agricultural areas, there were only 2.7 percent of private tube wells in 1968 (*Sayeed, 1980*). Even after the establishment of the National Awami Party-Jamiatul Ulama-e-Islam (JUI) coalition government in the Frontier in 1972, Pakhtun complaint relating to the pre-empting of the lucrative forces of revenue by the central government and their alleged unwillingness to make amends for this through generous allocation of central revenues to the province continued. These regional disparities were further heightened by the way the central government had allowed the industries to exploit the resources of the Frontier for the benefit of Punjab and Sindh (*Kukreja, 2003*). Although Since 1972 it has seen its economy grow in size by 3.6 times.

In the economy of the province agriculture is an important sector not just in monetary terms but also in terms of employment. In the Khyber Pakhtunkhwa only 30% of its land is cultivable and the main cash crops include wheat, maize, tobacco, rice, sugar, beets as well as fruits are grown with major horticulture crops such as apples, potatoes and tomatoes. In the year 2011-12 it produced 40.4% of the national output of wheat, 20.2% of maize, 18.6% of barley, 1.3% of rice, 0.6% of millet, 3.4% of gram, 8% of sugarcane and 8.3 % of tobacco. In fact, more than 75% of Pakistan's tobacco is grown in the province. However, the part of the economy that it dominates is forestry, where its share has historically ranged from a low of 34.9% to a high of 81%

giving an average of 61.56% (*David, 2009*).

The overall economy of Khyber Pakhtunkhwa has suffered for decades due to the fallout of the Soviet invasion of Afghanistan and today the province is being targeted for a different situation of terrorism. However, some manufacturing and high-tech investments in Pashawar has helped improve job prospects for many locals, while trade in the province involves nearly every product. Unemployment has been reduced due to establishment of industrial zones. Workshops throughout the province support the manufacture of small arms and weapons. By 2012, there were approximately 1,821 industrial units that were running in the province. Major industries include canning and preservation of fruits and vegetables, manufacturing and refining of sugar, cotton textiles, cement, furniture, and tobacco processing. Mineral production also contributes to the economy of the Khyber Pakhtunkhwa. Limestone, marble, rock salt and gypsum are a few of the major mineral mines.

Religion

The state religion in Pakistan is Islam, which is practiced by about 95.98% of the total population of the nation. Freedom of religion is guaranteed by the Pakistan constitution. Pakistani constitution established a fundamental right in which all Pakistani citizens irrespective of Religions have equal rights. The remaining 2.5% practice Christianity, Hinduism, Sikhism and other religions. Most of the inhabitants of Khyber Pakhtunkhwa profess Islam, with a Sunni majority and minorities of Shias and some Ismailis in Chitral district. Many of the Kalasha of Sothern Chitral still retain their ancient Animist/Shamanist religion. Animism is the religious belief that objects, places and creatures all possess a district spiritual essence. Potentially, it perceives all things-animals, plants, rocks, rivers, weather systems, human handiwork and even words as animated and alive. While Shamanism is a practice that involves a practitioner reaching altered states of consciousness in order to perceive and interact with a spirit world and channel these transcend ental energies into this world. In addition, there are small communities of Hindus, Christians and Sikhs.

However, since the 1979 Afghan War, Khyber Pakhtunkhwa remained the geographical and ideological focal point for the religious extremism and also for the Islamist politics. The history of Pakistan tells us that from 1947 leaders use religions as a tool to strengthen the country's identity. These religious parties are supported by state to gain influence in political process or to support the military dominance in politics (*Jamshed, 2014*). The process of incorporating Islamist into formal politics started during the Zia regime, which provided strength and legitimization to his rule. Dictators are always supported by the Islamist throughout Pakistan's history (*Mukherjee, 2010*). Especially after the terrorist attack on World Trade Centre on September 11, 2001, Pakistan was forced to join the War on Terror when many of Musharraf's companions were not happy over this decision (*Khan, 2011*). The participation of Pakistan in War on Terror (WoT) created opportunities to the militants and for the religious parties a good time to expand its ideology and the result was the formation of MMM's government in Khyber Pakhtunkhwa and Baluchistan after the provincial elections of 2002.

Language

Urdu being the national and official language serves as a lingua franca for inter-ethnic communications, and sometimes Pashto and Urdu are the second and third languages among communities which speak other ethnic languages (*Claus, Sarah, and Margaret, 2003*). English is co-official and also used in education, while Arabic is used for religious purposes and education. In 2011 the provincial government approved in principle the introduction of the five regional languages of Pashto, Hindko, Saraiki, Khowar and Kohistani as compulsory subjects for the schools in the areas where they are spoken. In addition, there is some population in Pashwar city who speak Persian since nineteenth century; this population saw an increase during 1980s and 1990s due to migration form Afghanistan. The table below shows the speakers of different language in percentage.

Table-6

Language	Speakers in %
Pashto	73.9%
Hindko	18.0%
Saraiki	3.9%
Punjabi	1%
Khowar	1%
Kohistani	1%
Urdu	0.8%
Others	0.7%

Recent Government and Politics

The unicameral legislature, the Provincial Assembly of Khyber Pakhtunkhwa was established under Article 106 of the Constitution of Pakistan, made in the year 1973. The assembly has 124 elected members, 99 regular seats, 22 seats reserved for women and 3 seats for Non-Muslims. The last assembly election held in June 2013 and since 5 June 2013 Parvez Khattak with 61 seats, is the leader of House or Chief Minister of the province. Historically, the province perceived to be a stronghold of the ANP-a left-wing and pro-nationalist party. The Pakistan Peoples Party (PPP) also enjoyed considerable support in the province due to its socialist agenda. Khyber Pakhtunkhwa was thought to be another leftist region of the country after Sindh. It has a executive branch which consists of the Governor of Khyber Pakhtunkhwa appointed by President of Pakistan, subject to Prime Minister's advice, Chief Minister, elected by Provincial Assembly of Khyber Pakhtunkhwa and Cabinet appointed by Governor of the Province, subject to Chief Minister's advice. In judicial branch the High Court and Lower courts judges are appointed by Chief Justice of Pakistan with Supreme Judicial Council of Pakistan approval. It interprets laws and overturn those they find unconstitutional.

As significant change appeared in voters' mood in the election of 2002 when a plurality of electorates elected one of Pakistan's only religions-based party MMM during the period of military dictatorship of Pervez Musharraf. A groundswell of anti-American sentiment after the 2001 United States invasion of Afghanistan contributed to the Islamist coalition victory (*Simon,2008*). The 2002 was also in context of a ban by Musharraf against extensive canvassing by Pakistan's two most popular political parties, the Pakistan Peoples Party and the Pakistan Muslim League, with the heads of both parties having been barred from participation in the elections.

After coming to power, the MMM government introduced a range of social restrictions, though Islamic Shariah law was never fully enacted. Restrictions on public musical performances were introduced as well as a ban prohibiting music to be played in public places as part of the Prohibition of Dancing and Music Bill 2005- which led to the creation of a thriving underground music scene in Peshawar. The Islamist government also attempted to enforce compulsory hijab on women and wished to enforce gender segregation in the province's educational institutions. The coalition further tried to prohibit male doctors from performing ultrasounds on women and tried to close the provinces cinemas. In 2005 the coalition successfully passed the 'Prohibition of Use of Women in Photograph Bill, 2005', leading to the removal of all public advertisements that featured women. However, the religious coalition was swept out of power by the secular and leftist Awami National Party in the free elations of 2008 that took place after the fall of Musharraf, leading to the repeal of the Islamist social agenda.

In 2013, the centre-right Pakistan Tehreek-e-insaf was elected to power in the province. Public disapproval of ANP's leftist programme integrated in civil administration and popular opposition against religious programme promoted by the MMM swiftly shifted the province's leniency towards the right-wing spectrum led by the PTI in 2012. With PTI forming the government 2013, the Khyber Pakhtunkhwa serves as a stronghold of the rightist PTI and is perceived as right-wing spectrum of the country. In non-Pashtun areas, such as Attock, Abbottabad, and Hazara District, the PML (N), the centre right party, enjoys considerable support over economical and public policy issues and has a substantial vote bank.

In an important development the Government of Pakistan on March 2, 2017 considered a proposal to merge the Federally Administered Tribal Areas (FATA) with Khyber Pakhtunkhwa and to repeal the Frontier Crimes Regulations (FCR) which are currently applicable to the tribal areas. The Frontier Crimes Regulations comprises a special set of laws of Pakistan which are applicable to the FATA of northwestern Pakistan. The state states that three basic rights are not applicable to the residents of FATA- appeal, wakeel and daleel (the right to request a change to a conviction in any court, the right to legal representation and the right to present reasoned evidence, respectively. In the context, some political parties have opposed the merger, and called for the tribal areas to instead become a separate province of Pakistan.

References

Adeney, Katharine (2007). *Federalism and Ethnic Conflict Regulation in India and Pakistan*, Palgrave, p.116.

Ahmar, Moonis (1996). 'Ethnicity and State Power in Pakistan: The Karachi', Crisis, *Asian Survey*, Vol. XXXVI, No. 10 (October), pp. 1032-33.

Ahmed, Feroz (1985). 'Pakistan's Problem of National Integration', Mohammad Asghar Khan (ed.) *Islam, Politics and the State: The Pakistan Experience*, London, Zed Press, p. 234.

Ahmed, Feroz (1991). 'The Language Question in Sind', Akbar S. Zaidi (ed.), *Regional Imbalances and Regional Questions in Pakistan*, Lahore, Vanguard Books.

Ahmed, Ishtiaq (1991). 'The Politics of Ethnicity in Sindh: Changing Perceptions of Group Identity,' *Asian Societies in Comparative Perspective*, Nordic Institute of Asian Studies, Vol. 3, p. 809.

Andeney, Katharine (2007). 'Democracy and Federalism in Pakistan' in Baogang He, Brian Galligan and Takashi Inoguchi (eds.), *Federal in Asia*, United Kingdom, Edward Elgar Publishing, pp. 111-13.

Ansari, Sarah (1995). 'Partition, Migration and Refugees: Responses to the Arrival of Muhajirs in Sindh during 1947-48,' *Journal of South Asian Studies*, Vol. XVIII, pp. 95-108.

Ansari, Sarah F.D. (1992). *Sufi Saints and State Power: The Pirs of Sind, 1843-1947*, Cambridge University Press, p. 115.

Badar, Hammad, Abdul Ghafoor and Sultan Ali Adil (2007), Factors Affecting Agricultural Production of Punjab (Pakistan)', *Pakistan Journal of Agriculture Science*, Vol. 44, No. 3, pp. 506-09.

Bahadur, Kalim (1994). 'Ethnic Problems in Pakistan,' *World Focus*, Vol. XV, Nos. 4-5 (April-May), p. 27.

Baxter, Craig (1974). 'Constitution Making: The Development of Federalism in Pakistan', *Asian Survey* Vol. 14, No. 12, University of California Press, pp. 1034-85.

Bhavnani, Nandita (2016). 'Unwanted Refugees: Sindhi Hindus in India and Muhajirs in Sindh', Australia, *Journal of South Asian Studies*, Vol. 39(4).

Bose, Sugata and Ayesha Jalal (2004). *Modern South Asia – History, Culture Political Economy*, New Delhi, Oxford University Press, p. 177.

Burki, Shahid Javed (2012), 'Punjab's Economic Importance', *The Express Tribune*, 13 May.

Chakravarty, Sukha Ranjan (1976). 'The Paktoon National Movement', *Foreign Affairs Reports*, Vol. XXV, No. 1, p. 9.

Claus, Peter J., Sarah, Diamond and Margaret, Ann Mills (2003). *South Asian Folklore: An Encyclopedia: Afghanistan, Bangladesh, India, Nepal, Pakistan, Sir Lanka*, Taylor & Francis, p. 447.

Cohen, Stephen P. (2004). *The Idea of Pakistan*, Brooking Institution Press, p. 382.

Cole, Owen William and Singh Piara (1995). *The Sikhs: Third Religious Beliefs and Practices*, Sussex Academic Press, pp. 130-33.

Dalrymple, William (2015), 'The Great Divide', *The New Yorker*, 29 June.

David, Roman (2009). 'Pakistan's Taliban Fight Threatens Key Economic Zone', 15 May.

Eijazuddin, Chaghtai Mirza (2010). 'Sindh's Role in Pakistan Movement', *Dawn*, Karachi, 24 January.

Election Commission of Pakistan (2013). 'Party Position (National Assembly)', 24 May.

Express Tribune (2012), 24 March.

Frotscher, Ann (2008). *Claiming Pakistan: The MQM and the Fight for Belonging*, Baden- Baden, Nomos, p. 90.

Gandhi, Rajmohan (2013), *Punjab: A History from Auranzeb to Mountbatten*, New Delhi, Aleph Book Company.

Gayer, Laurent (2014). *Karachi: Ordered Disorder and Struggle for the City*, Noida, Harper Collins, Chapter 1.

Gibran, Peshimam (2009). '25 Years of MQM a Critical Analysis', *The News*, 6 August.

Hanif, Farhan and Hanif, Siddiqi (2012). *The Politics of Ethnicity in Pakistan. The Baloch, Sindhi and Mohajir Ethnic Movements,* Rutledge, p. 88.

Hanif, Muhammad and Khan, Muhammad Nawaz (2012). 'Eighteen Amendments Revisited', Nuri, Maqsud Hassan, Hanif Muhammad and Khan Muhammad Nawaz (eds.), *Eighteen Amendment Revisited,* Islamabad policy Research Institute, pp. 23-26

Haq, Farhat (1999). 'Rise of the MQM in Pakistan: Politics of Ethnic Mobilisation'. *Asian Survey,* Vol. 35, No. 11, University of California Press, pp. 990-1004.

Harrison, Selig S. (1981). *In Afghanistan Shadow: Baluch Nationalism and Soviet Temptations,* Washington, D.C., Carnegie Endowment, p. 283.

Hiranandani, Popati (1981). *The Golden and Silver Pages of My Life,* Delhi, Sindh Akademi.

Hurst, C.D. (1996). 'Pakistan's Ehtnic Divide,' *Studies in Conflict and Terrorism,* Vol. XIX, p. 189.

Hurst, C.D. (1996). 'Pakistan's Ethnic Divide,' *Studies in Conflict and Terrorism,* Vol. XIX, p. 181.

Husnain, Ishrat (2014). 'The Economy of Sindh', *Second International Seminar* on Sindh Through the Centuries, 26 March, pp. 4-10.

Imperial Gazetteer 2 of India (2013). *Imperial Gazetteer of India,* Digital South Asia Library, Vol. 19, p. 154.

Jalal, Ayesha (1995). 'Conjuring Pakistan: History as Official Imagining'. International *Journal of Middle East Studies,* Vol. 27, No. 1, pp. 73-89.

Jalal, Ayesha (1995). *Democracy and Authoritarianism in South Asia: A Comparative and Historical Perspective* Cambridge, Cambridge University Press, p. 37.

Kennedy, Charls H. (2006). 'Political Issues in 2004', Kennedy, Charles H. and Cynthia A. Botteron (eds.), *Pakistan 2005*, Karachi: Oxford University Press, pp. 1- 11.

Khalidi, Omar (1998). 'From Torrent to Trickle: Indian Muslim Migration to Pakistan, 1947-97', *Islamic Studies*, Vol. 37, No. 3, pp. 339-352.

Khan, Arif, Khan, Taj Moharram and Rehman, Ashfaq U. (2017). 'Government – Opposition Relations Amidst the Provincial Autonomy During Bhutto Regime,' *Journal of the Research Society of Pakistan*, Vol. 54. No. 2 (July-December), p. 42.

Khan, Jamshed (2014). 'The Rise of Political Islam in Khyber Pakhtunkhwa: The Case of Muttahida Majlis-e-Amal (MMM),' *The Dialogue*, Vol. IX, No. 3, p. 299.

Khan, Kamran Aziz (2011). '2002 Elections in Pakistan: A Reappraisal', *Journal of Political Studies*, Vol. 18, No. 1, p. 94.

Kripalani, J.B. (2004). *My Times*, Delhi, Rupa, p. 703.

Kukreja, Veena (2003). *Contemporary Pakistan – Political Processes, Conflicts and Crises*, New Delhi, Sage Publications, p. 138.

Kumar, Priya and Kothari Rita (2016). 'Sindh, 1947 and Beyond South Asia', Australia, *Journal of South Asia Studies*, 39 (4), p. 775.

Lorch, Donatella (2001), 'Afghan Refugees in Pakistan at Risk', *United Nation's Human Rights Commission Report*, 1 August.

Malik, Iftikhar H. (1996). 'The State and Civil Society in Pakistan: From Crisis to Crisis', *Asian Survey*, Vol. XXVI, No. 7, pp. 673-90.

Malik, Iftikhar H. (1997). *State and Civil Society in Pakistan: Politics of Authority, Ideology and Ethnicity*, New York, St. Martin Press, p. 217.

Matthews, J.A. and Briffa, K.R. (2005). 'The Little Ice Age': Re-evaluation of an Evolving Concept', *Georgia Annual*, 87A(i), pp. 17-36.

McGarry N. and B.O' Leary (1993). 'Introduction: The Macro Political Regulation of Ethnic Conflict', in John McGarry and Brendan O'Leary (eds.), *Past Conflict, Institutions in Ethnically Divided Society*, Montreal. Mcgill Queen's University Press, p. 18.

Mitra, Subrata Kumar, Mike Enskat and Clemens Spiess (2004). *Political Parties in South Asia,* Greenwood Publishing Group, p. 366.

Mukherjee, Kunal (2010). 'Islamic Revivalism and Politics in Contemporary Pakistan', *Journal of Developing Societies,* Vol. 26, No. 3, pp. 329-53.

Nazir, P. (1993). 'Social Structure, Ideology and Language-Caste Among Muslims', *Economic and Political Weekly,* Bombay, pp. 2897-2900

Parekh, B. (1992). 'The Cultural Particularity of Liberal Democracy', *Political Studies, Special Issue,* pp.160-75.

Planning & Development Department (2015). 'Punjab Growth Strategy 2018 Accelerating Economic Growth and Improving Social Outcomes', *Government of Punjab* (PDF), Lahore, March.

Robert, J. (2003). *The Origins of Conflict in Afghanistan,* Greenwood Publishing Group, pp. 92-94.

Sana, Haroon (2008). 'The Rise of Deobandi Islam in the North-West Frontier Province and Its Implications in Colonial India and Pakistan 1914-1996', *Journal of the Royal Asiatic Society,* Vol. 18, pp. 66-67.

Sattar, Babar (2012). '18th Constitutional Amendment and Need for Passage of the 19th Constituional Amendment', Nuri Maqsud Haussan, Hanif, Muhammad and Khan, Muhammad Nawaz (eds.). *Eighteen Amendment Revisited,* Islamabad Policy Research Institute, pp. 74-87.

Sayeed, Khalid Bin (1980). *Politics in Pakistan. Nature and Direction of Change,* Praeger, Praeger Publishers, p. 123.

Schimmel, Annemarie (1986). *Pearls from Indus Jamshoro, Sindh,* Pakistan, Sindhi Adabi Board, p. 150.

Selig, S. Harrison (1986). 'Ethnicity and the Political Stalemate in Pakistan', Ali Banuazizi and Myron Weiner (eds.). *The State, Religion and Ethnic Politics*, New York, Syracuse University Press, p. 290.

Shah, Ali and Vaqar Sgayyid (1993). *Afghanistan and the Frontier in Marwat*, Fazal-ur-Rahim Khan (ed.), Emjay Books International, p. 256.

Simon, Robinson (2008). 'Religion's Defeat in Pakistan's Election', *Time*, 29 February.

Sindh Board of Investment (2017). 'Sindh Economy', *Government of Sindh*, Karachi.

Singh, Upinder (2008). *A History of Ancient and Early Medieval India: From the Stone Age to the 12th Century*, New Delhi, Pearson Education. p. 137

Verkaaik, Oskar (1994). *A People of Migrants: Ethnicity, State, and Religion in Karachi*, Amsterdam, V.U. University Press, p. 13.

Verkaaik, Oskar (2008). 'Cosmopolitanism: Culture, Cosmopolitanism, and Gender in Karachi Pakistan' Martina Rieker and Kamran Asdar Ali (eds.), *Gendering Urban Space in the Middle East, South Asia and Africa*, New York: Palgrave Macmillan, pp. 207-8.

Wakabayashi, Judy and Kothari, Rita (2009). *Decentering Translation Studies: India and Beyond*. John Benjamin Publishing, pp. 122-25.

Waseem. Dr. Mohammad (2010). *Federalism in Pakistan*. Lahore, LUMS, p. 18.

Wright, Theodore P. (1974). 'Indian Muslim Refugees in the Politics of Pakistan', *Journal of Commonwealth and Comparative Politics*, p. 191.

Yusuf, Huma (2014). 'The Other Threat to Pakistan', *The New York Times*, 2 April.

4

Balochistan: Accession and Status

Brief History and Accession

When Indian Prime Minister Narendra Modi referred Balochistan, the troubled province of Pakistan, in his address from the ramparts of Red Fort on 15th August 2016, the occasion reminded many of us the multi-layered inside story of the days that unwillingly created the situation for Balochistan to accede with Pakistan. The concept of Balochistan as a nation-state was formed in 1410. Stretching till Iran to the West and Afghanistan to the North, it was an independent country before the British attacked and annexed it in 1839. Then it was British who arbitrarily sliced Balochistan into three pieces - Northern Balochistan, Western Balochistan and Eastern Balochistan through two artificial borders-the Goldsmith Line (1871) and the Durand Line (1895). Northern Balochistan and Western Balochistan were given to Iran and Afghanistan respectively, while Eastern Balochistan, now a part of Pakistan, remained independent and maintained treaty relations with the British (*Firstpost, August 20, 2016*). Till 1947 the British remained in Eastern Balochistan and at the time of their departure they recognized Balochistan as an independent state. Thus, in post-withdrawal phase Balochistan, like the State of Jammu and Kashmir, was an independent entity before whom there was a clear option to accede with any or remain independent. In a fast-moving development and change of attitudes, on March 27, 1948, Balochistan made a choice to accede with Pakistan with heavy heart.

History of Balochistan

With combined history the Baloch, Baluch or Balochi are a people who live mainly in today's Pakistan, Iran and Afghanistan. About 50% of the total Baloch population lives in the western province of Pakistan, 40% of Baloch are settled in Sindh; and a significant number of Baloch people in Punjab of Pakistan. They make up nearly 3.6% of the Pakistani population, about 2% of Iran's population and about 2% of Afghanistan's population (*Central Intelligence Agency, 2013*). Although exact origin of the word "Baloch" is unclear, the Balochi generally hail from Aleppo, now in Syria and are descendants of Hazrat Ameer Hamza, the uncle of the prophet Muhammad, who settled in present day Aleppo. The Balochi generally live in remote mountainous and desert regions, which have protected them from invasion and allowed them to form a distinct cultural identity. They are predominantly Sunni Muslims but a significant number in Balochistan region are Shia Muslim. Balochi customs and traditions are conducted according to codes imposed by tribal laws. From the 1st century to the 3rd century CE, the region of modern Pakistani Balochistan was ruled by the Paratarajas, a dynasty of Indo-Scythian or Indo-Parthian kings. In succeeding years Arab forces invaded Balochistan in the 7th century, converting the Baloch people to Islam (*Nasser, 2012*). Arab rule in Balochistan lasted until the end of the 10th century.

In Medieval era, shortly thereafter western Balochistan fell to Nasir-ud-din Sabuktagin. His son, Mahmud of Ghazni, conquered the whole of Balochistan. A little latter, western Balochistan, Iranian Balochistan, became part of the dominion of Sultan Muhammad Khan in 1219. Afterwards part of the history of Balochistan centered around Kandahar and it was in this area in 1398 that Pir Muhammad, the grandson of Timur, fought the Afghans in the Sulaiman mountains. In succeeding century, the Pakistani Baloch extended their power to Kalat, Kachhi, and the Punjab and the wars took place between Mir Chakar Khan Rind and Mir Gwahram Khan Lashari. Further from 1556 to 1595 the region was under the Safavid dynasty. The army of Akbar the Great then brought what is now Pakistani Balochistan under control of the Mughals of Delhi until 1638 when it was again transferred to Persia. However, Makran alone remained independent under the Maliks, Buledais, and Gickis, until Nasir Khan 1 of Kalat brought it within his power during the 17th century (*Imperial Gazetter of India:276*). In coming years as Mughal power declined, the British gradually became involved in Balochistan during the reign of Mir Mehrab Khan – a symbol of British opposition in the area.

British Arrival and the Baloch

Among the Balochs, the Khans of Kalat consolidated most of the Baloch country into a feudal state during the 18th century. Abdullah Khan, the fourth Khan (1714-1734) expanded his realm from Kandahar, across the Makran area all the way to Bandar Abbas and extended his dominion to embrace Dera Ghazi Khan District on the edge of Punjab (*Harrison:18*) while Nasir Khan 1 (the sixth Khan) became the most popular, powerful and dynamic ruler of the Khanate (1739-1795) who claimed sovereignty over all lands where Baloches lived. He brought Karachi and most of western (Iranian) Balochistan under his administration. At an early period, he consolidated his authority over an immense kingdom, the secret of his success being that he had influence enough to ensure the obedience of his feudal chiefs and discretion enough to refrain from interfering in their internal affairs. Possibly the most interesting aspect of the long reign of Nasir Khan was his skilful internal policy, directed towards strengthening the powers and figure of the Khan, though without destroying traditional political mechanisms of a society that was still eminently tribal and pastoral in nature. He was regarded as the greatest and most powerful Khan among all the rulers of the Khanate. As a result of his successful reformist policies, he is sometimes compared to Peter the Great of Russia in the Baloch nationalist circles (*Marri:131*). With the death of Nasir Khan 1 in 1795, the deterioration of the central authority in Khanate started, even though it maintained its independence until the arrival of the British on the scene in the mid-19th century.

Almost by the time the big power rivalry in Central Asia began and it resulted in the British invasion of Afghanistan. It also brought British forces into the Baloch region. The British supply routes to Afghanistan could not be safeguarded without securing Balochistan and it gained much importance in British Central Asian Policy. As a result, in November 1839 the British forces were ordered to subjugate Kalat where Khan Mir Mehrab Khan refused to surrender and fought back against the invaders. In the war he was killed with his four hundred men and the British installed Shahnawaz Khan, a fourteen-year-old distant relative of the deceased Khan, posted a Lieutenant Loveday as regent and started the dismemberment of the Baloch country. Soon thereafter, as the British army left Kalat, Baloch tribes revolted and Mehrab Khan's son, Nasir Khan II, was enthroned as the new Khan. Nasir Khan II (1830-1857) was recognized by the British in 1841 and thirteen year later (1854) Kalat signed its first twenty-five-year treaty. In persuasion of the treaty British political agents were assigned to the Khan, with an annual subsidy paid to the Khan for loyalty and Quetta was returned to the Khanate. In a new treaty with Kalat, which was ratified at the end of 1876 it was arranged that British troops might be stationed in Kalat territory. In the following year (1877) Robert Sandeman was appointed Agent to the Governor General, Chief Commissioner and put in charge of the Agency for Balochistan (*Buller, 1908*). His appointment opened a new chapter in relations between the colonial power and the Baloch. He introduced a new system called "Sandeman system" and in this respect, considered as the real conqueror of Balochistan by the British Chroniclers.

The new Sandeman system was aimed at establishing direct relations with the Sardars and tribal chiefs, bypassing the Khan. He managed to have his way, and earned the loyalty of the Sardars by granting them allowances; his personal charisma enabled him to establish a whole network of close personal relations, undermining the prestige and sovereignty of the Baloch central power. Although, the Baloch people did not like to live under a foreign rule and soon after the martyrdom of Mehrab Khan in 1839, the hostility spread throughout the Baloch tribes in Eastern Balochistan. Further under an agreement with the Khan of Kalat in 1883, the British leased Quetta, Bolan Pass, Nasirabad, Chagai, Marri-Bugti and certain other Baloch areas and attached those with the Pashtun regions to rename "British Balochistan". Under the British, the Khanate's administration was carried out through prime minister who was appointed by the British Government while the released regions (British Balochistan) were ruled by the Agent to the Governor General of India.

Thus, even under the British the State of Kalat held a unique position within the British Indian imperial system. In theory it was sovereign and different from the other states. The northern belt of the Khanate (British Balochistan) and the responsibility for its defense and foreign affairs were handed over to the British Crown on the basis of mutually agreed upon friendly treaties. The Khan, in general, was expected to regain these territories and rights when ever the British decided to leave. What the British had gained by the treaties was not transferable to a third party. However, during British hegemony, the Baloch country was arbitrarily divided into several parts. One portion was given to Iran, a small portion was with Afghanistan and the northeastern region remained with the colonial administration under lease. The rest of the country was left in possession of the Kalat State. The Kalat state was further carved into the agency's territories and the federation of Balochi States (Kalat, Kharan and Las-Bela) remained with the Khan of Kalat, as the head of the federation. As the prospect for the British withdrawal came closer the National Party and other nationalist organizations joined the Khan of Kalat to seek independence of Balochistan. The Khan made a strong legal case for independence, arguing that Kalat like Nepal enjoyed a legal status based on direct treaty relations. In the earlier treaty of 1876, the British was committed to respect the "independence of Kalat" and to protect its territory against external aggression.

Fast Political Developments

In a final bid to devise the methodology for the transfer of power in India, the Labor Party Government sent a three-member Cabinet Mission headed by Sir Stafford Cripps who arrived in India on March 24, 1946. With his case prepared by several eminent lawyers including M.A. Jinnah, Mir Ahmad Yar Khan, the then ruler of Kalat, approached the Mission on behalf of his government to discuss the future status of his state in the scheme of independence for India (*Khan: 255*). The main concern of the submitted official memorandum was regarding the future position of the Khanate at the time and to restore its independence with the British withdrawal. By this submission the Khan of Kalat expected to restore its pre - 1876 status by regaining its full independence. As stated by the memorandum, the state of Kalat "will become fully sovereign and independent in respect to both internal and external affairs, and will be free to conclude treaties with any other government or state. Earlier in 1872, Sir W.L. Merewether, who was in charge of the British Government's relations with Kalat, wrote "There cannot in my opinion, be the least doubt of the course which should be followed with regard to the Kalat or Baluchistan as it should be correctly termed. The ruler Khan is the de facto and de jure ruler of that country. We have treaty engagements with him under which he is bound to keep his subjects from injuring British territory or people to protect trade. But the treaty is with him as ruler only (*Khan:265*). In the above and many similar contexts in another petition prepared for the purpose the Baloch nationalists stated that Kalat, which is not an Indian state and which was brought in relation with the British Government on account of its geographical position on the border of India, is just like Afghanistan and Persia. The State had no intention of entering into a federal relationship with successive government or governments in British India and therefore it requested your Excellency to declare the independence of Kalat State. In addition, although the other surrounding Baloch chiefs and Sardars demanded their separation from Punjab and to be linked with the Kalat state, the British representatives failed to settle any of the matters put forwarded by Kalat.

Even earlier to the formal announcement of Kalat's independence on 15th August 1947, on the basis of the Standstill Agreement (11th August 1947), on April 11, 1947 the declaration of independence was published and distributed as a pamphlet that outlined the constitution of a Free Baloch State. It followed a round table conference held in Delhi which was attended by Lord Mountbatten, Jinnah, Liaqat Ali Khan, Prime Minister of Kalat, Chief Secretary of Kalat, and the Legal Advisor of Kalat State. The deliberations agreed, "Kalat State will be independent on August 15, 1947, enjoying the same status as it originally held in 1838, having friendly relations with neighbors. In case the relations of Kalat with any future government become strained, Kalat will exercise its right of self-determination, and the British Government should take precautionary measures to help

Kalat in the matter as per the Treaties of 1839 and 1841 (*India Office Record:352*). This "Standstill Agreement" which was formally announced on August 11, 1947, accepted the sovereign status of Balochistan. It stated "The government of Pakistan recognized the status of Kalat as a free and independent State which has bilateral relations with the British Government, and whose rank and position is different form that of other Indian states" (*Baloch:352*).

Short-lived Independence and Accession

As a follow, up of the Standstill Agreement the Khan of Kalat proclaimed Khanate's independence on August 15, 1947, and addressing the audience he announced. "Today our country is independent and I can express my views freely and openly." The lower house of the Kalat which was convened specially for the purpose in September 1947 overwhelmingly approved this move. The majority of the fifty-two assembly members voted for independence, but did not foreclose the possibility of a special relationship between the independent Kalat and the newly established state of Pakistan (*Baloch:150-66*). The traditional flag of the state in green over red color and the crescent and star in the centre was hoisted and in a prayer in the Jamia masque of Kalat, as independent ruler of the state, addressed the audience in a lengthy speech, expressed his determination to achieve three objectives:

- Complete independence of the country from the foreign yoke and domination.
- Promulgation of Shariat Law with a constitution based on the injunctions of Holy Quran as understood; and
- The unity of the Baloch as a nation spread over a large part of Asia in large numbers (*Nasir: 489-90*).

In line, the bicameral legislature, its composition, and Rawaj continued as unwritten constitution while the Kalat Act of 1946 was used as the written constitution. In the year

1947 the election was held in Kalat and Makkoran. It was the first general election in Balochistan's history in which the National Party won 39 seats out of 52 in the Lower House.

Soon thereafter, Kalat parliament and ruler as well began to work independently and in its first three-day meeting held in Dadar in December 1947 recognized Baloch as the "official and national language" of the state of Kalat and decreed that it should be taught in schools (*Nasir:499*). The decision was approved unanimously by the Lower House in its meeting of January 4, 1948 and a committee was formed to study and report on the adoption of measures and methods for the introduction of Baloch as a medium of instruction in schools. Earlier to this the Khan of Kalat visited Pakistan as the head of a sovereign state in October 1947 and was received as the King of Balochistan by thousands of Baloch in Karachi. By the time Pakistan's attitude began to change and in course of the visit M.A. Jinnah advised the Khan to expedite the merger with Pakistan. Khan, at the moment, refused Jinnah's demand and argued, "As Baluchistan is a land of numerous tribes, the people there must be consulted in the affairs prior to any decision. I take, according to the prevalent tribal convention, no decision, which can be binding upon them unless they are taken into confidence by their Khan (*Baloch:183*).

Following Jinnah's proposal on Kalat's merger the Khan of Kalat summoned the legislature's meeting in which both houses of Parliament not only unanimously opposed the merger proposal but also argued that it was against the spirit of the earlier agreement arrived between Kalat Government and the spokesmen of Pakistan on August 4, 1947, as well as against the Independence Act of 1947. Earlier to this in September Kalat's Prime Minister and Foreign Minister were sent to Karachi to meet the Secretary to the Government of Pakistan's Ministry of Foreign and State Affairs. Their meeting was not fruitful as the host (Pakistan) advised them a merger with Pakistan rather than a treaty relationship. On the other hand from there onwards Pakistani authorities not only started campaigning against the Khan to compel him to join Pakistan but also prepared to use coercive methods for a forced merger of the state. As per demand of the situation the Khan of Kalat instructed the General to reorganize force and arrange arms and ammunition. In December 1947 he also approached the Commonwealth Relations office for help but the British did not agree to supply arms without the Pakistan Government's approval. In the same time, the desperate Khan also requested Indian authorities and the Afghan King for help, but with no success.

At the time the State of Kalat was made up of four feudatories – Lasbela, Kharan, Makkoran and Kalat itself which was the largest of all. In a unfortunate development the Government of Pakistan announced on March 18, 1948, the accession of Lasbela, Kharan and Makkoran which robbed Kalat of more than half of its territory and made access to the sea. In a last attempt on March 25, 1947, the desperate Khan of Kalat summoned and tried to persuade his Sardars against accession but only two unimportant Sardars obeyed the call while others refused to attend. Although, in safe side a letter of 27 March form the Khan to Jinnah denied reports that he had attempted to urge Sardars and people against Kalat's accession to Pakistan. In it he also denied reports that he had entered into negotiations with India or Afghanistan. In this way the independence moves came to an end when the Khan of Kalat, Mir Ahmad Yar Khan acceded to Pakistan on March 27, 1948, defining the matter of signing the merger document as a "dictate of history". On April 1, 1948 the Pakistan army moved to Kalat with orders to overcome the resistance from the nationalists. The accession of Balochistan into Pakistan was one of the epoch-making events in the history of Baloch people and their country. On March 28, 1948, the Khanate became a part of Pakistan. By this, the legal entity of the Khan of Kalat was abolished.

Economy, Religion and Language

Closely connected to social set up is its economy. The economy of Balochistan is largely based upon the production of natural gas, coal and minerals. Agriculture and livestock also dominate the Bloch economy. Horticultural development is a fairly recent, yet growing phenomenon. Other important economic sectors include fisheries, mining, manufacturing industries, trade and other services being rendered by public and private sector organizations in the province. Tourism remains limited but has increased due to the exotic appeal of the province. Limited farming in the east and fishing along the Arabian Sea coastline provide income and sustenance for the local population Due to the tribal lifestyle of many Baloch and Brahui people, animal husbandry and trading bazaars throughout the province are important. People choose to live in regions that have water, roads, hospitals, electricity, and a congenial climate. Therefore, the population is concentrated around the highlands of Quetta and Kalat and in the districts bordering the plains of Punjab and upper Sindh. The other well populated districts are along the Makran coast and in the Kirthar hill ranges along the western border of Sindh. Lack of adequate rainfall throughout the province and availability of water only in certain belts of land decides the occupation of the people.

Today, the Baloch, despite occupying a vast and resourceful territory has failed to keep the pace of socio-economic development and modernity with other fellow nations in the region. The economic grievances of the Baloch are dated back to the British era. As the British developed industries and agriculture in Sindh, Punjab, and NWFP, they ignored Balochistan. There is a widely held view that the British rulers neglected the economic development of Balochistan *(Dawn, Delhi)*. A section of them also view that it was not merely a case of neglect, but what might be called purposeful sidetracking, even suppression. Of course, the British had their own imperial interest to protect. Aijaz

Ahmad, a Pakistani Marxist, wrote, "The British imperialist interest in Balochistan was not primarily economic; rather it was of a military and geostrategic nature *(Ahmad, 1998).*" Military experts also expressed the same view and maintained that Balochistan was the chessboard on which the Great Game was played *(Ahmad, 1992)*. The British rulers probably thought that an economically and politically enervated Balochistan would lend itself to be used more easily. On the other hand, a prosperous and united Balochistan could become recalcitrant and forge relations with undependable principalities in the neighborhood *(Nicholas, 1982)*. However, despite this neglect, in the course of time, the British rule encouraged commerce and trade and the administration had created an abundance of new professions. All these developments led finally to the rise of Baloch national consciousness and nationalism in eastern Balochistan in the 1920s.

As earlier, with annexation in 1948, Balochistan remained on the whole extremely deprived. Since the early 1950s, the Pashtuns took control of most of the commercial life previously controlled by Sindhi Hindus. Provincial administration was predominantly Punjabi and few of the higher civil servants were Baloch. According to preliminary surveys, underground water as well as mineral resources were available in large quantities in Balochistan. But the underdeveloped infrastructure of the province made them difficult to exploit. As a result, in the 1970s, compared to the other three provinces Punjab, Sindh and NWFP, Balochistan was the most neglected and impoverished province in Pakistan. In 1976, the annual per capita income was 54 dollars as compared with the 80 dollars for Punjab, 78 dollars for Sindh, and 60 dollars for NWFP *(Burki, 1980)*.

In 1977 the life expectancy in rural Balochistan was 42 years as compared with the national average of 60 years. Similarly, the national literacy average was 16 percent, while that of Balochistan was 6 to 9 percent (*Harrison,1981*). To the

Balcoh such an economic gap can hardly be justified in the light of Balochistan's rich maritime resources along the several hundred miles of coast as well as its land-based mineral resources. According to Baloch nationalists, the people of Baluchistan were not the beneficiaries of the huge resources and income the province provided to the Federal exchequer. The continued negligence has deepened the sense of deprivation and feeling of hatred against Islamabad. A section of the Baloch nationalists believe that the centralist nature of Pakistani federation is such that small nationalities like the Baloch would find it hard to accommodate within the federation.

Thus, the basic issue related to the economic claims of the Baloch is the right distribution of natural resources between the centre and the province. Balochistan is the richest unit in the federation of Pakistan as far as the natural resources like various types of minerals especially natural gas, copper, marble and gold. At the same time, it has a very significant geographical and coastal position (*Imran, 2016*). Now the problem is that Ports and Shipping are not only a federal subject but it is totally operated from Islamabad. The local population has always been complaining against their deprivation of the royalties concerning natural resources and their lack of participation in the development.

The state religion in Pakistan is Islam, which is practiced by about 95-98% of the people of the nation *(Library of Congress,2005)*. The remaining 2.5% practice Christianity, Hinduism and other religions. Muslims are divided into different sects: the majority of them practice Sunni Islam, while 5.20% are Shias and 2.2% are Ahmadi Muslims. At large, Baloch differ from their neighbors not only in their language, literature, religion, and feelings, but also in their traditions and habits. For example, Arab Islam failed to assimilate the Persians into Arab traditions. Iranians fought and resisted Arab domination and though they converted to Islam, they formed a new sect (Shia) in Islam. They maintained their separate language, literature and traditions. Turks and Afghans also refused the domination and influence of Iranian Islam. The same is true of the Baloch, who maintained their own traditions and customs, which are different from Punjabi, Sindhi, Iranian and Afghan Muslims. Likewise, in sphere of religion the Baloch people have a different perception than other nations in Middle East. They are not fundamentalist and do not believe in mixing religion with politics *(Baloch, 1987)*. The overwhelming majority of the Baloch adhere to the Sunni branch of Islam of the Hanafite rite. It is important to note that before succumbing to Islam the Baloch were mostly Zoroastrians. The remnants of some Zoroastrian tradition are still evident among some Baloch tribes *(Shaheen, 1980)*. The conversion of the Baloch to Islam had a sterilizing effect on their sense of nationhood. Especially since the Nasir Khan's era, the term "Balochistan" has meant more than just geography. It also refers to Baloch culture and is therefore social and political concept as well.

Language, culture, and perception are intimately intertwined and hence language has been a key element contributing to a sense of national identity as one scholar puts it, "Baluch identity in Baluchistan has been closely tied to the use of the Baluchi language in inter-tribal relations". In spite of almost half a century of brutal assimilation policy, both in Iran and Afghanistan, the Baluch people have managed to retain their culture and their oral tradition of story telling. The harsh oppression of the governments has strengthened the Baloch's will to pass on their heritage to coming generations. The Baloch language is both proof and symbol of the separate identity of the Baloch, and impressive efforts are made to preserve and develop it. In Pakistan the Balochi is generally classified as Eastern Balochi and western Balochi. Eastern Balochi is spoken mainly in the north eastern area of the province of Balochistan in Pakistan and in neighboring areas of the province of Punjab and Sindh.

Western Balochi is spoken in the Western and southern areas of the Pakistani province of Balochistan as well as in Karachi and other parts of Sindh and other parts of the region.

Balochistan, despite its scarce population, has an uncommon racial and tribal diversity. Most of the people in the cities and towns understand and speak more than two languages. In addition to Balochi, Pashtoo and Brahvi, the majority of the population understand and speak Urdu, the national language. In Kachhi and Sibi districts, people speak Seraiki and Sindhi. Quetta city, the confluence point of all linguistic groups accommodates not only Urdu, Balochi, Pashtoo, Brahvi and Sindhi speaking people but Darri and Persian speaking ones as well.

In fact, Baloch culture is opposite to the general perception about it. Though Balochistan is an area of barren lands, deserts and mountains, the Baloch culture is full of traditions, arts and crafts. Balochistan is also known for its tribes and festivals. Another distinct feature of Baloch culture is the storytelling tradition. Poats and storytellers are highly respected in Baloch culture. In Baloch culture marriages are different and unique than in the other provinces of the country. The marriages are according to the Islamic principles in presence of a Maullana along with the presence of witnesses. Usually the marriages are done in young ages but are arranged in early childhood or at birth. There is a very low or negligible ratio of love marriages as this is not appreciated across the culture in all tribes. Likewise, divorcé rate is very low in Balochistan as compared to the other provinces of Pakistan. However, dress, festival, music, food, and sports are almost the same as of other provinces of the country.

About the Province

Baluchistan, the province of today's Pakistan, originally comprises of three areas : One, the Chief Commissioner's Province of Balochistan directly ruled by the British India, which in August 1947, immediately became part of Pakistan, two, the four princely states of feudalistic nature, namely Makran, Kharan, Las Bela, and the Khanate of Kalat, who decided to accede to Pakistan in March 1948. The Khan of Kalat agreed to join Pakistan under the condition that only defense, currency, foreign relations and finance would be controlled by the federal government. The third part was the enclave of Gwader, purchased from the Sultanate of Oman in 1958. In line, the four princely states together formed the Balochistan States Union in October 1952. Three years later in October 1955 "One Unit" system was introduced which resulted in the merger of Balochistan States Union and the Chief Commissioner's Province of Balochistan. The enclave of Gwader, which was still part of the Sultanate of Oman was purchased in October 1958 and all together formed the then province of West Pakistan. Again, the province was officially dissolved in 1970 and the former Balochistan States Union and the former Chief Commissioner's province of Balochistan were combined to form the new province of Balochistan. In 1977, the then Balochistan province was expanded and Gwader was incorporated. Thus now, in its present form includes the three-the Chief Commissioner's province, the Balochistan States Union and the enclave of Gwader. In total the country Pakistan is comprised of four provinces-Baluchistan, Gilgit Baltistan, Khyber-Pakhtunkhwa, Punjab, and Sindh two centrally administered areas, a territory and a capital territory.

The province Baluchistan is one of the four provinces of Pakistan located in the southwestern region of the country. Its provincial capital and largest city is Quetta. It shares border with Punjab and the Federally Administered Tribal Areas (FATA) to the northeast, Sindh to the southeast, the Arabian Sea to the south, Iran to the west and Afghan to the north. Most of the province's inhabitants are Baloch people, Pashtuns and Brahuis, although there are small communities of Hazaras, Sindhis, Punjabis, and other settlers such as the Uzbeks, and Turkmens It covers an area of 347,

190 square kilometres, and is the largest province by area, constituting 44% of Pakistan's total landmass. In addition, it also borders the geopolitical regions of the Middle East and Southwest Asia, Central Asia and South Asia. The climate of the upper highlands is characterized by very cold winters and hot summers. In the lower highlands, winters vary from extremely cold in northern districts to milder conditions closer to the Makran coast. Winters are mild on the plains, with temperature never falling below freezing point. Summers are hot and dry, especially in the arid zones of Chagai and Kharan districts. The desert climate is characterized by hot and very arid conditions.

Gradually but very slowly the social composition of Pakistan's province Baluchistan is changing and getting a focus world-wide. Originally, they are constituted from a number of kindred groups. It has many subdivisions or clans who claim to have blood relations with one another through common ancestors. Kinship, which has its characteristic form in clan and family structure, provides the basic ordering mechanism for society. Even in the 19th century as modernization and urbanization reduced the importance of tribes and tribal organizations, the influence of tribal pattern is not destroyed *(Philip, 1990)*. The tribal patterns are existent and paternalistic methods of control through family networks continue to have relevance. Another expert on international economic development Dr. Nek Buzdar, also confirms that the Baloch society, by and large, adheres to traditional ways of life. He believes that despite the emergence of political parties in Balochistan, tribal organization and political leadership still play a dominant role in local and provincial administration *(Nek, 2000)*. Tribes in Balochistan are divided into *Shahri* (Sedentary) and nomadic units. The Shahris were the backbone of the feudal order, which was predominant in central, and southern Balochistan (Makkoran) while the nomads were the cornerstones of the tribal order prevailing mainly in the northern tribal areas. Both groups, however, were bound together by a set of historically evolved relationships based on economic, social, political, military, and lingual interactions *(Swidler, 1977)*. Of the both, the Baloch tribal system is segmentary which means that it is a set of equal lineages allied relatively and contingently for political action, decisions being made by assemblies and councils, with no offices and hierarchy of authority, and thus no top *(Philip, 1983)*. Therefore, centralized authority is absent in such a system. Keeping the fact in view, the colonial government exercised control over the Baloch tribes, the British themselves were light on the ground, and in return for the chieftains, loyalty, gave them a free hand to keep the tribal way of life largely unchanged.

In traditional Baloch society the most widely known institutions are the *Sardari* and *Jirga*. Under these systems, every tribe had its separate *Jirga* (council of elders) which acted as a court of law, *(Hassan, 1976)*. Jirga at the tribe's level operated under the leadership of Sardar and dealt with important matters concerning the tribes and distputes arising among them, the election of a new Khan or the eventual external threats. Providing the Baloch society, a historical, social and political structure, the Jirga remained intact for a long period and helped the Baloch deal with the situation of anarchy, chaos and emergency. In line, the constitution and powers of traditional Jirga was changed under the British rule in 19th century when Sir Robert Sandeman introduced a new kind of Jirga, called "Shahi Jirga" where only Sardars and aristocrats could sit. The meeting of Shahi Jirga was usually held once or twice in a year. Its powers were expanded in comparison to earlier and now it could impose taxes in property and labour and only the Political Agent could review the decision *(Dehwar, 1994)*. The new system was considered as a shrewd mechanism of indirect rule with powers vested in a few carefully selected tribal elders loyal to the British and ready to act against their own people.

Another traditional Baloch social system, "Sardari"

appears to have had its origin in the Mughal period of Indian history. In contrast to the system of Jirga, Sardari system is highly centralized and hierarchical *(Barth, 1969)*. Under it, at the apex of the system is the sardar, the hereditary central chief from whom power flows downward to waderas, the section chiefs, and beyond them to the subordinate clan and sub-clan leaders of the lesser tribal units. The sardar's extraordinary authority within this structure probably stems from the essentially military character of early Baloch tribal society. However, modernization has changed much of the tribal system. It was first challenged by the setting of international boundaries which partitioned into three states, dividing some of the large tribes between countries and prohibiting the traditional summer and winter migrations of nomads and semi-nomads.

The second challenge occurred between the world wars, when the British and Persians largely pacified Balochistan. The termination of the traditional nomadic economic system devastated the tribes and as a result they move into cities and towns. This increased chieftains' distance from the tribe. Over the course of time, the traditional social organization of the Baloch to a great extent has changed and now there is a widespread Baloch national consciousness that cuts across tribal divisions *(Harrison, 1981)*. In a tribal society, a political ideology such as Baloch nationalism would hardly gain support, because loyalties of tribal members do not extend to entities rather than individual tribes. Within the tribes, an individual's identity is based on his belonging to a larger group. This larger group is not the nation but the tribe.

Government and Politics

Balochistan is one of the four provinces of Pakistan, located in the southwestern part of the country. Its provincial capital and largest city is Quetta. In common with the other provinces of Pakistan, Balochistan has a parliamentary form of government. The ceremonial head of the province is the

Governor who is appointed by the President of Pakistan on the advice of the provincial Chief Minister. The Chief Minister, the province's chief executive, is normally the leader of the largest political party or alliance of parties in the provincial assembly. The unicameral Provincial Assembly of Balochistan comprises 65 seats of which 11 are reserved for women and 3 reserved for non-Muslims. The judicial branch of government is carried out by Balochistan High Court which is based in Quetta and headed by a Chief Justice. For administrative purpose the province is divided into six divisions. The six Divisions are further subdivided in 32 districts.

The government of Pakistan has been dealing with animosity among the tribes of Balochistan since the time the country came into existence in 1947. The causes of the conflict with Balochistan include a ripe ethnic nationalism along with feelings of economic and political exclusion *(TheIndianExpress, August 18, 2016)*. Demographically though it constitutes a mere 3.6 per cent of the total population of Pakistan, it is strategically extremely important to the country because of the high concentration of natural resources including gas, oil, copper and gold. However, despite the richness in natural resources, Balochistan continues to reain the poorest province of Pakistan. In addition, following the capture of Kalat on April 1, 1948, cases of military atrocities have been a recurrent occurrence in the province. Acts of ill treatment by officials in the region included torture, arbitrary, arrests executions and acts of indiscriminate violence. As a result, the people of Balochistan fell a sense of separate identity on account of a shared history, language, and other cultural aspects. This shared culture among the Balochs led to the ripening of a strong sense of nationalism that propounded for a larger political autonomy and a separate state for Balochistan.

In Pakistan's Balochistan province, insurgencies by Baloch nationalists have been fought in 1948, 1958-59, 1962-63, 1973-77 with an ongoing and reportedly stronger, broader insurgency beginning in 2003. Baloch separatists allege that the central government of Pakistan is systematically suppressing development in Balochistan to keep the Balochs weak, while their opponents argue that international business interests have been unwilling to invest in the region due to continuing unrest *(Kemp, 2010)*. Of the five Pakistan faced the first insurgency in 1948 when on April 1, the military invaded Kalat and Yar Khan, the then ruler of Kalat, signed a treaty of accession, submitting the federal government. At the time Yar Khan's younger brothers, Princes Agha Abdul Karim Baloch and Muhammad Rahim, refused to lay down arms and in coming years continued unconventional attacks on the army until 1950. Second conflict took place from 1958 to 1959 against the "One Unit" policy of the government which decreased their representation in government. This guerilla war was fought by Nawab Nauroz Khan and his followers and they were arrested, charged with treason and subsequently hanged on the charges. It followed the tension continued to grow amid consistent political disorder and instability at the federal level. Further, Sher Muhammad Bijrani Marri led like-minded militants into guerilla warfare from 1963 to 1969 by creating their own insurgent base. This insurgency ended in 1969, with the Baloch separatists agreeing to a ceasefire. In 1970 Pakistani President Yahya Khan abolished the "One Unit" policy, which led to the recognition of Balochistan as the fourth province of West Pakistan. In the fourth conflict (1973) which led to armed insurgency Pakistani military lost 300 to 400 hundred soldiers while a large number of Baloch militants and civilians were killed. The current conflict started in 2004 with an insurgent attack on Gwadar port and their stated demands include greater control of the province's resources and a moratorium on the construction of military bases in the area. In the context Pakistan accused India, and occasionally the US of supporting Baloch rebels.

Effects of Centralised Balochistan

Unfortunately, at the time Balochistan was annexed to

Pakistan, there was no legislative assembly existed in Balochistan, because earlier, the colonial administrator's reforms towards representative rule in India did not include Balochistan and in terms of centralization Pakistan's treatment was worst than the colonial regime. Jinnah, one in all at the moment, in keeping with the colonial tradition, constituted a governor general's advisory council for Balochistan to be ruled direct by him (*Chaudhri, 1973*). Further to strengthen his grip on Balochistan and other frontier areas, the governor general created a ministry of states and frontier regions and, in an unparliamentarily manner, kept the ministry under his own control. The rule of the governor general in Balochistan was considered as a dictatorial form of government. It culminated in 1955, with the imposition of "One Unit" scheme in Balochistan which amalgamated the four western provinces into one. The new scheme was vehemently opposed in Balochistan than anywhere else, and it was the first defiance of central government's authority. This is why the army moved first in Balochistan, in 1958, just before the imposition of martial law. It was the beginning of a repressive regime in Balochistan. The unrest further increased when the army demanded that weapons should be handed in at police stations and the tribesmen refused to comply. And after 23 years of the creation of Pakistan, in 1970, Balochistan was granted the status of a province. It led to the formation of a pro-Baloch government of the National Awami Party (NAP), in alliance with Jamiat Ulema Islam (JUI), a religious party.

In line, centralized tendency of Pakistan continued in Balochistan even after coming of a democratic government in 1973, in country's history. However, it found no relief in the new regime and as earlier, centralist tendencies continued. As a result, the province faced the worst repressive measures during 1973-1977 when a strong and violent opposition was raised against the central government. Z.A. Bhutto's centralist tendencies and his support base in Punjab warranted that a check be placed on the reforms of Balochistan which raised further tensions in centre-state relations. Bhutto, in his letter to the governor of the province, among other things, wrote, "every effort should be made to preserve national integrity. Fissiparous tendencies are not only harmful to the nation but also affect our international relations. Therefore, movements like Azad Balochistan movement, however nebulous, should be firmly put down, and not be permitted to affect our relations with foreign powers, particularly friendly rightwing countries. In fact, from the very beginning the Pakistani state has been insensitive to provincial grievances and oversensitive to the voice of dissent.

As a result of abruptly changed scenario the Baloch people became a part of the independent state of Pakistan yet colonial policies for controlling these tribes continued. The policy of offering incentives to tribal chiefs at the cost of common man has alienated Balochistan with the rest of the federation. The political leadership of Balochistan argue that the British government always treated them differently and they enjoyed special status and relationship with the British Indian government. In the years 1947-1948, because of rapid, unfavorable political developments they accepted the amalgamation with the state of Pakistan, but got apprehensive about the fact that Baloch population was only a small fraction of the total population of Pakistan and hence in a serious danger of loss of identity if not duly protected. Their apprehension was strengthened by the imposition of "One Unit" system, and later on, political arrangements under long military rules existed in the country. This forced them to rally under the banner ship of nationalism. The Baloch had voiced strong grievances about their lack of representation in the Pakistani bureaucracy, and armed forces, or in the provincial administration of Balochistan. Relations between Baloch nationalists and the central government have been confrontational since the creation of Pakistan, periodically turning violent.

Recently, in last two decades, the understanding between

Baloch people and the central government has worsened further, specially during the military rule of General Pervez Musharraf and thereafter. In 2004, the long-simmering tensions broke out into renewed insurgency. The conflict stems in part from the central government's imposition of a historical narrative of the creation of Pakistan as a religiously homogeneous country into the ethnically distinct Baloch (*Kupecz, 2012*). The military coup in 1999 that brought Pervez Musharraf to power increased general alienation among the Balochs. This is because Balochs see the army as lacking Baloch representation due to its domination by the interests of the Punjabi-the main ethnic group in Pakistan that counts for approximately 45 percent of the country's population (*Livingston and Hanlon, 2011*). The transition from the military government of Musharraf to the civilian government of President Zardari in 2008 till today under the premiership of Nawaz Sharif almost nothing has been done to assuage Baloch discontent. Even today, in the year 2016, as reports appeared in various newspapers and periodical reports, arbitrary arrest and detention, torture, extra-judicial and summary execution, disappearances and the use of excessive and indiscriminate violence by Pakistan's police, military, security intelligence forces have created a war-like situation in the country (*First post, 2016*), Very recently, this trouble-torn province of Pakistan has caught world attention and likely to become a potential political issue of region and the world as well.

Concerns of Baloch in Pakistan are one of the most serious threats to country's federal structure. The history of their relationship (between center and Balochistan) shows a long story of political inaptitude, economic exploitation and unfulfilled promises. Centre in its successive policies and measures have overlooked the sociological and anthropological peculiarities of Balochistan people and harsh economic realities under which they pass their lives, and which over 70 years, have given birth to deprivation. In the years, the deprivation amongst Balochis has caused a number of uprisings against the federal government. Unfortunately, being kept away from the mainstream politics of Pakistan, the Baloch have a number of serious grievances, which over the time; have developed into nationalistic feelings, posing threat to the federation of Pakistan. The situation in Balochistan during last years evoked concern, with deteriorating law and order situation and strident political demands that threatened the destabilization of Balochistan with a growing sense of deprivation in that province.

At the moment, the Baloch nationalism which to a large extent, is within the precinct of constitution of Pakistan, is trying to retain the Baloch identity while safeguarding the rights of common man in making the developmental efforts of the provinces and the country. It is the high, and perhaps the most suitable time to address this issue seriously which otherwise may foster into separation given the increasing pressure from the sentimental youth of Balochistan. Nationalist terrorism has mainly been witnessed in province of Balochistan at regular intervals and mainly revolves around the issue of exploitation of resources and threat to the political identity and culture of minorities, sub-nationalities.

Under the circumstances what needs to be done is the wholesome response. The most fundamental and urgent requirement is for trust building and the only way this can even begin is, by governance measures from the centre that are urgent, transparent and reach the door step of ordinary masses. For its part, Pakistan needs to learn that the problem of Balochistan must be given urgent attention and top priority in good faith and measure. The governing elite in Pakistan have to be sensitive to the genuine demands placed on the federal government by the Balochis.

The government has to adopt a multi-pronged anti-insurgency strategy to placate the Baloch people. The use of force will not lead to a peaceful solution. History is witness to the fact that suppression further ignites such movements. By taking serious and urgent socio-economic measures and by providing justice and fair play as basis of governance, the back of the insurgency can be broken. This can be achieved if the federal government in conjunction with the provincial government, applies the will to ensure that the legitimate rights of the people of Balochistan are granted and delivered immediately.

To solve the various problems of national interest through wide consensus, government should work on creating and implementing concrete policies that will lead to socio-economic development and problem resolution. Provincial and ethnic autonomy could enhance the participatory approach which will help to have wide consensus over national affairs. The legitimate grievances of Baloch people must be addressed as of all other deprived areas. For the broader peace and security program in the region, the government must invest in human development, and politically empower the people to take part in economic development through modern but decentralized governance mechanism.

However, the real solution lies in the strong political commitment to implement independent policy decisions in the best interest of Pakistan. Peaceful resolution of the conflict in Balochistan is improbable in the near future because neither side is likely to change its behavior. The military will maintain its strategy of targeting recalcitrant Baloch leaders, while some nationalists will continue to use violence as a means of extorting concessions from the federal government. The state will attempt to negotiate with those it sees as moderate in order to buy as much peace as possible. Failure to do in positive direction could have serious repercussions for Pakistan.

References

Ahmed Feroz (1991). "The Language Question in Sindh", in Akbar S. Zaidi (ed.), *Regional Imbalances and Regional Questions in Pakistan*. Lahore, Vanguard Books.

Ahmed, Feroz (1998). *Ethnicity and Politics in Pakistan*. Karachi, Oxford University Press, p. 180.

Baloch, Inayatullah (1987). *The Problem of Greater Baluchistan: A Study of Baluch Nationalism*. Stuttgart, Steiner Verlag Wiesbaden, p. 75.

Barth, Fredrick (1969). "Pathan identity and its maintenance", in Fredrick Barth (ed.) *Ethnic Group and Boundaries*, Boston, pp. 117-34.

Buller, R. Hughes (1908). *Baluchistan*. Calcutta, p. 43.

Burki, Shahid Javed (1980). *Pakistan Under Bhutto*. London, Macmillan Press, p. 94.

Central Intelligence Agency (2013). *The World factbook: Ethnic groups*. November 3, 2014.

Central Intelligence Agency, 2017.

Chaudhary, Mohammad Ali (1973). *The Emergence of Pakistan*. Lahore, Research Society of Pakistan, p. 252.

Dawn (1946), February 1.

Dehwar. M.M.S. (1994). *Contemporary History of Balochistan*. Quetta, Third World Publication, p. 260.

First Post, August 20, 2016.

Harrison, Selig S. (1981). *In Afghanistan's Shadow: Baluch Nationalism and Soviet Temptations*. New York, Cartegic Endowment for International Peace. P. 16.

Hassan, Mohammad Usman (1976). *Balochistan: Mazi, Hal aur Mustaqbel*. Karachi, Indus Publications, pp. 174-175.

Imran, Muhammad, Akram-ul-Haq Muhammad (2016). "Pakistan federation and Baloch nationalism: A Prospect for economic development and political challenges. *Canadian Social Science*, Vol. 12, No. 3, March 26, pp. 56.61.

Kemp, Geoffrey (2010). *The East Moves West: India, China and Asia's Growing Presence in the Middle East*. Bookings Institution, p. 116.

Khan, Baluch, Mir Ahmad Yar (1975). *Inside Baluchistan*. Karachi, Royal Book, pp. 150—66 and 255.

Kupecz, Mickey (2012). "Pakistan's Baloch insurgency: history, conflict drivers and regional implications". *International Affairs Review*, Vol. XX, no.3, (spring), pp. 96-97.

Livingston, Ian and Michael O' Hanlon (2011). *Pakistan Index*. Brooking Institute, December 29, p. 12.

Marri, Shah Mohammad (2000). *Baloch Qaum*. Lahore, Takhliqat, p. 131.

Nasir, Gul Khan (1952-54). *Tarikh-e-Balochistan*. Quetta, p. 487.

Nasser, Dashti (2012). *The Baloch and Balochistan: A historical account from beginning to the fall of the Baloch state*. Trafford, pp. 63-67.

Nek, Buzdar (2000). Social Organisation, resource use, and economic development in Balochistan". *Balochi Labzank*, Balochistan (monthly), March-April, p. 82.

Nicholas, Mansergh (1982). The Transfer of Power 1942-47, Vol. XII, London, Her Majesty's Stationary Office, August 2, p. 480.

Philip, S. Khoury, Joseph Kostiner, eds (1990). *Tribes and State in the Middle East*. Berkeley: University of California Press, p. 136.

Philip, C. Salzman (1983). "Why tribes have chiefs: A case from Baluchistan", in Richard Tapper (ed.), *The Conflict of Tribe and State in Iran, and Afghanistan*. London, p. 267.

Shaheen, Mozaffar (1980). *The Politics of Cabinet Formation in Pakistan: A Study of Recruitment to Central Cabinets*. Ohio, Miami University, p. 180.

Swidler, Warren (1977). "Economic Change in Balochistan: Process of integration in the larger economy of Pakistan", in Ainslie T. Embree (ed), *Pakistan's Western Borderlands: The Transformation of Political Order*. Durham, Carolina, Academic Press, p. 91.

The Indian Express (2016). August 18.

5

Role of Military Rulers in Modern Pakistan

Initial Politico-religious Developments

The foundation of an Islamic state was laid down by a proposal of the first Constituent Assembly in March, 1949, called 'Objectives Resolution'. Among other things it noted, whereas the sovereignty over the entire universe belongs to Allah alone, and the authority to be exercised by the people of Pakistan within the limits prescribed by Him is a sacred trust; whereas the founder of Pakistan, the Quaid-e-Azam Mohammad Ali Jinnah, declared that Pakistan would be a democratic state based on Islamic principles of democracy, freedom, equality, tolerance, and social justice as enunciated by Islam...... wherein adequate provisions should be made for the minorities freely to profess and practise their religions and develop their culture........ so that the People of Pakistan may prosper and attain their rightful and honoured place among the nations of the world and make their full contribution towards international peace and the progress and happiness of humanity'. The dictum of 'Objective Resolution', since then, became a core of Pakistani politics and society as well. The later constitutions of 1962 and 1973 promulgated during the regime of Ayub Khan and Zulfikar Ali Bhutto, respectively were structured on the basis of these parameters.

Detail discussions were held on this Resolution and it met with two kinds of criticism. The Congress members of Eastern Wing held the view that it was a mixture of religion and politics while others criticised it because there was no provision for social change and no guarantee of the fundamental liberties of the people. From the start it was pointed out that protection of non-Muslims' "rights, privileges and statuses was one of the duties enjoined on the Muslim by Islam. Religious freedom is an important component of Islam. An Islamic society worth its name must follow the Quranic dictates like 'Let there be no compulsion in religion'. This is a message that has been repeated in the Holy Quran in different and from a variety of angles. Then there is an entire Sura (109) devoted to the message of co-existence of all religions. It concludes: Lakum Deenokum Waleya Deen, that means, to you be your faith, and to me mine. This same message is repeated in a different context in the verse of the Holy Quran (3:84): The Prophet is told that Muslims must believe in the revelations brought by all previous prophets and asked to say: We make no distinction between any of them (*Shahin,1999*). Thus, suppression of other religions or making any distinction among them is akin to Kufr (disbelief) in Islam. Apart from this, the Hadees and the Sunnah of the Prophet as well as books of Islamic law show clear preference for untrammelled religious freedom. The concept of religious freedom is dear to Islam.

The founders of Pakistan had thought about the application of Islamic principles in the new state, but they were essentially Westernised secularists, who treated the Islamist parties as nuisances, to be placated with occasional concessions. However, in both the constitutions definite provisions were made to give the structure a pro-Islamic theme. Part X of the constitution of 1962 made a mandatory provision for the establishment of an Advisory Council of Islamic Ideology. The Council was to consist the number of members neither less than five nor more than twelve as the President decided. The members to be appointed by the President on such terms and conditions as he may decide. The functions of the Council were to make recommendations to the Central Government and the Provincial Governments as to the means of enabling and encouraging the Muslims of Pakistan to order their lives in all respects in accordance with the principles and concepts of Islam and to advise the National Assembly, the Provincial Assembly and the President, or the Governor on any question referred to it. Further under Article 270 of the Constitution, Islamic Research Institute was provided whose members were to be appointed by the President. Its duty was to undertake Islamic research and instruction in Islam for the purpose of assisting in the reconstruction of Islamic society on a truly Islamic basis.

Except for minorities such as Hindus and Christians, the promulgation of the first constitution of Pakistan was a disappointing one. Ayub received most of the congratulations from his basic democrats who had much vested interest in the new system. Maulana Ghulamullah who later became the Ulema to the President said in Rawalpindi on 8 March that he had not congratulated the President on the Constitution and that the document left much to be desired from the Islamic standpoint. Undoubtedly, thanks should go to the President for an act of courage that he did not seek to appease the religious orthodoxy by providing that all laws should be in conformity with the Quran and Sunnah. Only the more or less universally accepted Islamic principles were made the yardstick for assessing the laws. The non-Muslims were in theory guaranteed the right to profess, practise, and even propagate their religion, though this clause caused some heart-burning among the diehard supporters of Islam.

Christians, in particular, heaved a sigh of relief on seeing the constitution as it put an end to the practice in some Karachi schools of compulsory Christian religious instruction to non-Christian pupils. It also made it obligatory for all schools to provide for the teaching of the quran and Islamiat for all Muslim students. The Hindu population of West Pakistan praised the Constitution while the Hindus of Eastern part mostly refused to comment. It seemed that they were either indifferent or were with the mainstream of non-conformist opinion (*Bhargava,1969*).

As to the position of women in society, Islam presents clearly an inferior view. Believers are advised to be kind to their wives, not to keep or take back the dower at the time of casting them away. But the general position is unambiguous. The women is to obey. The man, if necessary, may admonish her, banish her, beat her. Women are looked upon as things to be enjoyed. 'The whole world is to be enjoyed, 'the prophet says, 'but the best thing in the world is a good woman' (*Shourie,1987*). In other words, the Quranic concept of women being a man's tilth, his field that he may go into when or how he will. It is also no wonder therefore that women are to count for half of men in inheritance, that the evidence of two women is equal to the evidence of one man – 'This, 'says the prophet in relation to the latter, 'is because of the deficiency of a woman's mind.' The notion also affirms further,' Never shall succeed such a nation as makes a woman their ruler (*Shourie,1987*). The manifest inequity of these laws and their obsolescence have led one Muslim country after another to reform them wholesale. The countries have decided that even after choosing one school of a particular point, they are not bound by the settled or dominant view of that school on that point, but will choose from among all of the views that have been expressed on that point by any of the adherents of that school.

Explaining further woman's status, as put in the

Sharia'h by Prophet Muhammad in relation to women, it rested on a view of women as dependent on men, not their equals, but entitled to considerations, economic as well as social, both within and outside marriage. Within marriage, a wife should be paid mehr. If Muslim marriage was a simple civil contract between two equal partners, there would have been no rationale for the provision of mehr, which would then appear to be an unreasonable condition in terms of contract law. It was provided because women were not seen as equal to men. Based on the same principle, the Sharia's enunciation by Prophet, ordained that when divorce took place the wife should be shown consideration by way of a fair and reasonable economic settlement in her favour (*Ahmad,2001*). The Islamic conception of the woman is not founded on the principle of gender equality. For this reason, the original message directed the husband to take care of her material needs and to make a fair and reasonable settlement with pro-woman attitude in the event of divorce. What is important here is to visualise the tendency inherent in the Quran and the Prophet's injunctions. They did not abolish slavery, true; but, it can be argued that they tried to humanise it. They did not abolish polygamy, true; but they prescribed a maximum where there had been none. Their view of women bears the stamp of the time, true; but they took a step forward by enjoining that the women should be treated well. They did not place women on a par with regard to property, true; but they incorporated in their institutes the right of a woman to have property of her own (*Shourie,1987*).

In the light of the inherent tendency, several countries have pressed forward with reforms. It is in two directions. First, they have laid down conditions that must be fulfilled before the husband can take on another wife, and, second, they have decreed that institutions or persons other than the husband – the courts, the Qazis, etc- must satisfy themselves that the conditions laid down are indeed met in the particular case. Different laws and codes were enacted, though mostly in Muslim countries, with a view to provide considerable concessions to women in society. For instance, in Morocco (1958), Iraq (1959), Singapore (1968), Iran (1975) and in South Yemen (1974). In country after country the law now provides that no divorce is to be effective or to be recognised until the courts have passed a decree to that effect.

In Pakistan the women were conscious enough from the start. They agitated in the early fifties against the Prime Minister when he married his secretary and took her as his second wife. The agitation continued until Ayub Khan, who had captured power in 1958, enforced the Muslim Family Ordinance in 961 which put certain restrictions on polygamy and oral divorce. The said Ordinance provides that no husband, during the subsistence of an existing marriage, can contract another one without the previous permission in writing of a government-appointed 'Arbitration Council'. Under it, the husband is obliged to state in writing his reasons for wanting to marry again, and also to specify whether the permission of the existing wife has been obtained. The Council then asks him and his existing wife to nominate representatives. Next, it ascertains whether another marriage is necessary and just'. Even if the council sanctions another marriage, the wife can apply to the Collector for a revision and says the law, 'His decision shall be final and shall not be called in question in any court (*Shourie,1987*). It also provided that a wife can sue for divorce where her husband has taken another wife in contravention of the provisions of the Ordinance. If the court finds that the temperaments of the two are irreconcilable or that the marriage has broken down it can decide on a divorce. This Ordinance could not be undone even during Zia-ul-Haq's regime when the orthodox Ulema was closest to state power in Pakistan. Muslim women are undergoing change the world over. The orthodox Ulema can hardly restrain this forward marching. More and more Muslim women are challenging medieval theological formulations or simply ignoring them (*Engineer,2008*).

The 1973 Constitutions of Pakistan was prepared in the background of the debacle of its Eastern Wing, resulting in the handing over of rule to Zulfikar Ali Bhutto. His was the first elected government in the history of Pakistan since its inception in 1947. Under this constitution vast fundamental rights were given to citizens without making any distinction on the basis of sex, caste, religion etc. In sphere of religion, as mentioned in part II of the constitution every citizen was free to profess, practise and propagate his religion. Even religious denomination and every sect thereof shall have the right to establish, maintain and manage its religious institutions. But like the Constitution of 1962 sufficient Islamic provisions were inserted in Part IX of the constitution. It is provided that all existing laws shall be brought in conformity with the injunctions of Islam as laid down in the Holy Quran and Sunnah and referred to as the injunctions of Islam. No law shall be enacted in Pakistan which is repugnant to such injunctions. Establishment of a Council of Islamic Ideology was retained and its number was fixed 8 as minimum but not more than 15, remaining its functions, more or less, same as was in the Ayub constitution. In the constitution of 1973 Bhutto specifically provided that Islam would be the state religion, and the head of state a Muslim.

Despite the fact that Bhutto and his government represented the people of Pakistan in a democratic way within months of the assumption of the new dispensation, orthodox fundamentalists began to overpower the government. Months after coming to power Bhutto allowed a record number of persons to go for 'Haj' – the annual pilgrimage to Mecca. He made Friday into a national holiday, founded various government organisations for propagating Islamic teaching, encouraged the Arabic language and introduced the Quran into school curricula. On 22nd February 1974 Bhutto organised the historic Islamic Summit Conference at Lahore. He fulfilled the religious demands before they could force his hand, as one of his opponents remarked,' Mr. Bhutto is the biggest maulana of them all. In fact, he should be called "Maulana Larkanvi" (*Taseer,1980*).

In the latter part of his rule Bhutto began to work under pressure of the conservative forces to stay in power. It was clearly due to their influence that Ahmadiya Community of Pakistan was declared in 1974 a non-Muslim minority. Though Ahmadiya settled all over the world, live mostly in Pakistan's Punjab province. They also live in India somewhere peacefully with Hindus but the Gurdaspur district of Punjab (India) is known as their headquarters since 1891. Ahmadiyas also called Qadians, as most of them were once living in Qadian near Gurdaspur. In fact, Ahmadiya was a movement in Islam founded by Hazrat Niza Ghulam Ahmed of Qadian in "obedience to the divine command". He claimed to be the promised reformer not only for Muslims but 'as the embodiment of prophecies about a grand reformer foretold in the religious books of the world". He exhorted mankind to hold in equal reverence and esteem of all spiritual reformers irrespective of religions and the place of birth(*Ghose,1987*). Bhutto was not a bigot and the incident left an unpleasant taste in his mouth. After much heart-searching, the question was thrown to the National Assembly which overwhelmingly declare them a non-Muslim minority. That was a decision that far more conservative political regimes had resisted in the face of much greater pressure. As regard to fundamentalists, Bhutto adopted a policy of appeasement and in 1977, banned serving of alcohol, closed casinoes and nightclubs, prohibited gambling and all social activities as prescribed in Islam. Just to stay in power he tried 'Islamist tactics in a crude, mechanical fashion, giving clear preference to conservative forces over democratic and secular principles. However, these steps failed to keep control over post-election unrest in Pakistan and ultimately a military take-over under Zia-ul-Haq, the Chief of Army Staff, assumed power on July 5, 1977.

Mohammad Ayub Khan: The First Military Ruler

Pakistan's eleven-year experience in democracy was aborted on the night of October 7, 1958, the day, Iskandar Mirza, the President and General Ayub Khan, the Commander-in-Chief, abrogated the Constitution, dismissed the central and provincial governments, dissolved the constituent and provincial assemblies, banned all political parties and proclaimed martial law. The significant reason given for the takeover was the collapse of law and order, such as the disgraceful scenes of violence in East Pakistan Assembly, the inflammatory statements of Qaiyum Khan and the attempted secession by Khan of Kalat. As alternative, the two leaders simultaneously announced that they intended to re-establish constitutional government once the situation had been stabilised. But the announced reasons for the coup were far from reality. Political equations and alignment went against the ruling clique in East as well as in West Pakistan. Mirza's chief enemy Suhrawardy had established a base in East Pakistan and was preparing for a general election in March 1959. In West Pakistan, the Muslim League, under the Presidentship of Qaiyum Khan, had conducted an efficacious mass contact campaign in the Punjab. For Mirza, the emerging scenario of the Muslim-Awami League coalition was quite unacceptable. He was fearful of the possibility that Suhrawardy would be successful in East Pakistan and come to terms with the new political reality and form a coalition with Muslim League if he wanted to become Prime Minister. The military-bureaucratic combine's hostility to Suhrawardy was garbed in ethnic terms, but the issue was one of power and domination. It was not simply a Bengali-Punjabi clash but part of a wider conflict between the Punjab and the rest of the country. Consequently, the declaration of martial law was designed to perpetuate the policies of the ruling group. Though the military takeover did not bring any fundamental redistribution of power, army officers became more important than the civil servants, the new regime represented the combined power of the big industrialists, landlords, bureaucrats and the army aristocracy. Soon, it was followed by the outsting of President Mirza from office by his aide General Ayub Khan on October 27, 1958, on the charge of the conspiracy against the latter.

Maxim Gorky, the famous novelist, in his assessment of Lenin remarked, "The duty of honest leaders of the people is superhumanly hard. It is impossible to have a leader who is not, to one degree or another, a tyrant" (*Bhargava,1969*). The example is also suitable for a good measure in case of Field Marshal Ayub Khan. He was honest in the sense public men are expected to be as per the judgement of most observers, including Indian diplomats, who watched him from a close range. The circumstances which catapulted him into power were different to that of Russia and Germany, and, due to no such philosophy at hand he was not hoped to be that. His upbringing in the British Indian Army made him temperamentally unsuited to be demagogue. Ayub called his declaration of October as revolution. Within him was the heart of a poet which reflected in the preface of his political autobiography when he wrote, "Pakistan is my passion, my life. A look of happiness on the faces of people thrills and sustains me. Just as a shade of anxiety in their eyes causes me anguish. I have woken up from sleep to see whether the sound on the window panes is of long-awaited rain. I feel parched inside when I see a drought-stricken field. The soil of Pakistan fascinates me, for it is my soil. I belong to it" (*Khan,1967*). However, it was too good to last long. Forces of tyrant in him erupted when he was trapped by the elements of public and military life of Pakistan. At a later stage, like other tyrants, Ayub began to identify the progress and prosperity of Pakistan with his own position and power.

The Military take-over in Pakistan witnessed the collapse of constitutional politics for years to come. It perished, not due to any inherent weakness but because of the coercive power of those who feared its success. The constitutional process did not die a natural death but was the victim of political assassination. Pakistan's experience in the system, has, however, been different. Its first constitution never saw the light of day; it was drafted and printed but was never released to the public. Its second one, the product ofdiscussions in a Constituent Assembly, was never faithfully implemented and was ultimately abrogated. The most unfortunate affair in the context was that the Constitution itself was blamed and criticized. No ruler of the country was ready to accept his own lust for power and position as a motivating force behind the constitutional failure. Mirza when abrogated the 1956 constitution, said, "Pakistan was not forsaking democracy permanently" (*The Dawn,1958*). In the similar fashion, when Ayub Khan ousted Mirza, rejected the constitution because it was "unworkable" and "full of compromises". He was convinced, as indicated in an interview that politics cost Mirza's ouster .... he had vague ideas .... I have definite ideas. He claimed that what he was practicing was also a democracy (*The Statesman,1958*).

Democracy as a form of government and the sentiments for it is uppermost. George Bernard Shaw, the famous poet and novelist wrote much before the creation of Pakistan, "When we see Parliaments like ours kicked into the gutter by dictators, both in kingdoms and republics, it is foolish to watch until the dictator dies or collapses, and then do nothing but pick the poor old things up and try to scrape the mud off them; the only sane course is to take the step by which the dictatorship could have been anticipated and averted; and construct a political system for rapid positive work instead of slow nugatory work made to fit into the twentieth century instead of into the sixteenth (*Bhargava,1969*). Pakistan, soon after partition marked a significant difference to the society of India. Both have the same racial stock amalgam; they have the same languages, historical and political experience. And yet their responses tend to be quite different. How is it that democracy is as safe in India as it is unsafe in Pakistan, although both the armies were trained under the British? During the freedom movement, the Congress took the position that all Indians are one nation. Later the Muslim League took the position that Hindus and Muslims are two nations. But the fact is that Nehru once rightly put it, if you feel one you are one; it you don't then you are not. Hindus and Muslims may or may not be one nation; but they are two societies. And these societies consist of many sub-societies. No Constitution can possibly take separate note of all these societies and sub-societies. Only a full-blooded democracy, with adult franchise and free elections, can take care of all these societies in proportion to their strength. Even in Pakistan the pre-partition euphoria has evaporated and now they know that apart from Pakistani they are also Punjabis, Sindhis, Balochis and Pathans – and Mohajirs. Also, Shias, Sunnis, Qadianis, Syeds, Khans, Arains and Jats (*Malkani,2001*). For reasons more than one, the emphasis was on leadership, preferably of the militant variety and not on the people.

General Ayub Khan while declaring the martial law in the country, promised to provide the people of Pakistan a new constitution. Addressing a public meeting in Karachi on the occasion of the birth anniversary of M.A. Jinnah, he said, "Our aim is to introduce a representative form of government, as much as can be understood and worked by our people. We shall have to ensure that such a representative government is so designed that its working is not marred by political instability. As soon as the major problems facing the country have been solved, the reforms will be put into operation and the administration rehabilitated. The best constitution brains in our country will be asked to apply themselves to the question of framing a constitution" (*The Dawn,1958*). The new ruler, through his constitutional provisions, wanted to keep away the old politicians of the country from politics who were the chief determinents of Pakistan's fate. It was more accurate to say that Ayub's emphasis on the workability of the proposed constitution was a reaction to the havoc of Parliamentary democracy which the country had experienced since its inception. However, the system itself was not faulty but the pro-centrist people of West Pakistan who were entrusted to do the job. Its eastern wing, now Bangladesh, was continuously demanding for a Parliamentary and federal form of government in which the Prime Minister becomes responsible to the legislature.

Soon after the declaration of military takeover, General Ayub constituted a civilian structure of government which was formally established with the introduction of the system of 'Basic Democracy'. His new brand of democracy was, in fact, a device to perpetuate the rule. Under this system the President was to be elected not through direct popular vote but indirectly through an electoral college of individuals called 'Basic Democrats' who, in turn, had been elected through elections to local bodies at the village level. Given the structure of political power at the village level, based on clan and biradris of the landed elite, the composition of this electoral college overwhelmingly favoured the interests of the landlords and rich peasants. These influential landlords who were instrumental in getting the Basic Democrats elected had direct link with the bureaucrats. They were to perform local government functions. They were also given crores of rupees to spend for the economic development of their respective constituencies through a programme called Works Programme. Actually, Works Programme was a mechanism through which the Government bribed the Basic Democrats to vote for its candidates. Thus, the new system, in effect, constituted an instrument through which the bureaucracy could have an outreach into the village level clans and biradris, and could maintain the political system of Ayub regime.

The first election of Basic Democrats was held in 1959. Forty thousand democrats were elected from each wing of Pakistan totalling 80,000. Each Province was divided into

40,000 territorial units known as electoral units. The election, more or less, was non-political in the sense that very few of the politically minded persons took interest in them. Initially the union councils and committees were regarded as no more than local bodies. However, when it was realised that the basic democrats would constitute the electoral college for the election of the national and provincial assemblies, there was a hue and cry by the politically inclined. Particularly the rural peasants of West Pakistan had missed the chance to teach a lesson to their landlords. The land reforms of the military regime touched merely the fringe of the problem. Consequently, the electors of Pakistan's legislatures were essentially feudal in class character and outlook. It was only with the promulgation of the Political Parties Act of 1962, that political life was revived in the country. Ayub Khan's search for a suitable vehicle to sustain himself in power culminated in the decision to appropriate the dormant Muslim League. As the Party responsible for creating Pakistan, the Muslim League still retained a special appeal (*Taseer,1980*).

People of national and international repute took pains to draft the constitution. On May 1, 1961, the Constitution Commission presented its report to Ayub Khan who appointed two committees to examine the report and give their recommendations. One committee was composed of bureaucrats and the other of seven cabinet ministers. These ministers presumably carried special expertise, or more likely, the special confidence of the President. The Cabinet Committee was chaired by Manzur Qadir, the Foreign Minister. Despite the fact that it was a military-dominated constitution, adamant to make the President most powerful, General had deep faith that the people had upon him but on the basis of development he justified the making of the new constitution. He went on to add on the eve of the announcement of the constitution. 'Even if I were to hold a universal referendum I believe 95 per cent of the people would have asked me: why are you bringing back the constitution? But I am doing it with my eyes open. You can take that as an earnest of my honesty. Without institutions which the Muslims have never been able to develop so far during the last 14,00 years society cannot move from one stage of progress to another stage of progress. This is my firm belief.' The overall situation in Pakistan was at its lowest, was clear from the fact that even the severest critics of President Ayub Khan admitted that the prospect of a constitutional regime would be a definite advance on the then existing state of affairs.

The constitution of General Ayub Khan came into effect in early 1962. It had a preamble wherein it was stated that sovereignty over the entire universe belonged to Almighty. The territories included in Pakistan formed a Federation, in which the provinces enjoyed as much autonomy as was insisted with the unity and interest of Pakistan as a whole. In the constitution an attempt was made to reconcile the regional demands of the people of East Pakistan who resented their domination by West Pakistan. The constitution provided for the establishment of the seat of the National Assembly at Dacca and the Headquarters of the Government of Pakistan at Islamabad in West Pakistan. Dacca was made the second capital of Pakistan. Both Urdu and Bengali were made the national languages of Pakistan in order to give satisfaction to the people of East Paksitan (*Mahajan,1982*). Apart from this the principles of democracy, freedom, equality, tolerance and social justice, as enunciated by Islam were to be fully observed in Pakistan.

But the most important feature of the constitution was the powers of the President. Under Ayub Khan's constitution the President was the sole repository of all executive powers. The President ruled the centre through a Council of Ministers and the Provinces through two Governors who were selected by him. The National and Provincial legislatures had no power; they could not even vote on the budget; all public expenditures were the responsibility of the President and the Governors. Article 8 of the constitution had given "the responsibility of deciding whether any action of an organ or authority of the state, or of a person performing functions on behalf of an organ or authority of the State was in accordance with the principles of policy was that of the organ or authority of the State, or of the person concerned" (*Bhargava,1969*). The Government of Pakistan, as one author put it, has emerged as a result of the Ayub constitution as 'a government of the President, for the President and by the President (*The Dawn,1963*).

Though a constitutional parity between the two wings of Pakistan was provided in the new structure and attempts were made to fulfil the demands of East Pakistan, the latter claimed more grievances. In West Pakistan, the Karachi-based newspapers, The Dawn and the Urdu daily Jung and Anjam generally supported the document in the tone which lacked enthusiasm, other launched a campaign through editorials requesting the President not to establish such an unhealthy democratic convention using, at all, such a vast power. The newspapers of eastern wing expressed a critical tone and commented on the changeover in other countries, not naming Pakistan directly. Several public figures including Maulana Maudoodi, the founder of Jamaat-e-Islami, described the constitution as disappointing from the democratic points of view and unsatisfactory from the standpoint of Islam. But after all the new set up gained the impression that with all its shortcomings, it had opened the only avenue for an ultimate return to democracy and should, therefore be worked. They were well aware of the fate of 1956 constitution, which was wrecked, despite all its liberal provisions.

The constitution of General Ayub Khan was put into operation and in pursuance elections were held in March 1962. The results of the election reflected the fact that the bulk of the government supporters in the National Assembly came from the West Wing while the majority of opposition members belonged to East Pakistan, however, Sardar Bahadur Khan was two-in-one, leader of the opposition and brother of President Ayub Khan. General Ayub's hope that the electoral college of 80,000 basic democrats would supplant the old political leadership was belied in this election, which was fought largely on party-basis affiliations. Almost all the elected candidates had previous party affiliations and were either inspired or sponsored by the old politicians who were disqualified from taking an active part in politics. In the changed circumstances, political parties became an integral part of the politics of Pakistan. Ayub Khan himself realised it impossible to keep party politics out of national assembly and began to think to cultivate a section of them and evolve a new kind of party system. He gave his pains a voice in course of addressing the first session of the National Assembly on June 8, 1962, 'The new system did not mean that he did not require in the legislature a group of determined patriotic men, inspired by him aims and ideas and willing to help him'. He cleverly exploited the division in the opposition ranks and struck a bargain with those elements who were prepared to work with some changes in the system. As a result of this compromise the Political parties were legalised through the Political Parties Act of 1962. Ultimately, he reconciled himself to the Party system and on May 22, 1963 formally announced his decision to join the Party, though he was less than happy and said that unfortunately his system has broken down at the pyramid level. In answer to the question why he has joined the Party responded quickly, 'I have failed to play this game in accordance with my rules and I have to play it in accordance with their rules and the rules demand that I belong to some body. It is an admission of defeat on my part (*Development of Films,1963*). The experiment of limited democracy as implemented by General Ayub was condemned on the ground that the Electoral college was no substitute for adult franchise. It was no guarantee that the members of the Electoral College would always make sober and independent decisions. There was always a possibility of influencing them or buying them.

As to the social condition and change, Ayub's regime had widened the gap between East Bengal and West Pakistan. Two Five Year Plans for economic development were implemented but its eastern part gained little from these. Seventy per cent of the nation's wealth was concentrated in the hands of about twenty capitalist families of West Pakistan. During the period East Bengal lagged behind in comparison to West Pakistan in almost all walks of life. The constitution of 1956 was better in the sense that it established the principle of equality of opportunity for all Pakistanis by prohibiting discrimination on the ground only of race, religion, caste, sex, residence, or place of birth to the service of Pakistan. Though like the earlier one, the constitution of 1962 accepted the principle of parity between the two wings, its operative side had been watered down by saying that Parity should as nearly as it is practicable be achieved. The East Bengal was far behind and remained so during General Ayub's period especially in import-export balance, industrialisation, banking system, employment, education, proportion in defence and civil services, etc. According to the Economic Survey of Asia and the Far East prepared by the ECAFE in 1966, the East Pakistan Farmers, beleaguered as they are by the uncertainty of farming operations, can not derive adequate incomes from farming and the majority of them are forced to borrow at exorbitant rates of interest from money lenders and traders. Although, the General himself realised the enormity of the problem of poverty in Eastern Wing and allotted a sum of Rs. 5,760 million for the economic development of the province during the Second Plan period. Some progress in industrialisation was also achieved but it failed to make any significant impact as a whole. Thus, while West Pakistan's economy reached the take-off stage in the late sixties, Eastern Wing remained poor and under-developed.

But from among these poor people a new class of exploiters emerged in East Pakistan through Basic Democracy and Works Programme. The resentment of the people against this class and domination of its Western part found violent expression in the anti-Ayub Movement initiated by the Dacca University students in 1968. Since 1966, Sheikh Mujibur Rahman, an ex-student leader of the Language movement and President of the Awami League started fighting for economic emancipation and political autonomy through his six-point Programmes. He made it an issue in an all-Party meeting in Lahore. The wholehearted support that the Programme had received, made the ruling clique nervous. The government levelled various charges on Mujibur Rahman and even concocted a case against him known as the Agartala Conspiracy Case.

According the Ayub constitution of 1962 as amended in 1964, the first Presidential election was to be held by 7 March 1965 and the process was further hastened fixing January 2, 1965 as the date for the election. Divided opposition as they were, felt difficulty in choosing an agreed candidate and hence, their gathering momentum could not reach a climax in such a short period. On the other hand, propaganda for Ayub had been going on ever since the promulgation of Constitution in 1962. Though selection of eighty thousand candidates for membership of electoral college as basic democrats was not an easy one even for a well-established Political Party, for the Muslim League of Pakistan it was more so because of vertical and horizontal divisions in the Party. The ruling clique took full advantage of the situation and even some key members of the opposition were arrested to ensure the re-election of Ayub Khan. However, despite these disabilities, the opposition had given a good account of itself in the election campaign. The personality of Fatima Jinnah was good enough to catch hundreds of thousands of persons attending meetings addressed by her. But, the franchise being limited, the people who admired her did not usually had the right to vote. The landlords, businessmen and others who constituted majority of the basic democrats were threatened to face dire consequences if they were sided with the opposition. The net result was the re-election of Ayub Khan getting 62 per cent of votes cast. He got main support from the tribal areas and former Sind Punjab provinces. Not only that the very composition of the electorate was interesting as of the 156 members of the National Assembly, 112 were either landlords or businessmen and industrialists.

Even the landslide victory of General Ayub Khan failed to check the rising tides of discontent against the regime. Especially on economic front, it had disappointed the public more, than they anticipated. Establishment put forward the argument that the migration of Hindus and Sikhs from West Pakistan had left a void in the industrial sphere which needed to be filled. On the other, it continued to take decisions in favour of private industries that ultimately made the regime most unpopular in Pakistan. In the circumstances the country was bound to face all the disadvantages of a loosely controlled economy minus the saving grace of public ownership of the means of production. Private industry was encouraged to pursue the full of its profit motive; in collaboration with corrupt bureaucracy that enforced a system of control in such a manner that profited a few, at the cost of the many. Consequently, in May 1967, the Pakistan Democratic Movement was started. Its object was to agitate for the restoration of Parliamentary institutions in the country based on adult franchise. President Ayub was not happy with the movement and described its activities as "Playing with fire." The Dawn also described it as "Pakistan disintegrating movement". But these anti-democratic remarks became unimportant as in November 1967, Zulfikar Ali Bhutto set up his People's Party which stood for the restoration of democracy and adult franchise, with a socialistic pattern of society. Widespread nature of mass movement erupted particularly in eastern wing and later in the whole of Pakistan. During the Ayub regime there was a power-sharing arrangement between the Army and bureaucracy, with the bureaucracy the dominant partner. One reason why the internal balance of power within the state structure shifted into the hands of the bureaucracy after the 1958 military coup was that both Ayub Khan and the military behind him recognised the experience and ability of the civil bureaucracy in wielding state power (*Hussain,1996*).

In a final bid to redeem his position General Ayub agreed to convene a Round Table Conference with opposition parties. It met in Rawalpindi on March 10, 1969 and the deliberations continued up to March 13 (*The Times,1969*). A large part of the conference was spent on allegations and counter-allegations but the General had accepted the opposition's demand for direct election on the basis of universal adult franchise and for return to the Parliamentary system. Acceptance of these two demands was largely welcomed and Nasrullah Khan announced the dissolution of Democratic Action Committee, saying that the purpose for which it was formed had been achieved. Other demands which included Mujibur Rahman's six-point were to be considered after passing of the above two by the National Assembly. His demand for full regional autonomy for the eastern wing was kept in abeyance. He was not happy with the dissolution of the Democratic Action Committee which failed to champion the main demand of the people of East Bengal. On the other Zulfikar Ali Bhutto, the founder of People's Party and who had been with Ayub for several years, began to accuse Ayub of bringing Pakistan 'to the brink of disaster' and demanded his resignation.

In a very difficult situation created, on the one hand, by the unrest and anarchy on the part of the people of Pakistan, and by a strategy hatched by the ruling clique, on the other, Ayub Khan announced over Radio Pakistan on

March 25, 1969, his decision to handover power to Agha Mohammad Yahya Khan, the then Commander-in-Chief. Restoration of democracy in Pakistan was the chief cause for people's movement in various parts of the country. But as to the ruling strategy, a close study of the prevailing situation in Pakistan gave rise to the impression that Yahya with the connivance of Ayub allowed the conditions in East Bengal to deteriorate to an extent which would justify the imposition of military law. Additionally, under no circumstance, the ruling group of West Pakistan was not ready to transfer power to the popular Bengali leader and they conspired with the industrial tycoons of Western part who were equally eager to exploit the former as earlier. With this change, history repeated itself in Pakistan after eleven years and the nation once again reached the point from where it started. It solved nothing but ushered the country in a more complicated political crisis of large dimension which resulted in the birth of a new nation, today called Bangladesh.

Mohammad Yahya Khan: An Era of Turbulence

General Ayub Khan relinquished Pakistan when it was at the cross-roads. The timing of the transfer of power was smooth sailing neither for Ayub nor for his nominated successor Yahya Khan, who, in an announcement to the nation on Radio Pakistan, conveyed, "I, General Agha Mohammand Yahya Khan, Commander-in-Chief of the Army, do hereby declare that the whole of Pakistan shall be under marital law with immediate effect, and I assume the powers of Chief Marshal Law Administrator and the command of all the armed forces of Pakistan' (*The Pakistan Times,1969*). This second time imposition of military rule in Pakistan was an anti-climax for the political fortune of the country and its society as well. It lost all, gained in last ten years since direct assumption of power by Ayub Khan in October 1958. Though he, too, was not liked by the common masses and was not a democratic system by long chalks out, but the system ushered in by the 1962 constitution who respected the will of the people on a limited scale through implementation of the idea of Basic Democracy. The last phase of Ayub's regime seemed to be providing an opening for a more broad-based set-up especially between December 1968 and March 1969; the voice of the people was being heard and even heeded up to a point as reflected in the partial success of the Round Table Conference. Consensus on two vital issues in the Conference had generated hopes of a popular regime emerging ultimately in Pakistan.

By the time of the second coup it also became clear to the ruling clique that Pakistan consisted a society, of two distinct people, particularly in sphere of economic status, political choice and cultural heritage. This time frustration of its eastern wing was well high with economic disparity at its peak. Economic exploitation of East Bengal was not a new one but now it touched an alarming proportion. According to a survey conducted by a group of scholars in Vienna, it was revealed that while East Bengal provided 60 per cent of the total revenue of the Government of Pakistan, it received only 23 per cent of its expenditure. In fact, West Pakistan, with about 45 per cent of the country's total population, received 77 per cent of the total development expenditure while East Bengal, with about 55 per cent of population, received a bare 23 per cent. West Pakistan's contribution to the total foreign exchange earnings was 41 per cent but it was allotted 70 per cent of these earnings. East Bengal, contributing 59 per cent, received only 30 per cent (*Taseer,1980*). Apart from this contribution-return ratio, it was hardly comparable with the unrelieved poverty of the people of East Bengal. "Unlike West Pakistan, the poverty in the East was manifest in equal measure in the towns and in the countryside .... Malnutrition was endemic. So are tuberculosis and other respiratory diseases and stomach complaining. Closely related to it was the issue of food and dress. Food in East was often a single meal consisting of a pan of boiled coarse rice topped with lentils or a piece of fish ...... in the West the village might not always got meat, but they somehow managed a daily quota of milk or lassi. Clothing in the East consisted of a lungi and a soiled or tattered vest for the men. The women had to do only with a saree used to cover both breast and loins. But the poorest village women in West Pakistan would have at least three garments – salwar, kamiz and dupatta (*Ministry of External Affairs,1971*). Despite the fact that the people of West Pakistan were undeniably poor, they appeared to live more happily than the people of its Eastern part.

In post-partition phase, the political discrimination of West Pakistan with East Bengal had multiplied the economic, social and psychological problems of the territory. Lesser opportunities of development for eastern part was taken by Bengalis as a problem willingly created for them by the rulers of Pakistan. All sections of society – the upper middle class which wanted to establish itself as the new bourgeois of East Bengal, people engaged in or wanting to do small business, highly educated young men who wanted a greater share in the civil and armed services of the country, the intellectual, the student, the poor worker, the grief-stricken peasant and the vast masses of the unemployed were increasingly smarting under this sense of great injustice (*Mascarenhas,1971*). In the circumstances, the talk of national unity was of no avail for the people of East Bengal, who suffered a lot on several counts, and in general, found their future to be totally bleak.

The prevailing situation demanded first class statesmanship to fill the ever-widening gap between the two wings of Pakistan. After assuming charge, General Yahya Khan declared the dissolution of the National Assembly and the Provincial Assemblies and placed the two wings of Pakistan under the charge of two Administrators. The Yahya regime decided to adopt a different line of action and its proclamation of martial law was very much a defensive manoeuvre on the part of the army to maintain its position that was threatened by the mass upsurge of 1968-69. To keep the law and order under control it first imposed heavy penalties for trouble-makers, strikers, demonstrators and anyone who even questioned the wisdom of martial law were liable to as much as fourteen years in jail (*Bangladesh Document,1971*). The initial responses of the regime were rather pro-democracy and it was waiting for situations to become normal. In his radio broadcast to the nation on 26 March 1969, the General said that his only ambition was the creation of conditions conducive to the establishment of a constitutional Government on the basis of adult franchise. He contradicted that he was resisting the national urge for a democratic government and added that what he wanted was to clean the administration, restore law and order and then proceed with the task of conducting the elections and establishing a democratic rule.

Now the question arises: "Why did Yahya, in the first place, sought elections and then took resort to an extreme action?" The only logical answer was that as a member of the ruling clique he could never had been interested genuinely in the restoration of democracy. He thought that no single party because of the presence of several parties in Pakistan would be able to gain majority in the Constituent Assembly; and taking the opportunity of their weakness and disunity. The ruler, through his first-hand impression, was able to dispel pessimism by inspiring a nation-wide trust in his authority and integrity. He realised that in order to remove doubts and suspicion from the minds of the public and the politicians, some of the demands of the more vocal groups involving in the mass upsurge of 1968-69 would have to be met. Imbued with this objective in view he proceeded to adopt a number of conciliatory policies especially designed to placate these groups. On the other hand, the leaders of the main political parties were also agreed to ruler's point of view and were hopeful that a democratic set up would be established in the country soon. Zulfikar Ali Bhutto, the leader of Pakistan People's Party supported the view and said, 'Unless the military get a taste for power themselves – and I do not think this likely – the prospects for return to democracy seem good (*The Sunday Times,1969*). Sheikh Mujib, leader of the Awami League, also agreed with this analysis and decided to continue the struggle on the basic of his six-point agenda. Yahya thought from the very outset that the basis social and economic problems could be solved by the politicians when political power was returned to them and that his only function was to keep things from boiling over in the meantime. The change of regime, in general, was taken as a relief and most Pakistanis welcomed it. Unlike Ayub, who called himself 'a man in a hurry', Yahya proved himself to be a shy, reluctant and cautious dictator.

With the coming of Yahya Khan, perhaps for the first time, the political activities started in Pakistan at the national level. As he was interested in restoring of democratic institutions, removed restrictions on political activities on 1st January 1970 as a prelude to elections scheduled for the end of the year. General elections were a new phenomenon for Pakistan. This was the first time that the direct elections were held on national level. Provincial direct elections had been last held in 1954 in East Pakistan; in 1953 in Sind and in 1951 in Punjab. In the first month of his assumption the General undertook a country-wide tour, meeting politicians and hinting that he would appoint civilian advisers. In course of the meeting in Lahore he said that he was the servant of the whole nation and that he would not be where he was if the politicians presented a consensus among themselves (*The Economist,1969*). He invited and encouraged media for open discussion on the merits of each party, alternatives, past political records and matters which had been dormant for many years. Conservatism, Islam, Socialism, provincial autonomy, capitalism, free press, constitutional principles, Bhutto's new politics and so on, the arguments continued tirelessly. Election fever began to grip the country.

Military ruler though he was, he had no dearth of democrative alternatives. On 28 November 1969, he came with his most significant speech in which he announced his plan for transfer of power. It could be in four ways the first being to have an elected Constitution Convention whose task would be to produce a new constitution and then dissolve itself. The second was to revive the constitution of 1956, but the proposal was likely to be opposed in both wings of the country because certain features of that constitution such as One Unit and parity were no longer acceptable to the people. The framing of a constitution and put it to have a referendum on it as the third alternative had certain difficulties and simple 'yes' or 'no' by way of an answer could not be given by the people to such a comprehensive document as a constitution was. The last and most suitable alternative for the President was to evolve a legal framework for general elections on the basis of consultations with the various groups and political parties' leaders as well as the study of the past constitutions of Pakistan (*The Dawn,1969*). After a careful thought Yayha decided to adopt fourth as his centre of activities. Earlier on 28 July 1969, the President appointed a Chief Election Commissioner, promised elections within eighteen months and subsequently on 4 August 1969, constituted a civilian council of ministers for the Central Government with the people selected from political, bureaucratic and academic fields.

For Yahya the main constitutional issues facing the country was no less important. He noted with regret the absence of consensus among the political leaders on major issues relating to the future constitution of the country but at the sametime took decisions on the basis of "generally accepted view" which included (i) "One Unit" in West Pakistan would be dissolved and four-fold provinces would be revived in that region. (ii) The principles of Parity between the two wings of Pakistan would be discarded and the principles of one man one vote would be accepted; and (iii) Maximum autonomy would have to be given to the two wings of Pakistan as long as it did not impair national integrity and solidarity of the country. The people of the two regions of the country should have control over their economic resources and development as long as it did not adversely affect the working of a national government of the centre (*The Dawn,1969*). However, these announced steps were both, tactful and balanced. The break up of 'One Unit in Pakistan, had, to a considerable extent, neutralised the potential support prevailing in the small regions of West Pakistan like Sind, NWFP and Baluchistan and for East Bengal's demand for very substantial autonomy. His acceptance of the principle of 'one man – one vote' went a long way to keep the great popular anger in East Bengal within a check, at least, for the time being.

Keeping in view the elections to be held soon and in pursuance of the principles announced, the General elaborated his plan of action by a promulgation of the Legal Framework Order (LFO), on 30 March 1970. It was a comprehensive document containing a preamble and twenty-seven articles with accompanying schedules. Details included the composition of the national and provincial assemblies; the election schedules with a time plan and eligibility for candidature; one man one vote; elections on adult franchise and a Constituent Assembly which had to enact the Constitution in one hundred and twenty days. But the most important portion of the LFO was noted in Articles 25 and 27 respectively. Article 25 stated that the Constitution would have to be authenticated by the President and the National Assembly would be dissolved if the President refused authentication. Article 27 vested the final power of interpretation and amendment of the Legal Framework Order in the President. Here was the implied wish of the General not to dominate but to dictate the future constitution of the country. Not being elected by the people he was fully authorised by the LFO to overtake the National Assembly, an elected body of people's representatives. The National Assembly could not change the basic features of the constitution as dictated by the President. If it tried to do so, authentication would be refused by the President and the National Assembly would stand dissolved. Under the new scheme, the President would be the sole authority to decide whether the Constitution, as framed by the National Assembly, faithfully incorporated all the provisions of the Legal Framework Order (*Chakrabarti,1978*).

As a result of the announced elections, in early 1970 the country's political currents, old loyalties and new thought waves criss-crossed in startling variety making any exact political assessment difficult. In the absence of any recent voting patterns, indicators such as polls or referendums, assessments were based on traditional considerations: pre-independence groupings, the politics of caste and community and the traditional feudal ties (*Taseer,1980*). In all, twenty-five political parties put up their candidates in the elections but out of these only eleven were well-organised. Of the total parties, eleven were in East Pakistan and fourteen were in West Pakistan. Even the eleven important political parties who participated in the elections were of different shades of ideology. They included religio-political parties, such as Jamaat-i-Islami (JI), Jamait-ul-Ulema-i-Pakistan (JUP), Markazi Jamait-ul-Ulema-i-Islam (MJUI) and democratic, social democratic and leftist parties, such as the Pakistan Democratic Party (PDP), the three factions of Muslim League, i.e. the CML, Qayyum Muslim League (QML) and the PML; the AL, the NAP and the Pakistan People's Party (PPP). The election manifestoes of the different parties revealed that there was a marked similarity in their programme although the change of emphasis differed according to their orientation.

The year 1970 was a year of elections in Pakistan. Election campaigning varied widely in East and West

Pakistan with the coming up of different parties having separate strategies based on separate issues. In East Bengal, the Awami League, under the leadership of Sheikh Mujibur Rahman launched campaigning and concentrated on the six-point formula and the eleven-point charter of the East Bengal students which emphasised both provincial autonomy and the establishment of a socialist order. Its election manifesto was committed to the implementation of the six-point programme as well as "the creation of a just and egalitarian society free from exploitation ...... of a socialist economic order......." (*Bangladesh Document,1971*). It was the main contestant in East Pakistan and it faced opposition from both the right and the left. Since East Pakistan was allotted a majority of seats in the National Assembly, the party wanted to win a commanding majority in the Assembly by maximizing support in the eastern wing. It favoured to bring about a revolution through the democratic process and thereby to replace the prevailing system of injustice by a new constitutional, political, economic and social order in which justice between region and region, and between man and man would prevail (*Manifesto Awami League,1970*). Sheikh called upon the people to 'finish' the 'Mir Jafars or traitors of Bengal through elections.

Once the campaign began, a highly charged political atmosphere developed. In the West Pakistan the Pakistan Peoples' Party, under the chairmanship of Zulfikar Ali Bhutto was relatively in comfortable position. Bhutto's strategy was based on a calculated appreciation of existing political patterns. Each of the five provinces of Pakistan had their own peculiar characteristics, and he intended to concentrate where the response was the greatest. The designated battle grounds were Punjab, Sind and to a smaller extent, the North West Frontier. Though unlike East Pakistan there were more contestants in the West but the main schism was between the old guards, political leadership and the newly emergent PPP. Its programme was summed up in the slogan:

"Islam is our faith; democracy is our policy; socialism is our economy" (*Documents of PPP,1967*). Throughout his election campaign Bhutto relied foremost on man rallies. In fact, the vast majority of people in Pakistan can neither read nor write and do not have the financial resources to own radios and television. Public meetings, therefore, are the primary platform across which a message must be expounded. Like Nehru, he was at his best in vast public meetings. As his crowd feel developed, he could increasingly understand the stimulus and response of mass politics. He once said to the gatherings 'Our politics is the politics of masses – it is the politics of the open....... if there was any conflict between Islam and socialism, I swear we would have rejected socialism. I am a Muslim first and need no certificate'. In essence, the PPP manifesto barely differed from that of several of the other major parties, but the others lacked Bhutto's resonance and ability to get it across. It was clear enough from the strategy of Bhutto that he aimed to attract the newly mobilised groups of students, intellectuals, businessmen, small zamindars and workers and thereby to create public opinion in favour of his party and against the regime.

In between the two was the position of General Yahya Khan. As the campaign advanced it was felt that the ruling group, depending on its intelligence reports, grossly underestimated the strength of the Awami League and expected an instable party position in the National Assembly which would help to lengthen indefinitely the direct rule of Yahya Khan. Not sure of his position, the General had made it clear on the eve of elections that martial law would continue if the proposed Constitution was not framed in conformity with the five basic principles contained in the Legal Framework Order. He also added further that the aim of these elections is not to transfer power to a few hands but it is to transfer power to representatives of all the people of Pakistan. He also supposed it almost impossible to have any agreement between the Parties of East Bengal and those of West Pakistan.

By the time the country was undergoing for elections, the regime was preparing for the formulation of the Fourth Five Year Plan and on 1 July 1970, it was finally launched. On the basis of its timing the plan was criticized by political parties belonging to rightist and leftist shades who demanded that the interim government of Yahya should not go ahead with the scheme, instead it should be left entirely with the people's government which was going to assume the office soon after the elections (*The Ittifaq,1970*). Implementation of the Plan was also marred by political discontent, labour unrest and economic chaos, devasting floods, cyclone disaster etc. However, the election manifestoes of political parties and contradictory programmes contained therein called for a new approach which was cornered wisely by Yahya's Fourth Plan. These parties openly spoke on many a nationalissues like nationalisation of industries, foreign aid and trade, foreign policy, labour policy and strategy for agricultural and administrative development. If these new ideas were to be incorporated in the Plan, many fundamental changes would have to be made in regime's Five-Year Plan.

The elections to the National and Provincial Assemblies were held on 7th and 17th of December 1970 respectively with exception to some 26 seats which were postponed earlier and to be completed on 17 January 1971. Of the 313 seats for National Assembly and 169 in East Bengal the Awami League captured 167, while in Provincial Assembly out of 310, it was declared gainer on 298 seats. The Pakistan People's Party got 88 seats in the National Assembly, nearly 70 were from the Punjab, while in the Provincial Assemblies of West Pakistan other than those of the Punjab and Sind, it did rather badly and, in fact, failed to secure a single seat in Baluchistan. In NWFP and Baluchistan, the NAP, which supported the six-point formula, emerged as the major Party. Even in the Punjab, the party's success could not be described as spectacular, and therefore, it had no correct claim to represent all the people of West Pakistan (*Chowdhury,1972*).

But the Awami League, had secured 80 per cent of the total votes polled in East Bengal and it could claim to represent all sections of East Bengalis. Thus, the completion of Pakistan's first even truly general election with complete freedom and order was the significant and successful first step towards the restoration of a genuinely democratic and civilian government in the country since its inception.

The results of the election in National and Provincial Assemblies were a shattering blow not only for Bhutto but for General Yahya as well. It falsified the calculations that led the regime to think over other alternatives. After the election the situation changed drastically. Bhutto now saw that Majibur Rahman with his majority of seats, could form a government even without support from West Pakistan and yet he was not a man to play second fiddle. With control of only two provincial governments out of five, he saw his position as far from assured. However, he was satisfied with his victory. Within four and a half years of leaving Ayub Khan's cabinet and barely three years after forming the PPP he had won overwhelmingly in West Pakistan, transforming the political heavens and creating a multitude of stellars' newcomers.

For the General Yahya Khan, the massive victory of the Awami League in the elections caught the regime by surprise and upset its plan concerning post-electoral alignments. Earlier the ruling clique had expected that the election would bring either the Pakistan Democratic Party or Right-wing parties with Islamic ideologies to power or that it would bring about a situation where no party would gain an absolute majority. In case of latter situation, the only way out as thought by the regime was to establish itself as a mediator amongst the different parties. All the pre-poll predictions fell short. The confirmed view of the regime was expressed by Professor G. W. Chowdhury, the minister for communication and unofficial constitutional adviser to President Yahya, who observed in London on 10 September 1970, that there is no likelihood of any one single Party emerging either from West Pakistan or East Pakistan. I am personally quite optimistic that there will be no such confrontation between East and West Pakistan ....So, there is no question of East Pakistan members forming one single group in confrontation – if that comes then it means that the state comes to an end, and we are quite optimistic that this will never happen (*Muhit,1978*). Post-election scene was extremely alarming to the vested interests of West Pakistan.

The outcome of the general election compelled the regime to adopt its second strategy of acting as a mediator among the parties, especially between the Awami League and the PPP. As the Awami League had fought the elections as a referendum on its six-points of provincial autonomy, it was within its rights to demand immediately after the elections that the future constitution of the country must be based on the six-point formula. Its members of National and Provincial Assemblies took an oath to remain faithful to the six-point/ eleven-point formula in a mammoth meeting in Dacca on January 3, 1971. Asserting the formula as the basis of the future constitution of the country Sheikh also sought the cooperation of the People's representatives of West Pakistan in framing the constitution, but without any compromise on fundamental policy matters. Though by virtue of its majority the Awami League was entitled to enjoy power, but this did not mean, he added, that one region of the country would receive the benefit at the cost of the other. He assured the people that he would strive for a fair and equitable share of the various regions of Pakistan and would consciously preserve the interests of Sind, the Punjab, NWFP and Baluchistan. The plight of the poor and the down-trodden throughout the country was almost similar; all of them were the oppressed lot and victims of vested interests (*Bhuiyan,1982*). However, despite the fact that the general mood in East Pakistan was one of confidence, Mujib described the electoral victory as only the beginning of the struggle. "You have set only one foot on the road of struggle and not even both the feet" (*The Dawn,1971*). Perhaps he was knowing the intricacies of the situation.

On the other was the views of Pakistan People's Party concerning constitutional future of Pakistan. Soon, after the results were declared Bhutto and the President of the PPP had demonstrated that they had other ideas about the political and constitutional set-up of Pakistan. In pre-election phase, while campaigning, Bhutto assumed that still Mujibur Rahman was a Pakistani politician and his Six-Points' representing a negotiating position which could be altered depending on prevailing political realities. Actually, he ignored the Six-Point formula till as late as November 1970, when was convinced that Mujibur Rahman would be in a position to win an electoral majority. But he was assured under the terms of the Legal Framework Order which provided that for conducting the 1970 elections and the handing over of power to a civilian government, a two-thirds majority in the Assembly was necessary to pass a constitution. The chances of Mujibur Rahman attaining such a majority were remote.

Having taken stock of the political realities Bhutto's new strategy was to bid for a role in the federal government. For the new role the PPP needed a strong base and, therefore, Bhutto decided to set about dramatising his hand and building up his negotiating strength by adopting an aggressive posture. In a series of speech delivered in December 1970 he led a massive procession through the streets of Lahore. Addressing one of the largest gatherings ever seen in the city, he said, 'Punjab and Sind are bastions of power in Pakistan. I have the key of the Punjab Assembly in one Pocket, and that of the Sind Assembly in the other pocket. I am the real voice of the people. If anyone wants to create hurdles in the way of the awami toufan, the consequences will be disastrous. I am prepared to go into another struggle and would even sacrifice my life for getting justice to the down-trodden.' Continuing his tempo, he again declared that no constitution could be framed nor could any government at the centre be run without my party's cooperation. He added that his party was not prepared to occupy the Opposition Benches in the National Assembly and intended that majority alone did not count in National Politics. Even after the results he had not reconciled on the issue of provincial autonomy and remarked, 'the quantum of autonomy could not be determined by the force of the majority in the House, as, in that case, the National Assembly would not be able to give a Constitution acceptable to both wings of the country'.

The results had also created a great problem for the regime of General Yahya Khan. If he was to accept the verdict given by the majority of the people, he was to face the consequences as, the Awami League would come to power and frame a constitution on the basis of six-point/ eleven-point formula; Yahya Khan's rule would be terminated and the Armed Forces would lose their preponderance in the administration of the country; the Punjabi-led bureaucracy and the West Pakistani capitalists would loose their decisive say in the business of framing administrative and economic policies of the Government and last, the net result of the above would be that East Bengal could no longer be exploited further (*Chakrabarti,1978*). At the sametime Yahya's difficulty was that he could hardly allow the Awami League to frame a constitution and then refuge to authenticate it because such a course of action would clearly reveal the dictatorial nature of his regime and might well give rise to a great popular upsurge in both wings of the country. In the situation one calculation was to bring about an open confrontation between East Bengal and West Pakistan and established his rule as the saviour of Pakistan and help to prolong his rule indefinitely. But at the moment Yahya avoided this option and at first, decided to test a democratic method of persuading the parties and leaders of the both wings of Pakistan.

The General went to Dacca on 11 January 1971, in search of a solution and reiterated his desire to transfer power to the elected representatives of the people as soon as the constitution making was complete. In the meeting both sides adopted a positive approach and it ended on an optimistic note. Yahya held discussions with Sheikh Mujib on 12 and 13 January 1971 and raised his concern for defence budget. He was rather anxious the future of military's position in Pakistan because in a constitution based on six-point formula had little to do with these things. This fear was sounded on the ground that on several occasions Mujib had expressed his determination to dismantle the military edifice so that it could never interfere with politics. But apart from this, Mujib on his part, was soft in the meeting. According to various commentators, he had always indicated his intention to modify 'Six Point' to an acceptable degree. 'The whole political dialogue between Yahya Khan and Mujib from 1969 up to their crucial meeting in December 1971 after the elections was based on Mujib's unqualified and repeated pledge to modify his Six Point (*Chowdhury,1980*). Even Bhutto admitted that Mujibur Rahman manoeuvred the government into believing that he would become more amicable after the elections (*Bhutto,1980*). Thus, there was no reason for Yahya to be dissatisfied with the outcome of the talks and on the eve of his departure from Dacca on 14 January 1971, Yahya said that Sheikh Mujib was going to be the future Prime Minster of the country (*Pakistan Observer,1971*). However, the announcement had made hardly any difference for Mujib because, in a secret message to Bhutto he had offered him the post of Prime Minister if only the former agreed to help the Bengali leader to frame a constitution based on six-point formula.

After his meeting with Sheikh Mujibur Rahman at Dacca Yahya went to Sind which followed his talks with Bhutto on 17 January 1971. Later, Ayub publicly supported

Bhutto's theory of two majority Parties. It meant that the majority Party of East Bengal and the majority Party of West Pakistan would have to come to an agreement before the constitution could be framed. And it was on the insistence of the President and his companions, General Hamid and Major General Peerzada that Bhutto agreed to come to East Bengal for talks with Mujib. Thus, Bhutto, as leader of the PPP and perhaps, with the consent of Yahya, was authorise to veto a constitution adopted by the majority of the members of the National Assembly.

As a follow up of this plan and his understanding with the ruling clique, Bhutto visited Dacca on 27 January 1971, to meet Sheikh Mujib. Though the leader of the Awami League did not consider it necessary to receive Bhutto at the airport, the latter was accorded a warm welcome at Dacca and large crowds turned up to see him, chanting Pro- Mujib and Bhutto slogans. Chances of a compromise seemed good and a general feeling of bonhomie prevailed between the people of the two wings (*Sham,1980*). The two leaders held three rounds of talks covering-wide range of subjects. The first round of their talks centred around constitutional issues. The second round began with a detailed examination of the Awami League's Six Point on 28 January. In course of their discussion, three primary issues came up for special review in talks and those were the centre's powers to raise revenues for its needs, foreign trade, and provincial control of para-military forces stationed in the provinces (*The Pakistan Times,1971*). Unfortunately, the discussion was not conclusive and differences on several issues between the two leaders remained as earlier.

Awami League and its leaders criticised the Pakistan People's Party on the basis that it had no definable negotiating position. They were of the view that the Awami League had been working on the implications of 'Six Points' for a considerable time, but the PPP was still uninitiated and were not prepared to discuss the minutiae. During the meeting Mujibur Rahman had clearly advocated 'Six Points' as the cornerstone of the Awami League Manifesto, the formula was not acceptable in its totality within the framework of a 'united Pakistan. Throughout the period Mujib remained intransigent and he became increasingly adamant in his public speeches.' We want to frame a constitution, and we shall frame it on the basis of 'Six Points'. Those who would accept it, let them accept it; those who won't let them not accept it. If anyone refuses to cooperate, it will be his responsibility' (*Rahman,1971*). On the other, Bhutto had always laid greater emphasis on his negotiating skills and paid less attention to the more mundane details which the Awami League wished to discuss. Bhutto's meetings with Mujibur Rahman were non-committal. No clear agreement or understanding was reached. Bhutto, in general, was not a man who had deep regard for democratic norms. Educated in the harsh school of 'Wadera' politics and Ayub Khan's democracy, his respect for the representative government was shifting and cynical. Another politician with more moral scruple and with a greater respect for democracy would have bowed before the will of the majority but not Bhutto, who possessed none of these gentle characteristics. Before his departure for Karachi Bhutto said that he was neither satisfied with the talks nor these talks were a failure. He added that the dialogue should continue and there was no deadlock in the talk. Regarding Sheikh's suggestion that the National Assembly should meet on February 15, 1971, the PPP leader commented that there was nothing wrong 'if we take time up to the end of February" (*Bangladesh Document,1971*). A little later the schedule date for the Constituent Assembly to meet was fixed on 3rd March 1971.

At this juncture Zulfikar Ali Bhutto was in great dilemma and was yet to decide further course of action. The leaders of Awami League were asked for an early session of the National Assembly and did not want to delay the task of constitution-making. They were fearful that delay in calling the Assembly session might provide room for manipulation and conspiracy by the vested interests. The Chief of the Awami League also made it clear that in calling the National Assembly session early, the inherent goal of the Party was not to capture power but to establish democracy and the rights of the people. While the Chief of the PPP urged delay in convening the Assembly session and was seeking opportunities for conspiring against the Awami League, Bhutto felt it necessary to meet the leaders of all shades of opinion in West Pakistan including those of the defeated parties and held the view that in view of the peculiar geographical position of Pakistan it was necessary to have a consensus on constitution-making before the convening of the Assembly (*Bhuiyan,1982*). The two were also poles apart when an Indian plane was hijacked on 30 January 1971. While Sheikh Mujib deplored the burning of the Indian plane and demanded an inquiry into the incident, Bhutto supported the cause of the hijackers. Consequently, Bhutto was hailed for lending his support to the freedom fights in West Pakistan, Mujib was criticised for his views.

Causes for Bhutto's dilemma were many. The date for the meeting of Constituent Assembly had already been announced. Through his speeches Sheikh Mujib was showing the rigidity of stand on the Six Point and was determined to frame the constitution only within this formula. Now it was only up to Bhutto to prevent the passage of a 'secessionist constitution'. It could lead to a deadlock type situation and if a constitutional formula failed to evolve in 120 days, then as per the terms of the Legal Framework Order the Constitution would stand dissolved that was another unpleasant alternative. It was also possible that the elected members from West Pakistan would give way to the Awami League's dominant position and compromise with them enabling Mujib to get two-thirds majority need to pass the constitution. In fact, fear and apprehension had shadowed the PPP and its leaders which led Bhutto to announce in Peshawar on the 15th of February 1971; My Party will not attend the National Assembly session starting on the 3rd of March at Dacca unless it is made clear to me and my Partymen that there would be some amount of reciprocity from the majority Party, either publicly or privately. We can not go there only to endorse the constitution already prepared by a Party, and to return humiliated.'

Bhutto's decision not to attend the meet was widely criticised. It was considered as a disruption of the whole constitutional process. Leaders of the political parties belonging to East and West Pakistan condemned it unequivocally and refused to succumb to the pressure or threatening of anybody. Most of the leaders were of the view that the chances of compromise between the two political factions were not remote and for that matter democratic path should not be hampered. Wali Khan, the leader of the National Awami Party talking to Karachi airport, said, 'There was a difference in the 'Six Points' programme as a political slogan and the 'Six Points' which could form the basis of the constitution ...... let the Awami League give details of its constitution in the Assembly. If everyone began drafting and discussing the constitution in every part of the country, it might never solve the issue. We were voted to the Assembly by the people to form the constitution. If we sit in the Assembly and discuss this problem, only then will there be some understanding.' Even extremists, like Akbar Khan, went a step further and said that Bhutto wanted to push Bangladesh out of Pakistan.

Unrepentant at the controversy he had provoked, Bhutto was pretty adamant on the view as he told in a worker's meeting 'There are three forces in the country; the Awami League, Pakistan People's Party and the armed forces. We do not recognise any fourth power. The Awami League is a party of the people as is People's Party. We accept Sheikh

Mujibur Rahman as our elder brother. The elder brother should also listen to the younger brother. My party will not go to affix its thumb impression on a dictated constitution.' The situation between the two became so harsh that any offer, suggestion and modification put forward by Bhutto was considered by his Bangladeshi counterpart as a design to sabotage the rightful demands of the people of East Bengal. Gradually, the very word 'Bengla Desh' had now gained widespread currency all over East Pakistan. Politicians and student leaders were competing in extremism. A. S. Rab, the President of Dacca University Central Students Union, went to the extent of announcing, "The 1952 Bengali language movement was not merely a language movement, but laid the foundation of an independence movement. It seemed that all political parties, student unions and the people as well were united in the name of 'Six Points' and refused to bow to any pressure.

Despite the development of negative factors, the Awami League and its leaders were busy in preparing a draft of the constitution embodying their Six Point programme with a view to place before the Parliamentary Party for its consideration / approval thereby finally to be introduced in the National Assembly in the form of a Constitution Bill. However, the proposed draft had left it open to the provinces of West Pakistan to make any alternative provisions on the quantum of autonomy if they so desired. In this connection the Awami League Chief stressed that all members of the National Assembly should attend the session and take part in framing of a constitution and assured them that even if an individual member of the Assembly offered any reasonable proposal, it would be accepted. He also reiterated his assurance that the Six Points would not be imposed on any one (*The Dawn,1971*). Perhaps Bhutto's decision not to participate in National Assembly's session had compelled Awami leaders to become more liberal.

As the last resort to end the stalemate, Bhutto again on 28th of February 1971, while addressing a massive public meeting at Lahore, offered three alternatives as pre-condition for his participation; that Skeikh Mujibur Rahman should give some indication that on three of the six points – currency, taxation and foreign trade, he was prepared to reach some agreement before the National Assembly meets; the National Assembly session be postponed or the Legislative Framework Order provision that the Constitution be framed within 120 days should be waived. But the later part of his speech was a clear threatening, even use of coercive force. He added further that call of a strike would be organised from the Khyber Pass to Karachi – 'not a single shop would be allowed to remain open. He promised that the people of Pakistan would take full revenge from those who would go Dacca to attend or as he himself expressed 'he would break their legs. Thus, in the post-election period it was clear that there were three main political actors of Pakistan which had divergent and conflicting views regarding the political situation prevailing in the country. All the chances of accommodation and compromise, therefore, evaporated.

Again, in Pakistan democracy took a back seat. Faced with Bhutto's obduracy and Mujibur Rahman's intractability, General Yahya Khan on 1 March 1971 announced the postponement of the impending Assembly session sine die. He cited two reasons for such a step. Firstly, the major Party of West Pakistan, namely the PPP and certain other political parties announced their intention of not attending the National Assembly session on 3 March 1971. Secondly, the general situation of tension created by India further complicated the position as a whole that necessitated such a step. The announcement was followed by the removal of Admiral S.M. Ahsan, a popular figure, as Governor of East Bengal and in his place Shahabzada Yakub Khan, the Martial Law Administrator of zone B was appointed.

As soon as the news of the postponement of Assembly's session reached East Pakistan, it caused an eruption of twenty-five years of Bengali suspicions that power was to be denied to them yet again. The entire administrative and economic machinery of East Bengal was suddenly jolted to a halt. Almost the entire population of Dacca and other places of East Bengal were out in the street. A shrill serenade of protest greeted the decision and the huge groundswell of support rose for Mujibur Rahman, pushing the more extremist elements in his party to the forefront. As a result of the Presidential declaration, students, workers, small-shopkeepers and other sections of the Dacca population spontaneously brought out huge processions, raised slogans, demanding complete independence (*Mascarenhas,1971*). A meeting of the Awami League Parliamentary Party was held on 1 March 1971 and in response to public demand Mujib called for the observance of complete hartal in Dacca on 2 March, and throughout the province on 3 March. It followed the calling of an all Parties 'Meet' on 10 March 1971, which failed to give any result as Mujib refused to response Yahya and charged that the invitation was made on gun point and it came as cruel joke in the wake of widespread killings of the unarmed of the civilian population in Dacca and other parts of the province. Yahya Khan's announcement that the Assembly would meet on 25 March made no significant difference. The people showed an impressive display of unity and response to the call of Sheikh Mujib. Viewing the situation as critical and damaging the regime decided to adopt less and non-democratic methods which made the situation bad to worse.

Suddenly, Yahya found himself in a changed role. While the President and his advisers anticipated very adverse reaction in East Bengal to the announcement of postponement, they had hardly imagined the extent of the popular resentment. Despite government attempts to underplay the news, planeloads of non-Bengali refugees began arriving in West Pakistan with gruesome accounts of slaughter and mob violence. Indications from all sides showed that East Bengal was moving towards independence. Even Yahya's announcement that the Assembly would meet on 25 March failed to evoke a patriotic and constructive response from all the political leaders of the country. Preservance of absolute national integrity was at stake. In the circumstances, Yahya, in his broadcast issued a note of warning, "No matter what happens, as long as I am in command of Pakistan's armed forces and head of state, I will ensure the complete and absolute integrity of Pakistan. I will not allow a handful of people to destroy the homeland of millions of innocent Pakistanis (*Washington Post,1971*). As a follow up action, he replaced the civilian Governor and appointed Lt. General Tikka Khan as the military Governor and Martial Law Administrator of East Bengal. But even his appointment, who was best known as the butcher of Baluchistan, failed to improve the deteriorating condition of law and order problem in East Bengal.

In the changed and charged atmosphere the Awami League and its leader Sheikh Mujibur Rahman, who was at a time eager to attend the session now put forward four conditions for participation: the withdrawal of Martial Law; the sending of troops back to barracks; inquiry into killings, and transfer of power to the elected representatives of the people. Sheikh's speech in a gathering of over one million on 7 March 1971 was a clear indication what the people of East Bengal were fighting the war of independence under his leadership. At the conclusion of his speech Sheikh declared, "The struggle this time is the struggle for freedom; the struggle this time is the struggle for independence. Claring his position he added that he did not want to become the Prime Minister of the country; what he desired was the realisation of the rights of the people (*The Ittifaq,1971*). Soon after this historic speech political leaders of the two wings of Pakistan issued statements supporting Mujib's demands and urged the President to accept them so that the grave political crisis in the country could be solved. The Awami League leaders of Karachi requested the government, in particular, not to take any half-hearted measures and allow the National Assembly to be held in a peaceful and congenial atmosphere. They also criticised the President and the PPP Chief for conspiring together for postponing the Assembly session and said when the democracy loving people of East Pakistan protested against the decision of postponement, action was taken against them (*The Dawn,1971*). The leaders of Awami League began to move freely with red and green Bangladesh flags. On the 23rd of March 1971 mobs tore down the Pakistan flag all over East Pakistan, desecrated the picture of Pakistan founder Mohammad Ali Jinnah and shouted slogans for the freedom of Bangla Desh. However, the incident has vitiated the atmosphere of talks to be held on 25 March 1971.

Earlier, as a part of his last visible effort to produce a political settlement of the crisis Yahya took a trip to Dacca on 15 March and held discussions with Mujib on very next day. In fact, the opinion that Pakistan could be saved only through a political settlement between the two wings of the country was gaining ground rapidly. There was also a growing feeling in the close quarters of the army that Yahya Khan had no intention of going down in history as the man who presided over the liquidation of Pakistan nor the armed forces visualise for themselves the role of occupation troops in their own country. Sheikh Mujib, on the other hand, had agreed to hold talks with Yahya in spite of tremendous pressure from the many extremists inside and outside his party along with students and trade union leaders who wanted less than the independence. At the moment Yahya's difficulty was also multiplied due to the fact that Bhutto had made a demand for the lifting of martial law and the handing over of power to the Awami League and PPP in their respective provinces. Though a final talk with detailed discussions was held on 25 March 1971 among the three-Yahya Khan, Bhutto and Mujibur Rahman at Dacca which failed miserably to pave the path of further struggle. But till last Bhutto was insisting on a direct negotiation between his Party and the Awami League and said it was essential for breaking the prevailing deadlock. Thus, the end was approaching.

The period between 16 and 25 March 1971 was considered as decisive. The outcome of the meeting was a great disaster and allegations and counter-allegations were targeted at each other's views. It was clear from Bhutto's book The Great Tragedy, that there prevailed a complete breakdown of trust or mutual communication between the negotiating parties. Mujibur Rahman took first to Yahya Khan and then Bhutto into separate corners, whispering and asking for support against the other. All sorts of outrageous schemes were passed around. Already the chances of any negotiations for an agreement within a united Pakistan had become an impossibility (*Taseer,1980*). Outwardly, the President took an extremely conciliatory attitude and even gave the Awami League leaders to understand that he had no serious objections to accept the four demands put by them as preconditions for attending the National Assembly. On the otherhand, as the talks were going on, fresh military reinforcements were arriving everyday from West Pakistan to East Bengal. Yahya's very motive, at the juncture was in question. If he had been serious about a political settlement with the Awami League, he would have certainly issued appropriate orders to avoid the highly provocative incidents that were happening in East Bengal. His unwillingness to settle the issues indicated that the real purpose of his Dacca visit was to buy further time and supervise personally the preparations made by the military authorities to start the genocide in Bangladesh at a time of their choice.

Apprehensions about Yahya Khan began to unfold. It was a phase of great sensation all over Bangladesh. On the afternoon of the 25th of March 1971 Yahya flew to the West wing after giving instructions to his army to suppress the secessionist movement. Mujib again and again issued calls for discipline and non-violence but the situation did not improve at all. It seemed that the events were running out of his control. He termed it as unfortunate and, in a statement, said, 'We have done our duty and contributed our utmost toward the attainment of the political solution' (*The Dawn,1971*). He made a formal declaration of the Independence of Bangladesh before his arrest and said on 26 March 1971 in a broadcast, controlled by the Mukti Fauj, "In the face of an unjust and treacherous action by the military authorities in Bangladesh, I do hereby declare that from today Bangladesh is a Sovereign and Independent People's Republic. He urged the people of Bangladesh to defend the honour and integrity of Bangladesh" (*Bangladesh Document,1971*). With these developments Yahya's part in the political drama was over but his military role had just begun. The regime had in mind a military solution to the political problem and the Dacca talks were used only as a cover for the military build-up. Yahya, before leaving for Karachi on 25 March 1971, secretly ordered Tikka Khan to execute the plan. This was done to put down what he described as the legitimate attempt on the part of the Bengalis to assert their rights won in December 1970 elections. In his broadcast to the nation on 26 March 1971 he ordered the armed forces to do their job and finally restore the authority of the government and complete the ban of Awami League as a political party. The broadcast characterised Sheikh Mujib as the enemy of Pakistan and charging him with treason only infuriated the Bengali troops and the civilians (*Bhuiyan,1982*).

As a result of the civil war erupted at the close of March 1971, there had been a steady evacuation of refugees from East Bengal to India. Surprisingly the refugees who crossed the borders were mostly fleeing from army slaughter and included a fair portion of Muslims. They have been forced to leave their homes after having their properties systematically looted and burnt by the Pakistani army. The problem of refugees assumed an alarming proportion, not merely in size but also in political complexity. Political observers in India, Pakistan and abroad began to note the real danger involved in the refugee issue that was heading towards a crisis in India-Pakistan relations.

Ultimately, in the evening of December 3, 1971, the Pakistani Air Force undertook aerial raids on some of our airfields which were considerably damaged as the result of this action. The Government of India took it as an act of aggression on the part of Pakistan and in the early hours of December 4, 1971, the Indian Armed Forces were in action not only in Bangladesh but also in the Western sector. On 6 December 1971 it granted diplomatic recognition to the country as the People's Republic of Bangladesh. Swift joint action of the Mukti Bahini and the Indian Armed Forces led Pakistani army to surrender before the joint command on 16 December 1971. This historic event brought an end to the rule of Pakistan in Bangladesh. The people of Bangladesh decided to observe December 16, every year, as Victory Day and thus, East Bengal or East Pakistan as called so far, emerged as an independent, sovereign state of Bangladesh on the map of the world.

The humiliating defeat of Pakistan ensured the end of Yahya rule in the country. It made his position untenable. In desperation, Yayha Khan sent a message to Bhutto on the 18th of December to return to Pakistan and assume power. The plane of Pakistan International Airlines carrying Bhutto landed at Islamabad airport in the morning of 20th December and the same day of 2.45 PM Bhutto took the oath of office. His assumption to the office was greeted favourably by the world press, 'Zulfikar Ali Bhutto, who replaces Yahya becomes the first civilian to lead Pakistan since 1958, not only as a skilful politician ...... he knows the world, having been Foreign Minister' (*Washington Post,1971*). On 21

December Bhutto announced that Sheikh Mujibur Rahman would be released soon. He returned to Bangladesh on 10 January 1972 where he was received by his people with great jubilation. The birth of Bangladesh was a great event in history. With Pakistan's defeat, the power balance in the sub-continent had undergone a major change.

Advent of General Zia-ul- Haq

It was only thirteen months before the coup that Zia-ul-Haq was appointed Army Chief of Staff from the junior Corps Commander in Multan. He was the man, who, as a brigadier, had presided over the trial of army officers charged with the attempted coup in 1973 against Bhutto. His appointment over the heads of other more senior officers to replace the faithful General Tikka Khan, in 1976 came as no surprise as people knew Bhutto's style of functioning. But he himself was misplaced in evaluating Zia's loyalty and his political ambition for the job. The 1977 coup reflected the resurgence of military power within Pakistan. Despite its humiliating defeat at the hands of Indian army in 1971, the army of Pakistan recovered its strength and organisational network to such an extent. Anything else, the Pakistani state is stable. Ever since the country became independent, it has witnessed a constant battle to control the State between democratic forces and a military-bureaucratic elite that regards itself as the guardian of the Pakistani nation-state (*Jha,2000*). The event represented a major step forward for the politico-religious forces and a qualitative change from the preceding state of affairs. Zia-ul-Haq, the new ruler, was everything-Judge, jury and executioner, Head of State, Chief of Martial Law Administrator, Commander-in-Chief and honorary mullah. Though like Ayub and Yahya he did not wage any war with India but prepared the society of Pakistan for a long-proxy war, first in Afghanistan against the Soviet Union, and then in Kashmir against India.

When Zia-ul-Haq staged a coup, it was claimed that

Pakistan had been on the verge of civil war. He avowed an objective of ending political instability and threat to the country's survival. On the day of his assumption of power Zia pledged to hold elections within ninety days of that date and transfer of power to democratically elected people's representatives. But soon it became clear that the tasks undertaken by the Martial Law authorities were by no means easy despite the sincerity of General's Headquarters. In the post-1971 period the prestige of the armed forces declined so sharply that popular defiance of Martial law was an almost daily occurrence. It was an indication of the growing political consciousness of the people. Political issues raised in the constitution of 1973 were yet to be settled, though the said constitution was not abrogated but had kept in abeyance. The people of Pakistan were conscious about the constitutional terms, such as, a strong centre, Provincial autonomy, joint electorate vs. separate electorates, Presidential vs. Parliamentary government etc. He considered holding of elections and transfer of power to the elected representative as a very difficult task. Although the top political leaders belonging to the Pakistan Peoples Party including the Prime Minister Bhutto had been taken into "temporary protective custody", (*Lok Sabha Debates,1977*). Zia's dilemma was that a dead Bhutto may turn out to be more dangerous than the living one. Finally, he decided to postpone the elections and the removal of Bhutto from the political scene of the country. Under a new Plan "Operation Fairplay", it was announced that the new military regime intended to take judicial action against members of the previous administration, but the courts were kept open for those who wished to bring their own prosecutions. In the subsequent trials Bhutto was found guilty of the murder of Nawab Muhammad Ahmed Khan Kasuri, father of Ahmed Raja Khan Kasuri, a renegade member of the PPP and vociferous critic of Bhutto. Later, the first democratic Prime Minister of Pakistan was executed and buried on April 4, 1979.

Zia found the political situation which was beyond control, particularly, for a martial law administrator. In the initial period, as the coup took place, everywhere, the Pakistan armed forces reigned supreme. In the early hours of July 5, 1977, the army had subverted the entire mechanism of a civilised and democratic government. It had virtually destroyed the freedom and autonomy of every institution of value: press, parties, judiciary, bar, Parliament, trade unions, universities and even innocuous associations (*Bhutto,1983*). The painstaking written constitution of 1973 had been subverted, prostituted and finally consigned to the dustbin. However, the belief of the army and Zia that poor-handling of the post-election crisis the PPP had lost ground, proved wrong as it had failed to convince people and their weariness with military rule. At the juncture General Zia began to feel the need to legitimize his rule. He spent a year and a half in neutralising his regime's political opponents and at the sametime made efforts to isolate the PPP and its supporters from the mainstream of the national politics. Naturally the anti Bhutto elements in society and politics became pro-Zia under the new dispensation.

With a view to legitimize his rule Zia began to talk in terms of holding the 1973 constitution in abeyance rather than abrogating it and claimed to be working towards creating structures for an Islamic state and society within Pakistan. He started with a series of 'reforms' designed to bring law in various areas of activity in conformity with the tenets of Islam. The radical Islamisation of Pakistan began under Zia when he drafted the Ulema or mullahs to legitimise and extend his unconstitutional rule. In the process several controversial Islamic provisions were inducted in the constitution, which later proved to be so damaging to the Constitution and the rights of the people. It is widely held that they changed the very complexion of an otherwise non-violent Pakistani society. The shameful Hudood laws curbing the rights of the women, redefining law of evidence, amending the blasphemy law, establishing Federal Shariat Court and revising religious laws to create rifts among various sects were some of the more obscurantist changes (*Zaidi,2002*). Zia exploited religion to the hilt. Despite a solemn pledge, a defiance of which is strictly prohibited in Islam, he delayed the return of democratic government for eleven long years. He misused religion to prolong his despotic rule. Political workers were awarded harsher punishments including lashes for speaking against the government.

At political level Zia's supporters included fundamentalist and reactionary parties of Islamic attitude. Many of the changes had the imprint of the Jamaat-e-Islami, from which members were soon provided for the Zia cabinet. Support for Zia's 'Islamic' package was formidable, especially in the Punjab. It came from the lower middle class in the urban centres, part of the bourgeoisie that had been disenchanted with Bhutto's style of governance and policies, as well as artisans, petty shopkeepers and workers returning from the middle East and elsewhere. The latter had improved their economic standing but had remained socially and politically conservative. They felt more comfortable with Zia's Islamic, status quo, orientation as opposed to Bhutto's socialist rhetoric (*Rashid,1996*). Unfortunately, some sectarian groups, Sipah-i -Sahaba and Tehrik-i-Jafena also surfaced and flourished under Zia's patronage. Ethnic parties especially MQM and its rival group Haqiqi were also said to be creation of the martial law administration. The reactionaries astonishingly, were so naïve as to expect the army to make over power to them after it had overthrown a functioning democratic order. However, their minds were soon disabused and the Generals decided they deserved to rule themselves. Thus, their hopes soon belied as the Zia's regime began to beat the Islamic drum louder and louder. Some rightists felt pulled in his direction; others like the JI and Muslim League, despite their resignation from his cabinet, remained in his pocket (*Bhutto,1983*).

Zia's attempt to Islamise and legitimise his rule for a new lease of life had further polarised country's social segments. It came to be linked to the precepts of a particular brand of Islam and led to sectarianism, with religion becoming enmeshed within political controversies. He started a calculated move to part between Sindhi and non-Sindhi, Sindhi and Mohajir. The hanging of Bhutto had further widened the gap not only between the Sindhi in rural areas and the military regime but also with the people of Pakistan, in general. The new incident had created an overt hostility between the military and the Sindhi population. The Sindh province also witnessed the military increasingly as a Punjabi force acting against the interests of the Sindh and the power of central government became identified with a particular ethnic group (*Mazari,1996*). In order to undermine the political support of PPP in Sindh Zia encouraged the Mohajirs who constitute about 20 per cent to come together under one political platform, and it was for the first time that an All Pakistan Mohajir Students Organisation was formed in 1978. Though the dividing situation in Sind had its roots in history as well as in cultural and economic development, Zia was responsible overtly and covertly for the confrontation in both rural and urban region of the province. As the changes brought about by Zia were meant to provide legitimacy for his regime as well as strengthen his political constituency among the petit bourgeoisie as well as that section of the middle class and the feudals who favoured a strong centre.

Under a well-thought plan, Bhutto falsified the separatist movement of Pushtuns, essentially an ethnic struggle of the Pathans, in guidance of 'Frontier Gandhi', Khan Abdul Ghaffar Khan. The struggles of Pathans for a homeland was intense not only before Independence, but even after Pakistan came into being. But a vital factor that contributed to the downfall of the movement was that General Zia succeeded in assimilating discontented Pathans into Pakistan national politics. By doing so Zia targeted the Sindhis whose policies never suited the Pathans. However, the General had visualised the problem of regionalism existed in Pakistan because of the disparity in the pattern of economic development, his policy did pay rich dividends. Politically he went one step further, prominent Pushtun leaders were released from the prison and Zia even took the advice of its leaders on domestic and international affairs. Similarly, the government recruitment policy ensured that Pushtuns were employed in the military and bureaucracy. As a result of the policy of assimilation the Pushtun elite immediately ensured the cooperation of the educated middle class. They became an economically satisfied lot with the movement no longer holding any attraction for them.

But of all, the women and the minority segments of Pakistani society were the worst affected by Zia's Islamisation and his anti-minority policies. He promulgated and implemented several basic changes in existing laws of the country that had a direct bearing on social fabrics. For instance, under the Hadood Ordinance, which was made in 1979 and enforced in 1980-adultery became punishable by stoning to death, theft by amputation of the right hand and left foot, the drinking of alcohol and perjury with eighty lashes. Such hard laws along with public hanging and lashings, created an atmosphere that encouraged excesses in the name of Islam and a kind of vigilante mentality. The real intent behind these was to terrorize political opponents as well as potentially troublesome sections of society rather than to Islamic Pakistan.

As a follow up of the new Ordinance, many women were sentenced for crimes of Zina, which made no distinction between voluntary sexual intercourse and rape. More generally their position was weakened through laws of evidence promulgated in 1984, which equated the testimony of one man to that of two women. Similarly, protest demonstrations led by urban women's groups such as the

Women's Action Forum led to modifications. A ban was imposed on taking part in public sports, including the Asian Olympics and Pakistan's own national games, because sport clothes are skimpy. The Ministry of Education had ordered the wearing not just of a duptta as a head covering but of the chador as an all–enveloping overcoat (*Jensen,1983*). These anti-feminist proposals are in accord with what seems to be the basic psycho-pathology of the Muslim male, which is that woman is the wicked temptress, that man is incapable of resisting her wiles and must be protected against them by anti-woman restrictions imposed by the state (*Ghose,1987*). The whole set of laws had sent Pakistan's women back not merely to the early Islamic era but to the pre-Islamic one.

Among the minorities, the Ahmadiya community was most affected. The Bhutto government in 1974 had amended the Constitution to declare all Ahmedias non-Muslims, but the amendment was actually implemented during Zia's regime, through a Presidential Ordinance on 26 April 1984. It prohibited the Ahmedias from calling themselves Muslims or their places of worship "mosques". Their priests were also forbidden from calling the faithful for prayers through the Azan (*Nayar,1985*). The Ahmediya community resorted to wearing Kalima badges and the authorities began arresting those who displayed the badges. The Dawn, an English daily, reported the news in detail on 2 and 23 February 1985. Mashar Ali Khan, a distinguished Pakistani journalist, had taken up the case of the Ahmedias and had demanded an end to their persecution on the ground of religion. Strange lies here that how can a law stop a person from calling himself a Muslim? The Government of Pakistan may call the Ahmedias non-Muslims, but if they are firm in following the tenets of Islam, no one can take them away from this right. Similarly, separate electorates introduced in 1985 by Zia, alienated the Christians, Hindus, Parsis, Ahmedias and other minorities from the political mainstream.

In the same year (1985) the key constitutional amendment was made by President Zia was the insertion of Article 2A through Presidential Order No. 14 of 1985, making the Objective Resolution, which had formed part of the preamble of the Constitution, a substantive part of it. Further in 1986, the Blasphemy Law was passed which added Section 295C to the Pakistan Penal Code making blasphemy against Prophet Muhammad a criminal offence. It read whoever by words, either spoken or written, or by visible representation or by any imputation, innuendo, directly or indirectly defiles the sacred of the Prophet Muhammad shall be punished with death or imprisonment for life and shall be liable to fine. He also introduced Islamic legal code in 1988. In substance there was little in all such measures to distinguish Zia-ul-Haq and his regime from any other dictator or martial law regime. Am elaborate system of martial law courts and tribunals was put in place and the power of the higher judiciary drastically curtailed. He, like other Generals of the past, relied chiefly on the policy of divide and rule, sowing confusion everyday and using the media effectively (*Bhutto,1983*). The ruling elites continue to employ a combination of 'Islamic and secular innovations and 'reforms' to maximize their own power. The purpose is to avoid alienating the well-organized and potentially troublesome Islamist forces on the one hand, and the even more powerful wings of the army, bureaucracy and the bourgeoisie which remain secular (*Rashid,1996*).

At the social level Zia did not spare Pakistan's civil society and at its cost, encouraged purely Islamist political parties which not only commanded a strong base in the country but had international links too. To a large extent, the regime of Zia had militarised the civil society. With democratic political parties banned and all venues of protest through legal means closed, polarisation within society intensified. Cleavages and conflicts within civil society, which had already shown a violent trend under Bhutto's increasing use of the coercive elements of the state, grew worse under military rule. The ban on political parties led to an increasing focus on seeking identity through group membership based upon ethnicity, sectarianism and the traditional biradri system (*Mazari,1996*). Pakistan's civil society has been an increasing resort to violence to resolve all manner of conflicts. This militarisation of civil society – its preference for a violent course of action over other means of exercising influence became marked after the imposition of martial law following a military coup in July 1977. Militarism has not only expanded at the international level, in the form of arms buildup and in the use of force as an 'instrument of supremacy'; in the developing states it has also led to an increase in the role of the military establishment in domestic and foreign policy making and execution. In such a situation, as the case is in Pakistan, the military evolves its own doctrines of state and government which drive it to seek to influence state formation. This sense of purpose along with the desire to increase its power and privilege within the state leads the military to abuse its legitimate function and make inroads into the political structures of the state. In seeks legitimacy, in general, but it relies on force to perpetuate itself. As Zia stated,' martial law should be based on fear. The use of force becomes more pronounced where civil society as a whole, or critical segments within it, reject militarism.

In course of Islamisation Zia tried to mould educational system that is the soul of civil society in any country. He imposed several restrictions on campus education and gave an Islamic look to the education at primary level. In 1979, through an University Ordinance Zia reduced the role of the teacher to a menial government employee and allowed the government to victimise teachers for their political sympathies. Several teachers were either transferred to schools/ colleges in the interior of the country, sacked or incarcerated. As part of his educational reforms, Zia called for revising the curriculum and text books at various levels starting from the primary to make pupils more aware of the Islamic mainsprings of Pakistan's creation, its ideology and history of Islam. In addition, an Islamic University was established at Islamabad with the objective of fusing 'Islamic' and 'secular' education. To Zia's likings the University Grants Commission of Pakistan issued a directive for the benefit of prospective textbook authors spelling out the objectives of the new curriculum to demonstrate that the basis of Pakistan is not be found in racial, linguistic or geographical factors, but rather in the shared experience of a common religion; to get students to know and to appreciate the ideology of Pakistan (*Hoodbhoy and Nayyar,1985*).

General Pervez Musharraf

National humiliation at Kargil, deteriorating economic condition, Sharif's onslaught on the opposition, the judiciary and the press, etc. paved the way for another military coup in Pakistan. As expected the democratic government of Nawaz Sharif was overthrown in a military coup by General Pervez Musharraf. He took over on 12 October 1999, the day his dismissal was announced by the government. For a long time, the civil military relationship was plagued by the eternal conflict: civilian rulers wishing to assert civilian control by reigning in the army against the military insisting on an institutionalized role in state affairs. Any attempt to marginalize the army over key strategic subjects like J&K, nuclear capability, defense budget and Afghanistan would backfire. The establishment's political Philosophy is conservative one built upon three principles: the military's role as the 'guardian' of the ideology of Pakistan.' Parity with India and a highly centralized state of made that possible. The liberal leaders who tried to placate the Establishment by adopting its agenda were never trusted. They had an independent base and could "turn" when they grew strong. Puppets which tried to create an independent base for themselves could not be trusted either as the experience of Nawaz Sharif shows.

Like earlier this coup of Pakistan is a product of internal dissension among the ruling elites of the country whether civil, military or religious. The second inning of Nawaz Sharif's region which commenced in February 1997 was full of administrative contradictions and controversies. The Jamaat-I-Islami, which had earlier records of aggressive and militant postures and had a bitter experience of the authoritarian style of Sharif's leadership found little difference with the new dispensation from the start of the regime. It pressurized the government to maintain a relationship of parity with India in the sphere of nuclear energy and a s follow up of Indian steps, Pakistan exploded its first nuclear device at the end of May 1998 at Chagai hills in Baluchistan. In line the Jamaat did not like the growing understanding between India and Pakistan following Atal Bihari Vajpayee's visit to Lahore in February 1999 and persuaded the Government of Nawaz Sharif to undo the spirit of Lahore declaration. Naturally it also expressed displeasure when Pakistan declared for a pull out of the Mujahideen and militants from Kargil sector in the first week of July 1999. On the developments the Jamaat demanded immediate dismissal of Nawaz Sharif's government.

The state of Pakistan's economy under Sharif government was also a concern for all. The faltering economy constituted the most serious threat to the polity. The government was unable to muster enough political will and institutional capacity to cope with the culture of tax evasion, rampant corruption and extravagant government expenditure. The business community, the traditional stronghold of Sharif twice foiled the government's attempt to impose a general sales tax. Similarly, agriculturalists were not prepared to pay more than nominal taxes. The shortfall in revenue collection accentuated the existing resource gap and forced the federal government to cut back on the revenue share of the province (*Rizvi,1999*). It was facing a gloomy future as macro-economic fundamentals remained in a precarious position and recession continued to grip the country as a result of Pakistan's nuclear explosions in May 1998 and aggression at Kargil in 1999.

Nawaz Sharif inherited the ethnic and regional tension in a big way during his second term of office. Despite General Zia's military might and massive state imposed 'Islamisation Programme' they remained simmering and became more acute and formidable under the post-Zia democratic dispensation. The post-Zia regimes headed by Benazir Bhutto and Nawaz Sharif continued with more or less the same sort of highly centralized, repressive and negative approach as adopted by their predecessors to deal with the regional tensions. Political survival became the primary concern which overshadowed the larger issues of human rights, democratic freedom and national integration (*Kaushik,2006*). The already complicated scene in the Sindh province was wrecked by violence. Thousands of innocent people had fallen victim to the sectarian fanaticism of armed militias. The polarization ion of Muttahida Quami Movement (MQM), Pakistan Muslim League (PMC), Awami National Party (ANP) and other factions of Pakistan sharpened when the Sharif government unveiled its plan to introduced a constitutional amendment to amass more powers at the expense of the parliament, the judiciary and the provinces, under the pretext of introducing Sharia and mobilize orthodox Islamic groups to counterbalance his political adversaries. The Shariat Bill was introduced in the National Assembly in August 1999 without consulting his own party which led it to a mini rebellion.

Despite all odds the deciding factor for a coup in Pakistan has been the civil- military relations. The Sharif government's narrow based and personalised decision-making led to strains in its relations with the General Jehangir Karamat, the then Army Chief, who made several statements on the growing threats to the polity and talked about the adverse implicationsof the current economic deterioration and internal stability and external security (*The News,1998*). Sharif's tussle' with the military establishment began by this time and the Army Chief decided to step down three months ahead of his retirement. His departurein October 1998 signaled tough time in Pakistani politicswas replaced with Pervez Musharraf, an Urdu-speaking Muhajir from Karachi. With his appointment Sharif hoped that a Muhajir army chief presiding over a predominantly Punjabi-Pashtun high command would he weak and thus not able to build'pressure on the government. He, however, like Zia, was also a Deobandi in many ways which symbolises the ethos and religious orientation of the present-day army of Pakistan. During the regime of Zia, Musharraf had developed a close relationship with the ISI and Islamic fundamentalist groups like the Harkat-ul-Mujahideen.

After the debacle of Kargil Sharif made the grave mistake of attempting to place for the blame of Kargil fiasco on the military, hoping to mollify public criticism of the unconditional withdrawal which had adversely affected the internal coherence, morale and credibility of the armed forces. He also seemed determined to set about trying to divide the army's top command and used DSI as a tool in his strategy in this connection Sharif made the biggest blunder of his political career and decided to sack General Musharraf and appoint General Ziauddin as the new army chief. He was also mistaken in understanding the army as well Whatever the inner differences, the higher command of the armed forces remained united and loyal and committed to its chief. The military was also of the view that the army would have succeeded in Kargil had it not been pressurized to withdraw (*Kukreja,2003*).

With Pervez Musharraf's taking over the painful cycle of Pakistan was repeated again in 1958 it wasAayub Khan Who imposed martial law in Pakistan. The then Supreme Court in the infamous Dasso case endorsed field Marshal

Ayub Khan's military take over and for 11 long years civil liberties were suspended. Next the Supreme, Court unanimously validated toppling of Zulfikar Ali Bhutto's elected government that was looking to complete a second term in office. General Zia-ul- Haq emerged as the savior of Pakistan in November 1977 whose regime is considered a watershed in the polities of post-1971 Pakistan but especially for an amendment to the constitution of the country. The famous Constitution Eighth Amendment Act 1985 was passed. It was incorporated in the constitution to allow for the continuance of Zia's authoritarian rule with all the democratic paraphernalia. Article 58(2)(b) of this amendment empowered the president to dismiss an elected Prime Minister and Parliament without any obligation to consult with the Senate or the Supreme Court (*Bose and Jalal,2004*). Given the nature of the Pakistani state, the exercise of Presidential power, conferred by the clause was inconceivable without the approval of the military high, command. After the thirteenth amendment Article 58(2) (b) was omitted and this remained the position from 1997 to 2002. And again, the said article was reinserted in the constitution by the Legal Framework Order, 2002 (*Kashyap,2007*).

There is a basic defect with Pakistan that it has not been able to develop a responsive democratic liberal society. State survival became the primary concern of the rulers of Pakistan, who equated it with a powerful central government, strong defence posture, high defense allocations and an emphasis on monolithic nationalism. As a result, Pakistan shaped itself as a centralized administrative polity which stifled the growth of autonomous and viable political institutions and processes. There started the steady decline of all public institutions in Pakistan barring its military. As all institutions within the country lose their autonomy and become increasingly country lose their autonomy and become increasingly subservient to the military the prospects for the restoration of democracy become all the more dim.

Jack Snyder, an American political scientist has argued in his book, from Voting to Violence that in such a milieu, open elections might unleash ethnic, religious and hyper-nationalistic appeals on the part of various unscrupulous and unprincipled politicians (*Ganguly,2007*). Such an outcome. he argued further could come about because the norms and institutions that normally place restraints on the behaviour of demagogues would have been stripped and denuded during the authoritarian pasts (Ganguly,2007). For a country like Pakistan the steady weakening of all institutions except the military will pose the most overwhelming challenges of governance in the ethnically fractured, politically divided and economically fragile land.

General Pervez Musharraf having captured power in Pakistan started his search for the legitimacy of the regime. Initially it was done through the propagation of their self-image as a set of missionary progressives, neutral and patriotic guardians of the nation. He was aware that military solutions to social problems are counter-productive and guided by practical common sense, he sought a creative relationship with the civilian political groups. The scholar, touch of Henry Bienen has also emphasised that the term military regime is a misnomer as all military regimes have large civilian components. First because the military leaders want to give a degree of civilian colour to the new regime Second confronted with the practical task of running the government, as military leaders lack the requisite political and administrative skill they are forced to recruit appropriate talent from the civilian sector Thus the new military ruler of Pakistan opted for institutionalized technocratic politics, building on the models of both Ayub Khan and Zia-ul-Haq. He appointed a National Security Council and included Sharfuddin Pirzada, the attorney -general of the late Zia, and Atiya lnayatullah, another associate of Zia. A two-tier system of running the country was introduced: a national security council comprising the chiefs of the armed forces and civilian members of the government which will work as a supreme administrative body assisted by a group of advisors to help the country's day to day affairs (*Hussain,2000*).

Apart from political activities on the part of political parties headed by Benazir Bhutto and Nawaz Sharif there was a tremendous international pressure on the new regime for restoration of democracy in Pakistan. Pervez Musharraf gave the concept of real democracy and announced on 23rd March 2000, two days before the visit of US President Bill Clinton that he would hold elections in the local bodies later in the year throughout the country. He, as the Chief Executive of the country, addressed the national on 14th August 2000 coinciding with the Independence Day and announced his devolution plan and the scheme of party less democracy which was likely to be completed by May 2001. A second round of local elections at the district level were to be held in July 2001, effectively putting municipal governments back in power. He also made it clear that from her we will move up step by step to provincial and federal elections in due course (*Asian Recorder,2000*). Many observers and analysts had viewed Musharraf's devolution of power plan as ploy to consolidate his personal power, clearly designed to create a new power base for the military regime.

On 20 June 2001 Pervez Musharraf elevated himself to the presidency and reiterated his commitment to restore 'genuine democracy' in Pakistan while initiating reforms aimed at administrative and political decentralization, the General had no intention of relinquishing power. It seems that Musharraf wants an army-backed quasi-democracy and for which he will seek a permanent constitutional political role for the army and make it the guarantor of a quasi-democratic system by 2012. In a controversial referendum in April 2002 Musharraf declared himself elected president for another five years. The promised elections were held in October 2002 but not before the General had equipped himself with a Legal Framework Order which gave him powers to overrule the elected parliament and change the constitution to create a permanent role for the military in Pakistan's political structure.

Like predecessors the military regime of Pervez Musharraf confronted with the problems of ethno-sectarian violence. In spite of strict regimentation and imposition of official ban or sectarian outfits and sectarian educational centres, the entire society remains inflicted with the menace of sectarian violence and terrorism. The banned sectarian groups of both the Sunni and the Shia sects re-emerged with their changed name.

In a significant development a terrorist attack was made on the World Trade Centre and Pentagon in the US on September 2001 which resulted in all geo- political dynamics- international, regional and local. Earlier the American interest in Pakistan somewhat declined after the breakdown of the Soviet system and cessation of the cold war. But the event of 11 September had regenerated the US interest in Pakistan because it was at the centre of the world's worst Islamist terrorist network. The Bush Administration lifted all the sanctions' imposed in post-nuclear explosion period and it became an essential partner in the global war on terror. It also pushed the military regime of Pakistan in the biggest dilemma the country has ever faced. On the one side, the world's most powerful national, wounded and angry, was bluntly telling the General that if he did not act as a friend now he would be considered as the enemy. On the other were the Taliban leaders of the most brutish police state in the world and their hordes who threatened Jihad against the very country that had nurtured them.

General Pervez Musharraf was left with no choice and despite facing stiff opposition from the religious lobby, he boldly promised to curb Islamic militancy and restore Pakistan's image as a moderate member of the international comity of nations. With a weak economy, a polarized polity, China backing Washington and the Islamic bloc a virtual non-factor all taking together made Pakistan to side with the United States of America's global strategy against terrorism. In a televised address he tried to portray his US friendly act as strategic decision that was designed to prevent a proactive India from isolating Pakistan on the international scene in the aftermath of Pentagon episode. He also expressed country's concern for cooperation with the US on Pakistan's integrity, he states of economy. the sustainability of its strategic assists of nuclear weapons and missiles, besides the Kashmir issue (*Kukreja,2003*). Ultimately Musharraf decided to distance himself from the Taliban-ruled Afghanistan and agreed to provide help to Washington in such key areas as intelligence and information exchange, use of Pakistan's air space and logistical support which involved tremendous risks for his regime.

In return Pakistan got everything that is desired from the US and former's war against terror has changed country's destiny once again. Apart from lifting all sanctions related to the nuclear tests, aid has started to flow, inconvenient facts about cross-border terrorism have been brushed under the carpet. In the context of Pakistan supported cross-border terrorism in Jammu and Kashmir, the US did nothing more than listing the LeT and the JeM as foreign terrorist organizations. In fact, General Pervez Musharraf is considered by the US and his other Western allies as an important bulwark in the anti-terrorist fight, a moderate who needs to be supported and fortified. The US has also made it clear that it will stay in Pakistan till it is cleansed of terrorism. It will support Musharraf as long as he plays the role Washington wants (*Subrahmanyam,2002*).

However, the US Administration of late has become frustrated as Pakistan has not been able to wipe off the terrorist hideouts from its territory. Not only that, the Al-Qaeda is controlling the terrorist activities from their base in Pakistan. They have also reconstituted their positions on the Pak-Afghan borders. In previous years, General Musharraf has played that 'I am your final line of defence against the Jihadists taking over in this nuclear-armed country' card to win grace, favour, money, and arms from the US. Both Benazir Bhutto and Nawaz Sharif have warned of the perils of backing a duplicitous and unreliable General Pervez Musharraf. Washington, having invested so heavily in him (over $ 10 billion in aid since 2001) is seen as General's helper against the people (*The Hindu,2007*).

In Islamabad and Washington military officers of the Bush Administration have said that they believed much of the American money was not making its way to frontline Pakistani units. Money had been diverted to help finance weapons system designed to counter India not the Al-Qaeda or the Taliban. The $5 billion was provided through a programme known as Coalition Support Funds, which reimburses Pakistan for conducting military operations to fight terrorism under a separate programme, Pakistan receives $300 million per year in traditional American military financing that pays for equipment and training (*The Hindu,2007*). In December 2007, for the first time after six years the Pentagon has completed a review that produced a classified plan to help the Pakistani military build an effective counterinsurgency force. The US leadership, particularly in the Congress is expressing doubts in the intentions of Pakistan on controlling terrorist activities. The misuse of US funds in Pakistan has also reached to People's court and now the American citizen has started asking about the intelligent use ofits money, particularly when they dollar becoming more productive and yielding higher returns in India. A kind of rethinking on the issue was felt by the American government who is favouring he restoration of a democratic set up. It is true that Pakistan's government need greater popular legitimacy won through the ballot box in order to advances both long and short-term counter-terrorist goals.

But the fast-moving events and action of Pakistan have made the US options difficult to operate. The reasons are two. One the USA has become a hatedword The Pakistan and any leader who acquires power with the visible or even invisible support of America may not be acceptable to masses in the country. Second the army in Pakistan is too embedded in the political hierarchy and social fabrics. Markey, a famous scholar of the US, believes. Any attempt to crack down on Pakistan will exacerbate distrust resulting in increased Pakistani support for jihadists; coercive threats will undermine confidence without producing better results. Even for the present mess in the Pak polity West is more responsible than the Pakistan itself. Sixty years of pampering of the military dictatorships has brought about a strong military system that controls not only the political system but also the economy. In nutshell, the US has become a deciding factor in Pakistan whether civil or military. Washington can win the confidence of Pakistan, military establishment without accepting its exclusive political authority and it can help empower civilian leadership without jeopardizing the army's core interests.

Turbulence in Pakistan's national life erupted in 2007 when Pervez Musharraf's five years extended term as president expired. In 2007, the issue whether he could continue as an army chief and as a president was challenged in the court. In the meantime, on March 9, 2007, General Musharraf suspended the Chief Justice of Pakistan Iftikhar Choudhary and put him under house arrest. Justice Bhagwan Dass was appointed as the acting Chief Justice of Pakistan in his place on 25 March 2007 among wide protests from all sections of society Surprisingly, perhaps for the first time in Pakistan's judicial history the order of March 9, 2007, was set aside in a landmark judgment of the Supreme Court of Pakistan on 20 July 2007 which reinstated Iftikhar the Chief Justice of Pakistan. The court ordered that as a further consequence the petitioner the Chief Justice of Pakistan, shall he deemed to be holding the said office and shall always be deemed to have been so holding the same. The stand taken by the judiciary in Choudhary's case was a clear message that they were nobody's "Poodle".

General Pervez Musharraf, in order to safeguard his presidential post declared an emergency in Pakistan on 3 November 2007. With the declaration constitution was suspended, political leaders, judges, lawyers and many others were arrested. Public gatherings, rallies, protest meetings were banned. The general has now been revealed in his true colours as a ruthless military dictator, in the mould of Zia-ul-Haq and all his dismal predecessors who had kept Pakistan in a state of permanent Army rule (*The Hindu,2007*). In general, he has attempted to justify his imposition of Emergency by arguing that judicial intervention had led to a paralysis in civil administration even as Pakistan was 'on the verge of destabilization' because of rising militancy and extremism.

Imposition of an Emergency in Pakistan invited a deep concern from the country's worldwide but particularly from the US, the European Union, the Commonwealth, China and others Taking into consideration the position of the country all urged General Musharraf to restore normalcy in Pakistan as its future rest; on harnessing the power of democracy and the rule of law to achieve the goals of stability, development and countering terrorism. The US statement also called for prompt return to the constitutional force and made it clear that it would not support extra-constitutional means. Like Pakistan many countries have provisions for emergency powers in their law. These provisions are to be used during the times of national crisis such as war and other calamities. Emergency powers are expected to expedite relief measures, remove impediments and enforce strict security. History has shown that an Emergency, especially when declared for personal gains, was full of oppression. Freedom and rights were at peril and people had struggled. What people seek and cherish is democracy that cares for people interests, ensures freedom and where administrators can deliver and be accountable (*The Hindu,2007*). Perhaps under immense pressure from national and international sources Musharraf had lifted the emergency and restored the constitution with amendments made during this period in an address to the national he also promised holding of election, on January 8, 2008, but later it was deferred to 18 February due to an unprecedented event assassination of Benazir Bhutto during a election campaign in Rawalpindi on 27 December 2007.

A legend of the voice of democracy in Pakistan, its former Prime Minister and chairperson of Pakistan People's Party was killed in gunfire attack-cum-suicide bombing on 27 December 2007. Her assassination was condemned by almost all countries of the world including big neighbours and major powers who cherished Benazir as the last hope of democracy in Pakistan. They all held it as an odious act of heinous terrorist crime that took the precious life of Pakistan's most popular opposition leader of the country. With this it became clear that epic struggle lies ahead for its hard-pressed people. The political situation in Pakistan caught in a maelstrom, has been transformed overnight by the martyrdom of Benazir Bhutto, a courageous leader. Some analysts fear the assassination would spell the end of the tentative movement towards democracy witnessed in recent months. While such as outcome would suit the military establishment as well as the Islamists, it would have dangerously destabilizing consequences.

Benazir Bhutto was born in Karachi on June 21, 1953, into a powerful land-owning dynasty. She was the oldest of four children of her Westernized father and an Iranian Shia mother. She came from a political family steeped in Pakistan's turbulent history. After attending convent schools in Pakistan, she went to Oxford University and became the first Asian women to head its prestigious Oxford Union debating society. Educated at Oxford and Harvard in 1987 She entered an arranged marriage with businessman Asif Ali Zardari and after one year on August 17, 1988 became the first female premier of a Muslim country, when Zia-ul-Haq died in a mysterious plane crash. On the charge of corruption her government was dismissed in 1990 and she was replaced by Nawaz Sharif. Although again in 1993 she became the Prime Minister of Pakistan but three years later in 1996 her government was thrown out by President Farooq Leghari on further graft charges. Benazir Bhutto went into self-imposed exile in April 1999. After eight long years in exile she came back in Pakistan in October 2007 where she received a huge welcome.

Benazir Bhutto's return to Pakistan was followed by a controversial agreement with President Pervez Musharraf to withdraw corruption cases against her in exchange for her tacit support to him in the presidential election. She described the National Reconciliation Ordinance as the first step towards making changes in the way Pakistan governed. But at the same time, she also asserted that there is no questions of going back to the dysfunctional democracy of the past. The real issue for me is democracy. Being overwhelmed by the welcome she told. The Hindu in a brief interview, the message from this is that people want change, the people want democracy, they want jobs, they want security of lives and livelihood (*The Hindu,2007*).

The assassination of Bhutto gave a serious blow to US reconciliation efforts which the Bush Administration had started months ago. The power-sharing deal never came to fruition as the increasingly besieged president Musharraf had imposed a series of autocratic measures. Including a declaration of emergency rule and the dismantling of the country's Supreme Court, that left him politically weakened. Even during the emergency rule the officials of the US Administration continued to prod Benazir towards an arranged marriage with President Pervez Musharraf and hoped that they would form an alliance after Pakistan's January 8 elections. The new situation had left in ruins the delicate diplomatic effort to reconcile Pakistan's deeply divided political factions. It also highlighted George W. Bush's two main objectives iii the region—his quest to bring democracy to the Muslim world and his drive to force out the Islamist militants who have hung on tenaciously in Pakistan, especially in Pakistan-Afghanistan border.

The US policy in Pakistan was criticized by Stephen 1st, Cohen, a senior fellow at the Brookings Institute, who held the Administration responsible for not nurturing Pakistan's opposition for so long after president Musharraf's coup in 1999. He however, expressed the hope that the US could still urge moderate parties to ally themselves with president Musharraf, forming a governing coalition, assuming that the scheduled elections go ahead. A faction of experts in the US is believing that as Nawaz Sharif was, also a moderate and had worked withWashington in the war on terror with Clinton Administration in the 1990s, their country should not be suspicious about him (*Cooper and Myers,2007*). At the juncture it is it challenge for the US to find a trusted partner in Pakistan. Washington has been caught in a dilemma as Musharraf was a valuable ally of the West against the Islamist threat in the region, but his continuing indefinitely in rule Pakistan as a military dictator was becoming an embarrassment for the US.

Like any other politician of the time Bhutto's politics was full of complex and contradiction. She represented a liberalism both of the lifestyle kind as well as political liberalism yet it was she who built up the Taliban in Afghanistan. She approached the poor wearing her father's mantle, yet liberalised and privatised the economy, handing it over to the IMF and World Bank. She fought against one dictator in the 1980 refusing to compromise but reconciled to deals with another military man two decades later.

The Post-Benazir turmoil in Pakistan is considered as the worst crisis in its 60-years-old tempestuous history. In terms of its political and democratic future from now is the absence of the most important personality, who had been the public of dissent and hope for the last three decades. The loss of Bhutto as one of the most important vocal and courageous political figures on the Pakistani, and indeed global scene will be irreplaceable. Possibly, without her we will witness a different Pakistan in future.

References

Ahmad, Imtiaz (2001). 'Beyond the Original Message', *The Hindustan Times*, 31 May.

Asian Recorder (2000). New Delhi, pp.267-68.

Ayub Khan, Mohammed (1967). *Friends Not Masters*, London, p.157.

Bangladesh, Document (1971). Ministry of External Affairs, New Delhi, pp.15-22.

Bhargava, G.S. (1969). *Pakistan in Crisis*, New Delhi, pp.9-10.

Bhuiyan, Md. Abdul Wahud (1982). *Emergence of Bangladesh and Role of Awami League*, New Delhi, pp.153-54.

Bhutto, Benazir (1983). *Pakistan: The Gathering Storm*, New Delhi, p.5.

Bose, Sugata and Jalal, Ayesha, ed. (2004). *Modern South Asia-History, Culture, Political Economy*, New Delhi, p.195.

Chakrabarti, S.K. (1978). *The Evolution of Politics in Bangladesh 1947-1978*, New Delhi, pp.173-74.

Chowdhury, Subrata Roy (1972). *The Genesis of Bangladesh*, Bombay, p.58.

Cooper, Helene and Myers, Steven Lee (2007). 'A Serious Blow to US Reconciliation Effort', *The Hindu*, 29 December.

Department of Films and Publications (1963). Basic Democracies as Viewed by the President, Karachi.

Documents of Pakistan's Peoples' Party (1967). Lahore.

Engineer, Ali Asghar (2003). 'Look Ma No Purdah', *The Hindustan Times*, 24 July.

Ganguly, Sumit (2007). 'Dead End for Democracy', *The Times of India*, 28 November.

Ghose, S.K. (1987). *Muslim Politics in India*, New Delhi, pp.138-39.

Hoodbhoy, Pervaiz and Nayyar, Abdul Hameed (1985). *Rewriting the History of Pakistan*, Lahore, p.165.

Hussain, Akmal (1996). 'The Dynamics of Power: Military, Bureaucracy and the People', Kumar Rupesinghe and Khawar, Mumtaz eds., *Internal Conflicts in South Asia*, London, p.50.

Hussain, Zahid (1999). 'Day of the Generals', *Newsline*, October, Karachi.

Jensen, G.H. (1983). 'The Tyranny of Religion', *The Illustrated Weekly of India*, 16 October.

Jha, Prem Shankar (2000). 'General in His Rat Trap', *The Hindustan Times*, 26 August.

Kashyap, Shaunak (2007). 'Spectre of Emergency- Will There be a Resurgence of the Doctrine of Necessity', Dr. Subhash C. Kashyap, ed., *South Asia Politics*, Vol.6, No.5, September, New Delhi, pp. 49-50.

Kaushik, Surendra Nath (2006). *Contesting Identities in Pakistan, Region, Religion and the Nation*, Jaipur, p.17.

Kukreja, Veena (2003). *Contemporary Pakistan- Political Processes, Conflicts and Crises*, New Delhi, p.262.

Lok Sabha Debates (1977). Second Edition, Vol.4, 5-9 July, New Delhi, Colm.145.

Mahajan, V. D. (1982). *Select Modern Governments*, New Delhi, p. 520.

Malkani, K. R. (2001). 'Wish You Were Here', *The Hindustan Times*, 3 July.

Mascarenhas, Anthony (1971). *The Rape of Bangladesh*, New Delhi, pp. 21-22.

Muhit, A. M. (1978). *Bangladesh: Emergence of a Nation*, Dacca, p.184.

Mazari, Shireen M. (1996). *'The Militarisation of Pakistan's Civil Society*,' Kumar Rupesinghe and Khawar, Mumtaz eds., London, pp.101-2.

Nayar, Kuldip (1985). 'The Tragedy of Pakistan's Ahmedias,' *Sunday*, 31 March-6 April.

Rashid, Abbas (1996). *'Pakistan: The Politics of Fundamentalism*,' Kumar Rupesinghe and Khawar, Mumtaz eds., London, p.65.

Rizvi, Hasan Askari (1999). 'Pakistan in 1998: A Polity Under Pressure,' *Asian Survey*, Vol.39, No.1, January-February, pp.181-82.

Shahin, Sultan (1999). 'Bigotry in Pakistan,' *The Hindustan Times*, 14 December.

Shourie, Arun (1987). *Religion in Politics*, New Delhi, pp.78-80.

Speech of Mujibur Rahman (1971). Dacca, 9 February.

Subrahmanyam, K. (2002). 'Washington's Waiting Islamabad's Tokenism will not work,' *The Times of India*, 11 February.

The Dawn (1958). 16 October.

The Dawn (1958). 26 December.

The Dawn (1963). 2 April.

The Dawn (1969. 29 November.

The Dawn (1971). 5 January.

The Dawn (1971). 1 March.

The Dawn (1971). 26 March.

The Economist (1969). 7 June.

The Hindu (2007). 19 October.

The Hindu (2007). Editorial, 5 November.

The Hindu (2007). 6 November.

The Hindu (2007). 7 December.

The Ittefaq (1970). Dacca, 8 June.

The Ittefaq (1971). 8 March.

The Newsweek (1969). 7 April.

The News (1998). Lahore, 7 October.

The PakistanObserver (1971). 15 January.

The PakistanTimes (1969). 14 March.

The Pakistan Times (1971). 29 January.

The Statesman (1958). 18 October.

The Times (1969). 11 March.

The Washinhton Post (1971). 7 March.

The Washington Post (1971). 21 December.

Zaidi, Mubashir (2002). 'Jehad in Retreat,' *The Hindustan Times*, 20 January.

6

The Current Challenges of Modern Pakistan

Changing Nature of Pak Society

The new state called Pakistan was a creation of the Muslim League that was founded in 1906 to oppose the Indian National Congress (INC) and therefore, the former had hardly any members who had fought for the independence of the country. The result was that the power came into the hands of either to retired officials or man who had been brought into public life under British patronage. It created a wide gap between the ruler and the ruled in the newly formed nation while the public or society of it was a bewilderingly patchy. There are classes within class, castes within caste, social groups, ethnic groups, linguistic groups, urban modern educated elite, rural, feudal benighted masses, opulent industrialists, rich feudal lords and the seedy hangers-on the fundamentalists with the arch conservative and orthodox outlook, and the secular, democratic enlightened and liberal sections of society with the modernist view of man and society. In 1947, all Sikhs and nearly all high-caste Hindus left Pakistan. Cities and villages became totally Muslim. The resultant confessional homogeneity in Pakistan created favourable environment for Islamic folk culture. The situation of that time was also characterised by the low level of religious education.

The perception of "Fundamentalism" has come to imply a dogmatic adherence to tradition, orthodoxy, in flexibility and a rejection of modern society, intellectual innovations, and attempts to recreate a golden era. Essentially the term suggests going back to the basic texts and reproducing as closely as possible the laws and institutions found in its domain. Apart from its more ominous aspects, it also suggests bypassing the clergy and going back to the original sources for guidance. In the confusion engendered by modernisation, it means authenticity and rootedness which gives it strength and resilience. That all of this is not enough for it to grapple with contemporary reality, to respond to that challenge or even to release the full potential of its adherents is another matter altogether (*Chandra, 1999*). However, the term 'Fundamentalism' has been used in Western discourse to designate the moribund and hostile 'other'. The assessment is frequently made about Third World Muslim societies which in general lacks appreciation of the dynamic populist movement.

It is in the name of Islam that the country has created an image of being the most potent source of religious terrorism, which poses a threat to peace and stability in large parts of the globe. This conception of a Pakistani ideology and Pakistani identity based on Islam was put forward by the religious circles rather than the founding fathers of the nation. At the time of independence even the secular ideologists were also looking at Islam as the key symbol which consolidates the newly born and somewhat anomalous nation (*Nehru, 1989*). The motive force for Pakistan came largely from the middle-class Muslims of North India, many of whom had been educated at Aligarh. At some level, they identified with the ideas of Syed Ahmad Khan and Mohammad Iqbal along with the leaders of Muslim League including Mohammad Ali Jinnah. They all thought sincerely about the application of Islamic principles, but they certainly did not regard the movement for Pakistan as an effort to re-create some kind of a 'golden age' in Islam or to re-establish Wahabiism. The large number of Muslims who opted for somewhat secular leadership of the Muslim League accepted the Islamic values but denied the belief that the *Ulema* derive their authority from within the Quran and Sunnah. According to them there is in Islam no Church or priestly class, counterposed to the state and enjoying a kind of divine sanction.

This situation of Islam in new-born nation disappointed a large number of people mostly *Ulemas* who had migrated there to establish themselves and as a result from the start they challenged the leadership on the Islamic nature of the Pakistani state. The *Ulema* were in favour of Islam playing a dominant role in Pakistan. However, they were never clear and unanimous about what the role should be. In contrast to this view, the modernist, Western-educated political leaders and intellectuals sought the Pakistani state to be based on the Western parliamentary model with Islam playing a role only in the personal lives of the people.

The new nation, starting with this position allowed the debate on the kind of state but soon Pakistan shifted significantly in favour of the Islamist lobby. The pro-Islam Objective Resolution was introduced in the Constituent Assembly in 1949 which with some modifications became the preamble to the Constitution and eventually was made a substantive part of the Constitution. The Objective Resolution affirmed that 'sovereignty over the entire universe belongs to God Almighty alone' that therefore the people of Pakistan were to exercise power only 'within the limits prescribed by Him' and that Muslims would be enabled to order their lives' in the individual and the collective spheres in accord with the teachings and requirements of Islam as set out in the Holy

Quran and Sunnah (*Akhtar, 2003*). In the circumstances the leadership that had assumed control of the new state, though committed to Islam in broader terms, was largely Westernised and secular in outlook, it however, faced a widespread disturbance in the Punjab in 1953 which showed a remarkable strength of the Islamists on the one hand and weaknesses of the government on the other. From there onwards the Islamist parties of the time became keenly aware of the potential for agitational politics under the cover of sensitive religious issues. As a result, successive civilian governments sought the short-cut of adopting an Islamic formalism to assuage what they saw as potentially disruptive forces in society. At various points of time in Pakistan's history, religion has been exploited by the ruling elite to gain popularity and legitimacy and fight political opponents. Even the modernisaion of Islam by Ayub Khan and later by Z.A. Bhutto failed to outplay the conservative Islamist circles which did not trust them and their policies.

Islam started as a great revolutionary movement based on equality, human dignity and justice. These ideals were partly acceptable to the tribal society of Mecca. Equality and human dignity were acceptable in a limited way within tribal social boundaries. Members of a tribe could be accepted as equals, but not those of other tribes. Members of other tribes could be accepted only as a client, not as an equal. Radical Islam is what Prophet Muhammad is believed to have given to the citizens of Medina after his fight from Mecca. He outlined an ideology, couched in religious terms, from which an escape was next to impossible. The ideology offered no accommodation except on its terms, ruled out all compromises, and demanded an allegiance any violation of which was declared blasphemous, inviting instantaneous annihilation (*Gallagher, 1982*). As radical Islam spread far and wide beyond Mecca and Medina, often in the shadow of the sword, it did encounter powerful ideas which sometimes mellowed it and some times led to the emergence of new sprouts. In the circumstances, the concept of universal brotherhood and inter-tribal equality created social tension throughout the Islamic history. Even within Arab society these became explosive after the death of the prophet. By the time the prophet died, different tribes of Arabia had embraced Islam.

Thus, the ideas of radical Islam are in contrast to the message of Quran that the mystery of divine mercy is also being experienced in other traditions. Prophet Muhammad accorded the world - view and encouraged the Muslims to approach non - Muslims with respect and know how the mystery of God found expression in older traditions. With their internationalist attitude and travelling to foreign countries either in connection with their overseas and overland trade or in search of knowledge, the Muslims became the pioneers in starting inter - religious dialogue. In fact, the desire on their part to understand what other cultures might have to offer enriched their cultural heritage. However, the lofty ideals of Islam received a setback when the tribe of Quraysh claimed the Caliphate quoting a 'hadith and superiority over other tribes.'

Islamic society soon transformed into a feudal society. The reasons for embracing a religion could be quite varied. Some embrace it collectively along with other members of the caste or tribe or nation; some embrace it for political or economic advantages; and some after studying the religion. In its historical march to its present expanse, Islam has destroyed empires, countries, religions, cultures and people. In the process it even opposed the Sufi Islam which toned down the hard features of the original and introduced new concepts. Sufi Islam conditioned the Islamic mindset to acceptance of co-existence with other cultures and religions. Islamic extremism is invariably been politically driven and seldom a purely religious movement. It has no sanction either in Quran or in the practices of the holy Prophet of Islam. Distorted interpretation of various historical events by some Islamic clerics led to violence against non-Muslims in the past. The creed of tolerance compassion, charity and civilised behaviour preached and practised by Prophet Muhammad were forgotten soon after his departure from the scene. The stern commands in the holy Quran pertained to particular situations such as murderous attacks on Muhammad and his followers by the pagan tribesman. These were later misinterpreted or used by vested interests to wage wars against political opponents. The terrible massacre of Karbala, in a battle for political supremacy and power illustrated for ruthlessness of the tribal customs to achieve political ends.

In course of its spread far and wide Islam came to India with Arab invasions, Sultan Mahmud, of Ghazni, in particular. Initially the Islam that settled down in India was not so radical. Its core got impacted by Hindu philosophy, bhakti movements which provided Islam a broad-based co-existence with all religions of India. For over 300 years, Islam remained peacefully as a religion and taken its place among the many religions of India without trouble or conflict. Before Islam, Jainism and Buddhism had been absorbed by Hinduism. Also, there were Christianity and the Hebrew religion which had reached India probably during the first century after Christ, had found a place in the country. Historically, Hindu society had shown a peculiar ability to absorb and culturally assimilate groups which entered its fold from outside, even with military power (*Samad, 1995*). But Islam was the first exception. Islamic groups had much greater cultural self - confidence, and clearer self-recognition in terms of doctrines and observances. This prevented an absorption into Hindu society in the treacherously insidious way that had been the common fate of earlier intruders. The new approach produced powerful psychological reactions among the people and filled them with bitterness. There was no objection to a new religion but there was a strong objection to anything which forcibly interfered with and upset their way of life.

As a result of the industrial revolution more or less

world over, large sections of the population from their original surroundings, resulting in a deep sense of dislocation and alienation. At the same time, it fails to provide an alternative set of values and along with it, a sense of belonging to these people. To offset this deficiency, they try to reclaim and assert their traditional identities more stridently. The alienation generated in the process of modernisation provided the material for the growth of orthodox religious forms. It is said that this modern phenomenon of terrorist movement is born out of frustration and despair. Despair caused by social marginalisation, economic decline and political defeat. Leon Trotsky once described the two emotions central to terrorism as being despair and vengeance. The betrayed hopes, one talks of are, as we are aware, the hopes of diverse communities to obtain their fair share of the cake (*Sen, 1983*). In nutshell, the Islamic fundamentalism or pristine puritan Islam had lost its original dynamism and failed to meet the challenges of the time.

Delayed and Detained Democracy

Strong degradation of the Constituent Assembly, a democratic institution, was itself an indication that its future in Pakistan is bleak. It also proved an inherent contradiction that intelligentsia of the Muslim League and its mass represented. The three layers of society – leadership feudal elements and the common masses had fixed their eyes on power, self interest and welfare of all respectively. Among these, the first two had been in close contact in the national movement and the third was exploited in early and mid-forties in the name of Muslim nationalism and religious ideologies. As a result of this peculiar composition the august body had failed to create a political elite in Pakistan as a mark of modern democratic polity with social justice. It gave birth to a political elite that generally preferred narrow personal gain to national interest and have engaged in internecine quarrels fuelled with greed in situations which required unity and self sacrifice for the nation.

While struggling for the creation of Pakistan, with intervals, the two expressed the vision of the type of society they stood for. As most of the leaders of the Muslim League belonged to a liberal Westernised, they carefully articulated the aspiration of the Muslims in different parts of India for substantially improved material conditions and an absence of Hindu economic and cultural domination. Earlier Sir Syed Ahmad sought a rational exposition of Islam that represented a qualitative change from the past into the modern era. He held the Quran to determine our understanding of Islam and brought out its relevance to the new society of his day, he rejected the canonical traditions and the authority. Mohammad Jqbal as a step further rejected the static traditionalist interpretation of Islam and asserted that the quran provides an essentially dynamic world-view for Muslims. As a proof of this assertion he pointed to Ijtehad and wrote .... eternal principles when they are understood to exclude all possibilities of change which, according to the Quran is one of the greatest signs of God, tend to immobilize what is essentially mobile in its nature .... What then is the principle of movement in the nature of Islam? This is known as Ijtehad*(Iqbal, 1960)*. Though Iqbal conceded the need of some representation at the level of Muslim Legislative Assembly, his emphasis on representative democracy within the framework of Islam was clearly evident.

Further, the leaders of Muslim League including Jinnah, the founding father, may have thought sincerely about the application of Islamic principles, but they certainly did not regard the movement for Pakistan as an effort to recreate some kind of a 'golden age' in Islam. In the minds of most, whatever the other inducements underlying the demand for Pakistan, the project certainly had an idealist element involving the issue of identity and Islam (*Abbas, 1996*). As early in 1913 Jinnah himself articulated an ideal when he said, "When you find that Europe consisting of different nationalities and powers can maintain what was known as 'Concert of Powers' during the recent war, it is too much to ask and appeal to Hindus Mohammedans, the two great communities in India, to combine in one harmonious union for the common good." (*Ganguly, 2000*). But miserably Jinnah failed to keep his own advice, either in undivided India or in 'mouth-eaten' Pakistan. In pre-partition period and particularly from 1937 onwards, the Muslim League under the leadership of Jinnah repeatedly asserted that democracy was not suited to India as it would lead to a permanent Hindu majority. It operated with an extremist communal ideology which increasingly took a fascist form based on hatred and irrationality.

After the formation of Pakistan, it is true that Jinnah tried to make a turnaround and argued in favaour of secularism and democracy. The Constituent Assembly of Pakistan came into existence on August 10, 1947, and a day after, Jinnah in an inaugural speech adopted a more practical approach:

You may belong to any religion or caste or creed that has nothing to do with business of the state .... We are starting in the days when there is discrimination between one community and another, no discrimination between one caste or creed and another. We are starting with this fundamental principle that we are all citizens and equal citizens of one state. You will find that in due course of time Hindus would cease to be Hindus and Muslims cease to be Muslims, not in the religious sense, because that is the personal faith of each individual, but in the political sense as citizens of the state (Constituent Assembly Debates, 1947).

This statement of Quaid-e-Azam Jinnah was treated for a long time as the 'Magna Carta' of minority safeguards in Pakistan. No doubt, it was a very good beginning and an excellent ideal. Thus, the founder of Pakistan had formulated the principle of equality of all citizens irrespective of caste, creed and religion, and the framers of the Constitution followed this principle. Except for the provision that the head of the state must be a Muslim, there is no discrimination in the Constitution on the grounds of race, caste or religion in respect to citizenship or rights in the constitution (*Choudhury, 1971*).

Apart from the religious basis of Pakistan, there was a strong philosophical cause backed by the socio-economic-political backwardness of the Muslim community. In the pre-independence days, the Muslim League was so mush absorbed in the fight for Pakistan that it could never develop any social or economic programme. It was likely that the upper strata of the Muslim League did not want any social change because that would have affected their social position. In Pakistan, the leadership that had assumed control of the new state, though committed in broad terms of Islam, was largely Westernised and secular in outlook. It represented the emerging Muslim bourgeoisie and the feudal elite which had internalised the ideals and the idiom of Western secularism. They held religion to be a largely private matter between man and God. Along with intelligentsia they believed that it was only a matter of time before the forces of modernity and secular liberalism would completely marginalise such elements in society. Leaders of the Muslim League especially Jinnah due to his ultimate commitment to Islam, conceded its central theme while formulating the broad principles, 'Islam is not only a set of rituals, traditions and spiritual doctrines, Islam is a code for every Muslim which regulates his life and his conduct in all aspects, social, political, economic, etc. It is based on the highest principle of honour, integrity, fairplay and justice for all. One God, equality and unity are the fundamental principles of Islam (*Abbot, 1968*). But even Jinnah, the tallest of leaders, could not shift political and ideological gears after having inculcated year after year a certain ideology and practised a particular type of politics.

These were too good to last. The initial efforts of these secular minded leaders did not yield any positive result because it was nipped in the bud by a nexus of feudal forces religious fundamentalism, bureaucracy and the army as well. In undivided India the British had nurtured the tribes, jurgas and the feudal lords just to keep precarious peace and the colonial empire intact. In Pakistan, to make a feudal system viable, it was necessary that all civil liberties be denied to the people. To deny civil liberty we need an undemocratic system. And to justify and legitimise an undemocratic system we need religious fundamentalism and majoritarianism pretending to be nationalism. This use of fundamentalism is also evident in those Muslim countries where a few controls all national wealth. Though the eilte dole out crumbs to the ordinary citizen in these countries, no civil rights exist. At least fundamentalism or theocracy has one thing in common with fascism that both believe in the total disruption of the basic rights and civil liberties of citizens. Especially in post-partition phase the Muslim League leadership found itself with a nation-state on its hand and a people who sought to order their lives according to Islam in a broad sense but with very little agreement on what Islam required of them. Though it was not a pressing issue for the great majority, it was a situation that affected the ulema or religious teacher who had, with very few exceptions, opposed the founding of Pakistan but had migrated in great numbers from India, to establish themselves in the newly formed state.

Partition based on communal line had forced the religious parties to reconsider their old goals and project a new agenda. The religious groups, particularly those who had supported the All India Muslim League, had expected that Pakistan would lead to the establishment of the sharia. The subsidiaries championed the ideal of an Islamic state. In it, all power belongs to Allah and the Quran and the Shariat are the ultimate source of authority. There is an absolute transcendental certainty as far as the Islamist view of the scriptures is concerned. Nothing is left to chance and nothing is attributed to the growing knowledge of the universe, and the changing perception of man, society and the institutions human ingenuity brings into being. In the initial years there was no Political Party in Pakistan except the Muslim League. Since the Muslim League was the architect of Pakistan, any opposition to the Muslim League was tantamount to treason. But unfortunately, from this position in the first heady days of Independence in August 1947, the League leadership allowed the debate on the kind of state Pakistan was going to be to shift significantly. At this juncture the leaders of the Muslim League appeared in a great dilemma to the future course of action based whether on secularism or on religious fundamentalism.

The West-influenced leaders of the Muslim including Liaquat Ali Khan and others were of the view that the two contradictory elements can be one. Soon the ethnic composition of the military-bureaucratic oligarchy faction along with divines led by Maulana Usmani, the most important alim in the ruling hierarchy began to put pressure to adopt an Islamic state as an ideal for Pakistan. Liaquat's first reaction was to try to hoodwink the religious opposition, and concede to their demands in appearance but not in substance. The premier called the Objective Resolution the embodiment of the Islamic principle, as it invested all authority in Allah and it was accepted by Usmani as a statement of good intent. The proposed constitution attracted hostility from the ulama, who objected the secular character of the state, and the regional elements who opposed the unitary features. Liaquat's solution was to use Islam to widen the support base of the ruling group. He tried to do this by propounding that the Pakistan state would be built on Islamic principles(*Pakistan News, 1948*). This was not in contradiction to Jinnah's commitment to secularism and rejection of a state based on confessional faith (*Choudhury, 1967*). Liaquat agreed on the secular approach, but used the term Islam and Islamic socialism rhetorically to describe a society based on social justice and equality. It was largely criticised that its provisions particularly those relating to fundamental rights as it was directly opposed to the principles of an Islamic state. The premier had misjudged the mood and depth of the opposition, and the publication of the Interim Report provoked a furious response from the religious teachers and other religious factions whose view on Islamic state tallied with the former.

Death of Jinnah in September 1948 and assassination of Liaquat Ali Khan in October 1951 were a major blow to the establishment of democracy, though worth in name, and affected adversely the future course of action. Jinnah was the person who could have guided the Muslim League through the political mine-field and consolidated the leadership's position was gone. Liaquat's death marked a distinct change in the government's attitude to the religious opposition. The greater the expansion of democracy world-wide, the better would be our chance of ensuring security and peace. The downfall of democracy in Pakistan started with the assassination of Liaquat in 1951. Thereafter, Pakistan was governed without any reference to the popular will. Democracies are less likely to fight one another, less likely to encourage terrorism and more likely to cooperate on issues of common concern (*Swami, 2001*). In 1941, there were only about a dozen democracies in the world. The last quarter of a century has been democracies quadrupling worldwide. But dictatorship have thwarted democracy's effectiveness and expansion in many Islamic nations where they managed to create military influenced regimes. The 'will of the people' is the basis of authority of a democratic government.

The anti-democratic elements of Pakistan now began to challenge the leadership on the issue of the Islamic nature of the state. In less than six years after Pakistan's inception, the Islamists were able to put up a remarkable show of strength and exposed the weakness of the government and the modernist liberals. In post Liaquat period the more conservative Bengali group who had sympathy for the ulama was inducted in the cabinet and resulted in some gains for the divines. These concessions included the provisions that only Muslims were qualified to be the Head of the State, and that an advisory body of the ulema would be established to consider whether the laws already approved were compatible with the Quran and Suuna. The divines, however, were not interested in cosmetic changes and wanted a specific five-man bench of clerics attached to the Supreme Court to vet laws (*Weekly Pakistan, 1949*). They aspired to become the sole arbitrator of Islamic matters, but such a position was not acceptable to the government who saw its implications very clearly. The Muslim League leadership knew that if they gave a Constitution to the country at this stage it would mean their own elimination. It was one of the reasons, that they lengthened the life of the Constituent Assembly in one pretext or another.

Constitutionally making Pakistan an Islamic state had presented before the country a complex and difficult problem. What would be the rights and status of non-Muslim citizens in an Islamic structure? The supporters of the Islamic state pointed out the broad principles of Islam towards the minorities. It is in favour of democratic principles in politics and confers on the state a flexible constitution based on human rights and human duties. It makes every one equal in the eyes of the law and establishes a control over the sovereign power by rendering the executive authority subordinate to the law. Thus, Islam was involved from the beginning with political power. The Prophet himself established the state at Medina, and administered it in a manner which became a model (*Sheik, 1981*). While, on the other, critics of the Islamic state maintained that whatever may be the theory of tolerance in Islam, history belies it. They argued that in an Islamic state the best status that the non-Muslim can have is that of the Dhimmi, whose have their lives, laws and property assured to them, but they have a definitely inferior status;

they are not full citizens, but enjoyed the status of protected wards. According to some Ulama, the Non-Muslims in Pakistan cannot be full-fledged citizens (*Choudhury, 1971*).

The Western liberal idea in Pakistan was constantly undermined by the fact that those who professed to support it were content to leave unchanged a system that incorporated the worst excess of feudalism and an unjust social order. The reference made to the Islamic Constitution in Pakistan was not to claim that it had conferred all the protections and privileges to the non-Muslim citizens, but to affirm that there is nothing basically wrong in having an Islamic Constitution in state like Pakistan where there is non-Muslim minority. Whether they are treated well or whether their fate is no better than that of the Muslims in India, depends not so much on having an Islamic or a secular constitution, as on the attitudes and behaviour pattern of the majority community. After the conference on minority problems, held at New Delhi in 1950 between Liaquat Ali and Nehru, the latter told Indian Parliament that Liaquat Ali had declared that Pakistanis looked upon their ideal of an 'Islamic state' in exactly the same sense that Indian referred to 'Ram Rajya' as the goal of their government. Satirically, it may be treated that according to Liaquat Pakistanis did not associate the term 'Islamic state' with the Muslim religion in the narrow sense, any more than Indians associated the slogan 'Ram Rajya' with the Hindu religion in an exclusive sense (*The New York Times, 1950*).Ultimately, as Professor Wilfred Smith has remarked while analysing these complexities in Pakistan, "It is fundamental to remember that the rights accorded to any minority or other non-powerful group in any state depend on the ideal of those in power .... A state may be democratic in form but unless it is democratic also in ideal, unless the majority of its citizens are actively loyal to the transcedent principles of democracy recognizing the ideal validity of every man's status as a man, then the arithmetical minority has, through the democratic form, no rights at all (Smith, 1951).

It rests with the ideal of the centres of power. Thus, democracy in its truest form, became a dream for the people of Pakistan and the world. To quote Gunnar Myrdal that a drama is unfolding in South Asia. The basic theme of this drama is the high-pitched aspirations of the people and their bitter frustrations. The gap between the expectations and reality is leading to a dramatic tension which, Myrdal hopes, would not lead to a tragic end if those who shape the destiny of these countries can adopt a wise course of action. His hope has been belied at least in case of Pakistan (*Sen, 1983*).

The widespread disturbances that erupted in the Punjab in March 1953 continued till May that year made many things clear from the political points of view. First, at the level of civil society there was no response from the powerful section of Westernised liberals, including those many who saw Islam not just a set of rituals but who emphasised its broad principles and spoke for modernity and bourgeoisie. Secondly, the Islamist Parties, including the Jamaat-e-Islami which at the time had a membership of very few persons became keenly aware of the potential for agitational politics under the cover of sensitive religious issues (*Abbas, 1996*). However, the Jamaat-e-Islami remained an important factor in Pakistan's politics, not because of the numbers it commands, but by virtue of its ability to strengthen or undermine governments through its hold among the petit bourgeoisie, its presence in the civil and military bureaucacy and its manipulation of certain trade unions and campuses.

Jamaat-e-Islami was famous, from the beginning, for its religious fanaticism and took credit for steps the Muslim League had adopted or announced for Pakistan being an Islamic state. It claimed its first victory in 1949 when the League introduced in the Constituent Assembly a resolution defining the 'Objectives' of the new state, which, with some modifications became the preamble to the Constitution. Liaquat Ali Khan, the then Prime Minister of Pakistan, while introducing Resolution, said, "The State is not to play the part of a neutral observer wherein the Muslims may be merely free to profess and practise their religion because such an attitude on the part of the state, would be the very negation of the ideals which promoted the demand of Pakistan, and it is these ideals which should be the cornerstone of the state which we want to build. The state will create such conditions as are conducive to the building up of a truly Islamic society, which means that the state will have to play a positive part in this effort." (*Smith, 1957*). Further, the passing of the Resolution was a confirmation of the faith that sovereignty over the entire universe belongs to Almighty God only and therefore the people of Pakistan were to exercise power within the limits prescribed by Him and the Muslims would be free to lead their lives as per requirements of Islam.

When the Resolution was okeyed and became an integral part of the preamble of the Constitution. Maulana Abul Ala Maududi, the leader of Jamaat-e-Islami, claimed that it was a result of their efforts. Now it was a well-placed religious turned political organisation in the Constituent Assembly and started dominating its proceedings. Maududi had been writing copiously on the principles of an Islamic constitution, and his views were accepted by other religious groups. He formulated twenty-two principles for the establishment of an Islamic state. His narrow, but logically coherent interpretation of the Islamic law and his theory of the Islamic state held a certain kind of appeal for a section of middle-class and lower middle-class Muslims. In underlying the broad elaboration of what an Islamic state should be was the assumption that Islam was engaged in a conflict with the West, and that modernisation, as dictated by the West, meant also a surrender of Muslim identity and culture. Hence, genuine improvement of the Muslim lot meant less, rather than more, Westernisation which had become, erroneously, a synonym for modernity.

Maududi's thesis of civilization conflict was

diametrically opposed to the unity concept based on a multicultural polity. The latter had also come under increasing threat because of Pakistan's degeneration into a terrorist state and the appearance of Islamic fundamentalism in the aftermath of the Iranian 'revolution'. The central idea in his formulation is sovereignty, in the sense of absolute power and authority, which belongs to God. In political sphere the concept had clear meaning that the Islam is against the division of power into temporal and secular segments, so conspicuously present in the modern democratic states. The Islamic state is a theocratic state, a religious state where God-ordained laws as codified in the Sharia based on the Quran, hadith and ijma are supreme. Thus, according to the Islamic proposition there is a sharp difference between the democracy in an Islamic state and the democracy as practised in Western and other secular countries. "As the West understands it democracy incompasses the concept of sovereignty. And what we Muslims call democracy refers only to Khilafat (vice-regency).

In their democracy, to run the state, the government is formed and changed by popular vote. So, too, in our democracy. The difference is that in their conception the democratic state enjoys absolute sovereignty, whereas a democratic Khilafat is bound by the Law of God." (*Maududi, 1981*). However, elaborating the idea Maududi proposed that the elected head of the state should be the supreme head of legislative, executive and judiciary alike. In his view, non-Mulsims are not eligible for key posts and should be allowed to exercise franchise only under a system of separate electorate. He was also not opposed to the establishment of such state in India where Hindus are in majority and maintained in his addressed to the founding conference of Jimaat-e-Islam on 26 August 1941 held at pathankot when said, "If a Hindu government based on Hindu law came to India and the law of Manu became the law of land as a result of which Muslims were treated untouchables and were not given any share in the government—not only that, they did not even get the citizenship rights. I would have no objection." (*Yechury, 2003*). The proposition paid much later on.

Both, the threat and misinterpretation of democracy in Pakistan had hampered its due development in the country. Yousuf Mehralli, a socialist leader in his book '*An Imaginary Trip to Pakistan*', remarked very appropriately that Pakistan is a land where impossible always happened and inevitable never. The legal and political institutions left in tact are present today but are totally out of democratic context. To make things really difficult it is tumultuously an Islamic country where Islamic ideology and secular values are fiercely battling each other and bedevilling the democratic process. The majority is openly intolerant of minorities and the minorities have neither love nor understanding amongst themselves nor for the majority. The minorities have been systematically marginalised politically and decimated numerically (*Mathur, 2001*). Especially in case of Pakistan, continuous intervention by the military-bureaucratic oligarchy had serious long-term implications. It retarded the emergence of an alternative leadership, broke up the Muslim League into numerous opposition parties and it all prepared the ground for the Governor-General's assault on Parliamentary democracy itself.

Unfortunately, for a model role Pakistan always looked towards West Asia and the Gulf –countries and not to South Asia that had narrowed down the choice to military dictatorship or some form of authoritarian government. Most Muslim countries are either monarchies, one-party governments or military dictatorship, except very few which are precariously democratic such as Malaysia. There is also an inherent fact that what happens in the Muslim world is usually blamed on Islam. But it is not so and all Muslim do not behave what the theologians or even the teachings of Islam say. Second, social customs, traditions and social milieu exert their own pressures. Third, there are multiple interpretation of Quran. Fourth, the modern world view always plays an important role in determining one's point of view and behaviour. For example, the quran makes a clear pronouncement in favour of equal rights for both sexes, this vision of Islam could not find practical implementation for a number of reasons. Those who embraced Islam were the products of a fiercely male-dominated society. On the other hand, quaranic pronouncement was an ideal that required very different cultural milieu. The Arab culture to which Pakistan looked for, was patriarchal and had set its own understanding. What is worse is that Islam spread through deeply feudal societies like those of Iran, parts of Roman Empire and India. The ulema could not transcend the cultural norms of these societies. Thus, Shari'ah formulations came into existence mainly in Iraq, Egypt and Medina. Iraq and Egypt formed the confluence of ancient cultures with age-old traditions of their own. These milieus greatly influenced the Muslim theologians in their understanding of quranic pronouncements (*Engineer, 2003*).

In Pakistan religious parties have always been in cahoots with the armed forces and have helped them to come to the helm of affairs repeatedly. After all religious intolerance and fanaticism do not jell with democratic process and institutions. Between 1947 and 1954, between independence and the assumption of total power by an ex-bureaucrat-dictator, through the three constitutional draft constitutions that were presented and the third had been agreed to. But before its formal passage, the authoritarian head of state pre-empted it by a palace revolution because it threatened his own power and he was in cahoots with the army bureaucracy and West Pakistan's aristocracy. This combination to which captains of business, finance and industry were cooperated, continues to provide the basis of dictatorial regimes (*Bhutto, 1983*). They opted for military dictatorship because while Pakistan was politically always a chaos, armed forces were the only well organised and coherent entity to restore order and keep the state from disintegrating. There have been brief, lucid democratic interludes only to be scuppered by the authoritarian forces waiting to strike at the right moment.

Dominance of Muslim Laws

The foundation of an Islamic state was laid down by a proposal of the first Constituent Assembly in March, 1949, called 'Objectives Resolution'. Among other things it noted, whereas the sovereignty over the entire universe belongs to Allah alone, and the authority to be exercised by the people of Pakistan within the limits prescribed by Him is a sacred trust; whereas the founder of Pakistan, the Quaid-e-Azam Mohammad Ali Jinnah, declared that Pakistan would be a democratic state based on Islamic principles of democracy, freedom, equality, tolerance, and social justice as enunciated by Islam...... wherein adequate provisions should be made for the minorities freely to profess and practise their religions and develop their culture........ so that the People of Pakistan may prosper and attain their rightful and honoured place among the nations of the world and make their full contribution towards international peace and the progress and happiness of humanity'. The dictum of 'Objective Resolution', since then, became a core of Pakistani politics and society as well. The later constitutions of 1962 and 1973 promulgated during the regime of Ayub Khan and Zulfikar Ali Bhutto, respectively were structured on the basis of these parameters.

Detail discussions were held on this Resolution and it met with two kinds of criticism. The Congress members of Eastern Wing held the view that it was a mixture of religion and politics while others criticised it because there was no provision for social change and no guarantee of the fundamental liberties of the people. From the start it was pointed out that protection of non-Muslims' "rights, privileges and statuses was one of the duties enjoined on the Muslim by Islam. Religious freedom is an important component of Islam. An Islamic society worth its name must follow the

Quranic dictates like 'Let there be no compulsion in religion'. This is a message that has been repeated in the Holy Quran in different and from a variety of angles. Then there is an entire Sura (109) devoted to the message of co-existence of all religions. It concludes: Lakum Deenokum Waleya Deen, that means, to you be your faith, and to me mine. This same message is repeated in a different context in the verse of the Holy Quran (3:84) : The Prophet is told that Muslims must believe in the revelations brought by all previous prophets and asked to say : We make no distinction between any of them (*Shahin, 1999*). Thus, suppression of other religions or making any distinction among them is akin to Kufr (disbelief) in Islam. Apart from this, the Hadees and the Sunnah of the Prophet as well as books of Islamic law show clear preference for untrammelled religious freedom. The concept of religious freedom is dear to Islam.

The founders of Pakistan had thought about the application of Islamic principles in the new state, but they were essentially Westernised secularists, who treated the Islamist parties as nuisances, to be placated with occasional concessions. However, in both the constitutions definite provisions were made to give the structure a pro-Islamic theme. Part X of the constitution of 1962 made a mandatory provision for the establishment of an Advisory Council of Islamic Ideology. The Council was to consist the number of members neither less than five nor more than twelve as the President decided. The members to be appointed by the President on such terms and conditions as he may decide. The functions of the Council were to make recommendations to the Central Government and the Provincial Governments as to the means of enabling and encouraging the Muslims of Pakistan to order their lives in all respects in accordance with the principles and concepts of Islam and to advise the National Assembly, the Provincial Assembly and the President, or the Governor on any question referred to it. Further under Article 270 of the Constitution, Islamic Research Institute was provided whose members were to be appointed by the President. Its duty was to undertake Islamic research and instruction in Islam for the purpose of assisting in the reconstruction of Islamic society on a truly Islamic basis.

Except for minorities such as Hindus and Christians, the promulgation of the first constitution of Pakistan was a disappointing one. Ayub received most of the congratulations from his basic democrats who had much vested interest in the new system. Maulana Ghulamullah who later became the Ulema to the President said in Rawalpindi on 8 March that he had not congratulated the President on the Constitution and that the document left much to be desired from the Islamic standpoint. Undoubtedly, thanks should go to the President for an act of courage that he did not seek to appease the religious orthodoxy by providing that all laws should be in conformity with the Quran and Sunnah. Only the more or less universally accepted Islamic principles were made the yardstick for assessing the laws. The non-Muslims were in theory guaranteed the right to profess, practise, and even propagate their religion, though this clause caused some heart-burning among the diehard supporters of Islam. Christians, in particular, heaved a sigh of relief on seeing the constitution as it put an end to the practice in some Karachi schools of compulsory Christian religious instruction to non-Christian pupils. It also made it obligatory for all schools to provide for the teaching of the quran and Islamiat for all Muslim students. The Hindu population of West Pakistan praised the Constitution while the Hindus of Eastern part mostly refused to comment. It seemed that they were either indifferent or were with the mainstream of non-conformist opinion (*Bhargave, 1969*).

As to the position of women in society, Islam presents clearly an inferior view. Believers are advised to be kind to their wives, not to keep or take back the dower at the time of casting them away. But the general position is unambiguous. The women are to obey. The man, if necessary, may admonish her, banish her, beat her. Women are looked upon as things to be enjoyed. 'The whole world is to be enjoyed, 'the prophet says, 'but the best thing in the world is a good woman' (*Shourie, 1987*). In other words, the Quranic concept of women being a man's tilth, his field that he may go into when or how he will. It is also no wonder therefore that women are to count for half of men in inheritance, that the evidence of two women is equal to the evidence of one man – 'This, 'says the prophet in relation to the latter, 'is because of the deficiency of a woman's mind.' The notion also affirms further,' Never shall succeed such a nation as makes a woman their ruler. The manifest inequity of these laws and their obsolescence have led one Muslim country after another to reform them wholesale. The countries have decided that even after choosing one school of a particular point, they are not bound by the settled or dominant view of that school on that point, but will choose from among all of the views that have been expressed on that point by any of the adherents of that school.

Explaining further woman's status, as put in the Sharia'h by Prophet Muhammad in relation to women, it rested on a view of women as dependent on men, not their equals, but entitled to considerations, economic as well as social, both within and outside marriage. Within marriage, a wife should be paid mehr. If Muslim marriage was a simple civil contract between two equal partners, there would have been no rationale for the provision of mehr, which would then appear to be an unreasonable condition in terms of contract law. It was provided because women were not seen as equal to men. Based on the same principle, the Sharia's enunciation by Prophet, ordained that when divorce took place the wife should be shown consideration by way of a fair and reasonable economic settlement in her favour (*Ahmad, 2001*). The Islamic conception of the woman is not founded on the principle of gender equality. For this reason, the original message directed the husband to take care of her material needs and to make a fair and reasonable settlement with pro-woman attitude in the event of divorce. What is important here is to visualise the tendency inherent in the Quran and the Prophet's injunctions. They did not abolish slavery, true; but, it can be argued that they tried to humanise it. They did not abolish polygamy, true; but they prescribed a maximum where there had been none. Their view of women bears the stamp of the time, true; but they took a step forward by enjoining that the women should be treated well. They did not place women on a par with regard to property, true; but they incorporated in their institutes the right of a woman to have property of her own (*Shourie, 1987*).

In the light of the inherent tendency, several countries have pressed forward with reforms. It is in two directions. First, they have laid down conditions that must be fulfilled before the husband can take on another wife, and, second, they have decreed that institutions or persons other than the husband – the courts, the Qazis, etc- must satisfy themselves that the conditions laid down are indeed met in the particular case. Different laws and codes were enacted, though mostly in Muslim countries, with a view to provide considerable concessions to women in society. For instance, in Morocco (1958), Iraq (1959), Singapore (1968), Iran (1975) and in South Yemen (1974). In country after country the law now provides that no divorce is to be effective or to be recognised until the courts have passed a decree to that effect.

In Pakistan the women were conscious enough from the start. They agitated in the early fifties against the Prime Minister when he married his secretary and took her as his second wife. The agitation continued until Ayub Khan, who had captured power in 1958, enforced the Muslim Family Ordinance in 1961 which put certain restrictions on polygamy and oral divorce. The said Ordinance provides that no husband, during the subsistence of an existing marriage, can contract another one without the previous permission in writing of a government-appointed 'Arbitration Council'. Under it, the husband is obliged to state in writing his reasons for wanting to marry again, and also to specify whether the permission of the existing wife has been obtained. The Council then asks him and his existing wife to nominate representatives. Next, it ascertains whether another marriage is necessary and just'. Even if the council sanctions another marriage, the wife can apply to the Collector for a revision and says the law, 'His decision shall be final and shall not be called in question in any court. It also provided that a wife can sue for divorce where her husband has taken another wife in contravention of the provisions of the Ordinance. If the court finds that the temperaments of the two are irreconcilable or that the marriage has broken down it can decide on a divorce. This Ordinance could not be undone even during Zia-ul-Haq's regime when the orthodox Ulema was closest to state power in Pakistan. Muslim women are undergoing change the world over. The orthodox Ulema can hardly restrain this forward marching. More and more Muslim women are challenging medieval theological formulations or simply ignoring them (*Engineer, 2003*).

The 1973 Constitutions of Pakistan was prepared in the background of the debacle of its Eastern Wing, resulting in the handing over of rule to Zulfikar Ali Bhutto. His was the first elected government in the history of Pakistan since its inception in 1947. Under this constitution vast fundamental rights were given to citizens without making any distinction on the basis of sex, caste, religion etc. In sphere of religion, as mentioned in part II of the constitution every citizen was free to profess, practise and propagate his religion. Even religious denomination and every sect thereof shall have the right to establish, maintain and manage its religious institutions. But like the Constitution of 1962 sufficient Islamic provisions were inserted in Part IX of the constitution. It is provided that all existing laws shall be brought in conformity with the injunctions of Islam as laid down in the Holy Quran and Sunnah and referred to as the injunctions of Islam. No law shall be enacted in Pakistan which is repugnant to such injunctions. Establishment of a Council of Islamic Ideology was retained and its number was fixed 8 as minimum but not more than 15, remaining its functions, more or less, same as was in the Ayub constitution. In the constitution of 1973 Bhutto specifically provided that Islam would be the state religion, and the head of state a Muslim.

Despite the fact that Bhutto and his government represented the people of Pakistan in a democratic way within months of the assumption of the new dispensation, orthodox fundamentalists began to overpower the government. Months after coming to power Bhutto allowed a record number of persons to go for 'Haj' – the annual pilgrimage to Mecca. He made Friday into a national holiday, founded various government organisations for propagating Islamic teaching, encouraged the Arabic language and introduced the Quran into school curricula. On 22nd February 1974 Bhutto organised the historic Islamic Summit Conference at Lahore. He fulfilled the religious demands before they could force his hand, as one of his opponents remarked,' Mr. Bhutto is the biggest maulana of them all. In fact, he should be called "Maulana Larkanvi" (*Tasser, 1980*).

In the latter part of his rule Bhutto began to work under pressure of the conservative forces to stay in power. It was clearly due to their influence that Ahmadiya Community of Pakistan was declared in 1974 a non-Muslim minority. Though Ahmadiya settled all over the world, live mostly in Pakistan's Punjab province. They also live in India somewhere peacefully with Hindus but the Gurdaspur district of Punjab (India) is known as their headquarters since 1891. Ahmadiyas also called Qadians, as most of them were once living in Qadian near Gurdaspur. In fact, Ahmadiya was a movement in Islam founded by Hazrat Niza Ghulam Ahmed of Qadian in "obedience to the divine command". He claimed to be the promised reformer not only for Muslims but 'as the embodiment of prophecies about a grand reformer foretold in the religious books of the world". He exhorted mankind to hold in equal reverence and esteem of all spiritual reformers irrespective of religions and the place of birth (*Ghosh, 1987*). Bhutto was not a bigot and the incident left an unpleasant taste in his mouth. After much heart-searching, the question was thrown to the National Assembly which overwhelmingly declare them a non-Muslim minority. That was a decision that far more conservative political regimes had resisted in the face of much greater pressure. As regard to fundamentalists, Bhutto adopted a policy of appeasement and in 1977, banned serving of alcohol, closed casinoes and nightclubs, prohibited gambling and all social activities as prescribed in Islam. Just to stay in power he tried 'Islamist tactics in a crude, mechanical fashion, giving clear preference to conservative forces over democratic and secular principles. However, these steps failed to keep control over post-election unrest in Pakistan and ultimately a military take-over under Zia-ul-Haq, the Chief of Army Staff, assumed power on July 5, 1977.

Proliferation of Terrorism in Pakistan

Terrorism is defined as violence against innocent citizens to secure political ends. It is the tool used by groups seeking to force a government to yield on political issues. Attacking the citizens is the means by which the population is terrorised. This makes the government look helpless and incompetent. The citizens' pressure builds up and in due course the government capitulates and seeks to come to terms with the terrorists. The legitimacy of the government is then questioned by the citizens. The political cost of not being able to protect the citizens on the one hand, and the failure to tackle the terrorist threat on the other, is quite heavy. In response to the terrorists use of violence the state uses its military apparatus. In the process it alienates the population. The increasing reliance on the military can not and does not stop terrorist activity. It, in fact, increases the vulnerability of the citizens (*Raghvan, 1999*). The present-day Pakistan is a land where the problem rests on the belief of those that sustain terror through the employment of State institutions. The problem resides in the precincts of power in Islamabad-Rawalpindi that justify the covert and overt employment of violence and terror as a tool of diplomacy.The problem, ultimately, lies in the environment created by these institutions of the Pakistani state in which the various nihilistic terror groups can raise funds, set up camps, arm, train and launch their drugged cadres onto their deaths. It is this all-pervasive environment that spawn's terror with global reach, not an Al-Queda cave or Taliban camp. Ultimately it is this environment that supports terrorism psychologically, while it also provides the physical space for it to operate from.

In general, the intellectual contact of Islam with Europe was renewed many times throughout the history but none was more significant than that which occurred in the nineteenth century. The Islamic political thinkers and their successors had put Islam in contact with the main currents of modern European political philosophies: population sovereignty, nationalism, liberation, socialism, technology, individual rights, secularism, in short, European modernity. Despite this intellectual background the society of Pakistan has adopted a different path and the kind of terrorism that proliferated in its social segments, has appeared to owe its allegiance to a form of religious fundamentalism that aims at subjugating members of their religious communities to conservative norms and practices, selectively excerpted from their traditional religious scriptures and systems on the plea of restoring the fundamental purity of their respective religions. It often enjoys various degree of popular support – prompted at times by admiration, at times by fear – ranging from those who see terrorism as mere retaliation against the states' oppression, to those who support it as a means of achieving independence.

In this connection the Soviet intervention in Afghanistan at the close of 1979 was a significant event that we can hardly ignore. The year between 1977 and 1987 saw a steady inflow of Afghan refugees into Pakistan and the use of Pakistan as a conduit for arms for the Afghan war. As a result of these two trends emerged to fuel the crisis of civil society a large proportion of weapons meant for the Afghan guerillas filtered into the illegal arms market and, a rapid growth of the heroin trade. Powerful Mafia-type syndicates emerged to operate the production, domestic transportation and export of heroin. Many Afghan refugees, who had taken over a significant share of inter-city overland Cargo services, also became integrated into the drug syndicates. In 1980s the states' authority weakened over the basic functions of the state. Cultivation of opium in Afghanistan provided a fertile land there to flourish drug trafficking in the region. The Government of Pakistan and its army had been encouraging this business with a view to take maximum advantage (*Singh, 2001*). Afghan Mujahideen with the active support of drug smugglers of Islamabad, Pakistani government and its army began to spread the drug-trafficking in the region.

The Islamic Jehad, like any other multinational, is now truly a globalised entity, and it has no love for soft Islamic parties that rule elsewhere. Even the origins of al-Queda and other terror groups during the Afghan war of 1979-92, their fight against the Soviet army and the role of the US, Pakistan, Saudi Arabia and others is well known. Its mentor and chief Osama bin Laden started a drive to recruit Muslim volunteers worldwide. US officials estimate that tens of thousands of foreign fighters were trained in bomb-making, sabotage and guerilla warfare tactics in Afghan camps that the CIA helped set up between 1985 and 1992. Taliban and Al-Queda are not merely the names of organisations. They stand for an aberrant mental outlook and a highly regressive socio-political agenda, which rejects the ideals of pluralism, secularism, freedom and democracy and has no respect even for national boundaries. For the pursuit of its goal to establish global hegemony, it considers the use of terrorism domestically as well as its aggressive export to countries near and far entirely legitimate (*Vajpayee, 2002*).

Beginning from 1979 Pakistan became the most important ally of USA in this part of the world and the weapons for Afghan Mujahideen were passed on through Pakistan. It enabled Pakistan to receive substantive military aid as well as quite acceptance of its indulgence in nuclear technology extended by China. Pakistan's involvement with Islamic terrorism has made it a global offender. The Pan-Islamic Wahabite agenda of the Taliban movement which was born and nurtured by the Jamaat-e-Ulema-e-Islami and by Pakistan's Inter-Services Intelligence (ISI) in the madrasas of Pakistan's North-West-Frontier Province and Baluchistan, today threatens all the countries of the region. Neither the West-Asian countries with their incipient transition to somewhat more liberal societies, nor Iran, the Central Asian Republics, India nor even China remains unaffected by this militant agenda.

Thus, terrorism, religious bigotry and drug-trafficking made for a deadly cocktail and Pakistan began to move in the direction, previously unknown to its social and economic system. These evils are like a balloon. We squeeze it at one end and it reappears at the other. The people of Pakistan are caught in the crossfire of a war not of their making, living like feudal serfs under the shadow of the mullahs, gangsters and mercenaries, a force that clearly seems more feared than respected. The land is now increasingly in the grips of a coterie of retired Generals who occupied the top posts in the army during 1980s Afghan operation. They made billions out of the CIA during that period and set up madrasas to create a cadre of Islamic militants. Even though the Generals have retired, still they call the shots. They influence appointments in the army and their protégés run the ISI. Pakistan's meddling in Afghanistan led to Talibanisation of parts of Pakistan itself. It released a miasma of terrorism from which most of the world now suffers. Pakistan is no exception.

Death of General Zia in August 1988 in an air crash was followed by the formal end of the Soviet takeover in Kabul in February 1989. After his death the military establishment quickly found a set of politicians, collected under one banner by ISI, with General Hamid Gul, the then Chief, in the name of Islamic Jamhoori Ittehad (IJI) to disrupt democratic process in the country. The nexus saw Afghanistan as its strategic backyard. At the other end, the Soviet withdrawal marked the end of an era. The supply of US arms which were given to Afghan rebels to fight the Soviet army and Pakistan to protect itself from Soviet influences were suddenly came to a halt. The US was not in favour of establishing the kind of government in Kabul that Afghan rebels wanted. Further the pro-US element in Kabul also suffered a set back on account of Gulf crisis that prevented them to be famous internationally but, more so to Soviet disintegration which marked the end of cold war between the two superpowers and made US least interested in Afghan affair.

In the situation where the Soviets had left and the CIA lost interest, Islamabad took over. Seeking strategic depth, Pakistan turned Afghanistan into a colony. It was a brilliant foreign policy initiative wrecked by inept execution. It brought Pakistan dangerously close to being branded a terrorist state. Soviets' exit was followed by the installation of a communist regime headed by Najibullah. The Generals of Pakistan wanted to send troops to overthrow the Najibullah government. They backed the Taliban and the communist regime collapsed in 1992. In the post-Afghan period, though Pentagon helped during 1992-95, with the movement of thousands of mujahideen and other Islamic elements from Central Asia, even some Turks, into Europe to fight alongside Bosnian

Muslims against the Serbs, a large number of Afghan mujahideen became irrelevant to the US. Once the Afghan jehad was over, the Generals did not know what to do with the fighters being turned out by the madrasas. One option was to turn them into private militias and to use them to terrorise Pakistan's minorities. The other, more attractive alternative, was to export them to Kashmir to try and repeat the so-called Afghan jehad.

However, many perceptive Pakistanis express serious concern over their government's appeasement of terrorism fueled by religious extremism. They have voiced alarm over how Pakistan's social fabric and its institutions have been grievously affected by its government's policy of creating and systematically promoting the Taliban, ostensibly to gain strategic depth in Afghanistan and a force multiplier for its anti-India campaign in Jammu and Kashmir. Benazir Bhutto in her book, *Pakistan the Gathering Storm,* published in 1983, had also criticized the government's role in continuing disturbances. "Pakistan can not sustain its present role in the Afghan insurgency. It is creating unacceptable security risks for the country. The coterie of Generals headed by Zia cannot cope with this situation. At any rate, his role in promoting extreme right-wing religious obscurantism everywhere inside Pakistan, South West Asia and Afghanistan – is sowing the seeds of much evil to come." (*Bhutto, 2003*). She also laid emphasis on total freezing of Pakistan's role in the affair.

In subsequent years, Islamabad extended substantial support to the Taliban Government formed in Kabul. Every Afghan felt over Pakistan's role in propping up the Taliban and holding it up there. For most Afghans, the Taliban were just a bunch of village idiots forced upon their country by Pakistan. And it was actually Pakistan – and not Osama bin Laden or his Al-Queda network that wrecked their country in the name of the Taliban. There is also an evidence that Pakistani nationals had held senior positions, including in the Cabinet, in the Taliban regime. As revealed recently Mullah Razaq, the Taliban interior minister, equivalent to the Minister of Home in India, was actually a Pakistani and so was the governor of a critical province. The Taliban were the creation of Pakistan and it did all it could to keep them going. But what the common man of Afghanistan was thought of the regime, was the worst. In Afghanistan, everything that the rest of the world blamed the Taliban for was attributed to Pakistan. The banning of girls from schools and colleges, for instance, was said to have been Pakistan's intention of keeping Afghanistan illiterate (*Raj, 2002*). In fact, all the retrograde edicts of the Taliban regime were blamed on Pakistan, which it is said, wanted to keep this country backward and dependent as a colony. No wonder, the regime collapsed as soon as Pakistan pulled the plug at the close of the century.

Globalisation and Terrorism

In today's world globalisation, liberalisation and privatisation is gaining growing attention as a strategy for survival, competition and growth. True economic globalisation involves a qualitative shift towards a system based on a consolidated global market place for production, distribution and consumption rather than on autonomous national economies (*Mohanty, 2002*). It is an inexorable technology-driven process, which is bringing about an economic impact. The ship, the steam engine, the railroad, civil aviation and the Internet have reduced geographical distances and inspired global economic integration as never before (*Mukherji, 2003*). The compression of time and space triggered by the Third Industrial Revolution–roughly, since 1980–has changed our interactions with the international environment. For many, globalisation–the intensified cross border exchange of goods, services, capital, technology, ideas, information, legal systems, and people is both desirable and irreversible. In this age of increasing globalisation and interdependence, the national and international dimension of terrorism in fact, constitutes two facets of the same social phenomenon which infringes upon the interest of all states, not only as an assault against their public order and institutions that protect the liberty and security of their citizens but, also at the same time as a serious danger to peaceful international relations and cooperation, which is clearly understood as encompassing human rights and values as well as the principles of equal rights and self–determination of people. It is, therefore, that the transnational character of contemporary terrorist events has prompted international efforts to suppress them at the global regional and bilateral levels.

However, the concept and phenomenon of globalisation, in its first phase, dated back between 1840 and 1914 when it reached its height and ended shortly before the World War I. During the height of globalisation, tariff barriers were reduced and prices of goods travelling between continents came down because with bigger ships being used to carry good, transportation costs were lowered. There was also the huge migration of Europeans, about 60 million, for various destinations across the Atlantic. It swelled America's labour force and reduced Ireland's working population leading to a convergence of wage levels across the Atlantic. There was a greater volatility of funds travelling across the continents and those losing out from globalisation triggered a political backlash against it*(Babu, 2006)*. American wheat imports for instance hurt the interests of European farmers who protested and continental Europe closed its agricultural markets and imposed high import tariffs. The United States too raised tariffs to protect its infant manufacturing industry and migration was clamped because it threatened American workers, living standards. Other rich countries followed in becoming protectionist and the stage of globalisation came to an end.

In between the years the world in general made

achievements in all the spheres of human life and in the sixties the concept of global village was given by Marshall Mcluhan which is realising in the current phase of globalisation. There are several things in the concept of global village–an ideal, a destination to be reached and a conceptualisation of the ongoing transformation in the community. The earth in which we live is an integrated, interpenetrated and interconnected unit. The advances of communications and information technology have made the global village a virtual reality and this has paved the way for evolving frameworks of global governance. A major impact of the globalising world is that security can no longer be compartmentalised regionally or nationally and any analysis of the security environment of a region or area has to take into consideration global issues that have a direct or indirect impact on the region (*Kalkat, 2006*). In broader context the genesis of terrorism can be attributed to the development of exclusive instead of inclusive societies. Terrorism draws its strength from one of three sources: militant religious fundamentalism, ethnic intolerance or deprivation. Religion sans frontiers, therefore religious militancy, has to be addressed globally. Ethnic intolerance and deprivation are region specific, with the common thread of economies running through them, and are best dealt with regionally or nationally.

The current position and dark side of globalisation has reminded us the capitalist mode of production which always maintained a global reach whether in the form of colonies or as trading partners across the continents. The inherent logic of capitalist economic system pushes it towards borderless economic transactions and is characterised as 'centralisation–cum–globalisation of finance capital'. This is the epoch of finance capital and of monopolies and we are in a phase of imperialism-led-globalisation. The finance capital operates in the context of unity among the finance exporting leading capitalist countries in which every recipient country of this finance capital operates under a common sword of democles wherein foreign investments can be withdrawn without a moment notice to the recipient of such a finance (Patnaik, 2000). It proves the volatility of movement of finance capital and its most disastrous implication is that capital market of any country of the South can be destabilised by the investors who want quick and immediate profits and returns on investments. Joseph Stiglitz, an insider of the World Bank, published a seminal work on *Globalisation and its Discontents* (2002) in which he warned about the disastrous consequences of the present stage of capitalist globalisation. His brief description clearly indicated that national economy which is controlled and guided by a national state has been replaced and displaced by united globalisation capitalism (*Bhambhri, 2004*). Even in normal circumstances state systems of the peripheral developing countries are weak while dealing with the centre of capitalism, in the new context of highly mobile and volatile operations of finance capital the nation states have been completely marginalised under the impact of these new trends in global capitalist system. Marginalisation of the state and unity of the capitalist bloc is the reality of present phase of global capitalism.

Under globalisation the movement of people remains tightly restricted. The flow of capital is highly asymmetrical. Over the last two decades, overseas development assistance from the rich to poor countries has totalled $ 50-80 billion per year. In the same period, every year, $ 500-800 billion of illegal funds have been sent from the poor to rich countries. That is, for every one dollar of aid money over the table the West gets back $ 10 under the table (*Heine and Thakur, 2011*). The benefits and costs of linking and delinking are unequally distributed. Industrialised countries are mutually interdependent; developing countries are largely independent in economic relations with one another; and developing countries are highly dependent on industrialised countries. In addition, there is also a growing divergence in income levels between countries and peoples, with widening inequality among and within nations. Assets and incomes are more concentrated. Wage shares have fallen. Profit shares have risen. Capital mobility alongside labour immobility has reduced the bargaining power of organised labour. Professor Paul Krugman has admitted in his book The Return of Depression Economics that technical change and globalisation have increased the demand for highly skilled workers in the US while reducing the demand for the less skilled (Sengupta, 2000). He said that inequality of both wealth and income has increased to levels not seen before since real wages actually declined for many workers.

The emerging implications of the liberalisation process which had begun in the early 1990s, are far more evident in terms of the resultant of new economic policy and change in the historical–ideological orientation of our political economy. Though considerable progress has been achieved in terms of higher growth rate and GDP, the basic needs and the crucial concerns of the core sectors of Indian economy such as agriculture and textiles affected millions of people pose a challenge to the successive governments (*Singh, 2011*). Developed countries erect obstacles to trade in particular, barriers to trade in agricultural products and textiles. The West, under the guise of globalisation, pushes the developing countries to open their markets. But they raise barriers of entry into their markets. Globalisation, the way it is practised, encourages an unequal distribution of power and wealth among the countries of the world (*Reddy, 2007*). The rich agricultural countries fear that agricultural trade liberalisation will be harmful to their highly protected agriculture and the European Union and Japan are reluctant to open up their markets for agricultural products. The US has also retained a protectionist stance regarding its textile industry and has readily used anti–dumping laws. Even the South East Asian countries which became prosperous through globalisation have also witnessed a strong backlash against the trans–nationalisation and internationalisation of capital because trillions of dollars travel across the globe in seconds.

Like India in many traditional society's agriculture is not considered merely as an occupation but a major source of livelihood and for the vast majority a way of life. The traditional relationship between the people, land and agriculture has emotive overtones and any careless tampering with this delicate subject could unleash waves of violence and social disruption. Its direct result is the increase of insecurity of individuals, groups and nations in various domains–economic, financial, culture, employment, legal, social, health care, ecological, political and personal. And this is why the concept of globalisation is encountering resistance from various interest groups–environmentalists, labour leaders, cultural traditionalists, religious leaders of different persuasions and non–government officers (*Galbraith, 2002*). This apart, the influential international NGOs have been against multinationals and the fast pace of globalisation that they have triggered. They have also come to form an international civil society because national governments no longer have a monopoly on information and because civil society now has access to data on the workings of multinationals and governments around the world.

The new system of capital finance and the ideology of 'roll-back the state' which allows market forces and private domestic and global operators to manage the economy in society has a definite impact on social life of the country. Since, every capitalist society is class–divided, a socially disastrous impact of such social divisions is felt very acutely on the majority of peasant and working classes in poor developing countries especially if economy in such societies is handed over to domestic and external private capitalists. The scholars–James K. Galbraith and John Williamson have also criticised the new global economic policy. Galbraith observed that 'rising inequality after 1980 is the rule' and stated, 'The patterns strongly suggest that forces of globalisation, including high global interest rates, debt crisis, and shock liberalisation are associated with rising inequality in pay structures. John Williamson has also lamented that the 'Washington Consensus' as a policy manifesto of the New Age 'omitted a concern for income distribution' (*Williamson, 2003*). In the circumstances so long as there exists in the world poverty, strife, injustice and oppression, conditions will exist which terrorists can turn to their advantage. No doubt that the campaign against terrorism is one that must be mounted at various levels, including political, economic and humanitarian.

Even before the Global Financial Crisis (GFC), many developing countries were worried that globalisation would impinge adversely on economic sovereignty, cultural integrity and social stability. "Interdependence" among unequals translates into the dependence of some on international markets that function under the dominance of others. The deepening of poverty and inequality–prosperity for a few countries and people, marginalisation and exclusion for the many–has implications for social and political stability among and within states. The rapid growth of global markets has not seen the parallel development of social and economic institutions to ensure balanced, inclusive and sustainable growth. Labour rights have been less sedulously protected than capital and property rights, and global rules on trade and finance are inequitable. This has asymmetric effects on rich and poor countries.

Recently, globalisation has also let loose the forces of uncivil society and accelerated the transnational flows of terrorism, human and drug trafficking, organised crime, piracy, and pandemic diseases. Terrorism continues to be to be generated by recurrent social crises, arising from the increasing fear of marginalisation of some sections of society caused by the indiscriminate spread of capitalism and the free economy, through much publicised globalisation which may be perceived another dimension of religious fanaticism. Despair caused by social marginalisation, economic deprivation, and political defeat is another cause of this modern phenomenon (*Ahmed, 2004*). When the situation is thus monopolises by global power, when one deals with this formidable condensation of all functions through technocratic machinery and absolute ideological hegemony, what other way is there than a terrorist reversal of the situation. It is the system itself that has created the objective conditions for this brutal distortion. By taking all the cards to itself it forces the other to change the rules of the game. And the new rules are ferocious, because the stakes are ferocious. The terrorist groups are not ordinary civilians or some misguided youth but the paramilitary organs of militant extremism such as LeT, Naxalites, and the like who believe in the culture of extreme violence and whose objective is destruction of the established social system and structures, that is, the whole way of life of free societies. This virus does not take long to infect homegrown products and soon enough local criminal gangs get drawn into the terrorist's web.

Globalisation also cast a dark shadow on the governing pattern and civil society of the nation state system. The growth in transnational flows has not been matched by an equivalent growth in global governance mechanisms to regulate them. And yet the very nature of the structure of globalised network, which intertwine global actors and interests, ensures that no single power is able to maintain its position within the newly emerging global disorder without making compromises with other global players. The transfer of state functions to supranational forms of regional governance could enhance the capacity of individual states to combat uncivil society. The sharing of expertise, institutions, policy tools, personnel and other resources can go a long way in stemming the tide of unwanted activities. In this context justice is one of the strongest pillars for the Parliamentary democracy. Justice is truth in practice. Rule of law provides citizens a sense of protection and self–confidence. We should not forget that denial of justice breeds terrorism. It is not terrorist or terrorism who divided Ireland nor caused Israel-Palestinian problem. Terrorists did not separate India and Pakistan neither they carved out Bangladesh. As a result of the injustices and inequalities, a different kind of challenge is faced by countries of the world in general especially the developing and underdeveloped.

In the circumstances, the outright rejection of globalisation and a retreat into autarky is neither practical nor desirable. Opposing globalisation is like opposing the sun coming up every morning and about as fruitful. A country cannot ignore an absolute majority of its population which is poor and dissatisfied. A society cannot be peaceful if the majority of its poor population is socially alienated. Even a highly developed modern coercive apparatus of the state will not be able to deal with popular anger and the ruling classes will have to find some answers to meet the challenge of angry and alienated mass of society (*Bhambhri, 2004*). Jurgen Habermas, the German Philosopher, clearly brings out the 'Real Assumptions Underlying Globalisation' by mentioning I. that social inequality is a fate; or II. a necessary market outcome; that III. the state is no more than a corporation providing services; and IV. citizens are primarily entrepreneurs and customers. Thus, the message of globalisation is loud and clear that the poor should not expect anything from their society and state because market would create its own equilibrium. The Indian Prime Minister Atal Bihari Vajpayee also acknowledged that the experiment that began in 1991 has increased inequalities and his government has decided to give a new pro-poor, pro–village, and pro–employment orientation to the Indian economy.

The big gap which appeared due to globalisation and its offshoot social inequality turned the poor masses look toward the pre–capitalist system of the past for some security and succour. Tribal or caste or religious solidarities of the past attract the vulnerable and helpless poor of the present. In other words, the Western capitalist mode of production has not been able to shake the Asiatic social system based on caste or tribe, or religious loyalties and belief system. Religion is a common binding factor for the whole society in Hindu India, or Buddhist East Asia or Islam in the Arab world and other Muslim majority countries. Since religion exercises great influence over the whole societies of Asian countries, it plays significant role in the present crisis–ridden social order of these societies. However, at large, terrorism is motivated by a variety of inner drives ranging from financial gains to revenge, from fundamentalism to deprivation, political frustration, regional disparities, marginalisation of subnational groups, extremism, despair, injustice, discrimination, resentment against the existing regime, feeling of insignificance, intervention into personal freedom, weak government, separatism and oppression, inequality.

References

Abbot, Freeland (1968). *Islam and Pakistan*. New York, p. 188.

Ahmad, Imtiaz (2001). "Beyond the Original Message", *The Hindustan Times*, May 31.

Ahmed, Sheikh Saleem (2004). "Dimensions of Terrorism and Religious Extremism: Two Sides of the Same Coin, "in Mahavir Singh (ed.), *International Terrorism and Religious Extremism – Challenges to Central and South Asia*. New Delhi, Anamica Publications, p. 38.

Ali, Sheik B. (1981). *Islam-A Cultural Orientation*. Delhi, pp. 78-91.

Babu, Ramesh B. (2006). "The Liberal Capitalist West as the New Global State", *International Studies*, Vol. 43, No. 3, July-September, New Delhi, Sage Publications, p. 291.

Bhambhri, C.P. (2004). "Globalisation and Neo-Primordialism", in Mahavir Singh (ed.), *International Terrorism and Religious*

Extremism-Challenges to Central and South Asia. New Delhi, Anamika Publications, pp. 11-14.

Bhargava, G.S. (1969). *Pakistan in Crisis.* New Delhi, pp. 87-88.

Bhutto, Benazir (1983). *Pakistan: The Gathering Storm*, New Delhi, p. 24.

Chandra, Bipin (1999). "Tryst with Tyranny" *The Hindustan Times,* December 22.

Choudhury, G.W. (1971). *Pakistan's Relations with India.* Meerut, pp. 146-47.

Choudhury. G.W. eds. (1966). *Documents and Speeches on the Constituent Assembly*. Dacca, p. 21.

Constituent Assembly of Pakistan (1947). *Official Report*. Vol. 1, Karachi, pp. 3-6.

Engineer, Asghar Ali (2003). "Look Ma, no Purdah", *The Hindustan Times*, July 24.

Galbraith, James K. (2002). "Rising Inequality After 1980 is the Rule", *Foreign Affairs* July-August (New York), pp. 179.

Ganguli, Amulya (2000). "Politics of Conflict", *The Hindustan Times*, July 25.

Ghosh, S.K. (1987). *Muslim Politics in India.* New Delhi, pp. 138-39.

Heine, Jorge and Thakur Ramesh (2011). "The Dark Side of Globalisation", *The Hindu,* January 10.

Iqbal, Muhammad (1960). *The Reconstruction of Religious Thoughts in Islam*. Lahore, pp. 147-48

Javed, Akhtar (2003). "Beyond Real Estate". *The Hindustan Times,* July 15.

John, Gallagher (1982). *The Decline, Revival and Fall of the British Empire*. Cambridge, p. 155.

Kalkat, A.S. (2006). "Ensuring Security in the Age of Global Terror", *The Hindu,* September 13.

Mathur, A.B. (2001). *Administrative Change*, Vol. XXVIII, No. 2, and Vol XXIX, No. 1, January-December. Jaipur, pp. 103-4.

Maududi, Abdul Ala (1981). *Islamic State*. Lahore, p. 320.

Mohanty, J.C. (2002). "WTO and Implications for Indian Agriculture", in Ramesh K. Arora (ed.), *Administrative Change*, vol XXX, No. 1 and vol. XXXI, No. 2, January-December, Jaipur, p. 67.

Mukherji, Rahul (2003). "Noose Tightens Over Global Order", *The Hindustan Times*, June 30.

Nehru, Jawaharlal (1989). *The Discovery of India*, New Delhi, p. 351.

Pakistan News (1948). No. 30, December 17.

Patnaik, Prabhat (2000). V.I. Lenin, *Imperialism:The Highest Stage of Capitalism*. New Delhi, Left Word, p. 24.

Raghavan, V.R. (1999). "Response to Terror", *The Hindustan Times*, January 6.

Raj, Yashwant (2002). "Old Ghosts, New Hopes", *The Hindustan Times*, January 17.

Rashid, Abbas (1996). "Pakistan: The Politics of Fundamentalism", in Kumar Rupesinghe and Khawar Mumtaz (eds.). *Internal Conflicts in South Asia*. New Delhi, Sage Publications, pp. 58-59.

Reddy, Sheela C. (2007). "Globalisation – A Human Rights Perspective", *South Asia Politics*, Vol. 5, No. 2 (March), New Delhi, pp. 39-40.

Samad, Yunus (1995). *A Nation in Turmoil – Nationalism and Ethnicity in Pakistan, 1937-58*, New Delhi, Sage Publications, p. 15.

Sen, Anupam (1983). "The Political Elites of Pakistan: Their role in Pakistan's disintegration", in *The Political Elites of Pakistan and Other Sociological Essays*. New Delhi, pp. 78-80.

Sengupta, Jayshree (2000). "Threats of Globalisation", *The Hindustan Times*, February 4.

Shahin, Sultan (1999). "Bigotry in Pakistan", *The Hindustan Times*, December 14.

Shourie, Arun (1987). *Religion in Politics*. New Delhi, pp. 78-80.

Singh, Rajkumar (2001). *India's Foreign Policy: The First Study in Continuity and Change*. New Delhi, Samiksha Prakashan, pp. 137-38.

Singh, Rajkumar (2011). *Contemporary India with Controversial Neighbours*. New Delhi, Gyan Publishing House, p. 76.

Smith, Wilfred C. (1951). *Pakistan as an Islamic State*, Lahore.

Smith, Wilfred C. (1957). *Islam in Modern History*, London, p. 215.

Swami, I.D. (2001). "Wanted: Democracy in Pakistan" *The Hindustan Times*, December, 27.

Taseer, Salman (1980). *Bhutto, A Political Biography*. New Delhi, Sage Publications, pp. 152.

The New York Times (1950). April 11.

Vajpayee, Atal Bihari (2002). "We Shall Triumph Against Terrorism.", *The Hindustan Times*, January 1.

Weekly Pakistan News (1949). No. 35, February 19.

Williamson, John (2003). "The Washington Consensus and Beyond, "*Economic and Political Weekly*, Vol. XXXVIII, No. 15, 12-18 April (Mumbai), pp. 1475-1481.

Yechury, Sitaram (2003). "Fundamentally Flawed", *The Hindustan Times*, September 25.

7

Decadence of Democracy in Pakistan in Post-1971

Regime of Zulfikar Ali Bhutto

The emergence of Bangladesh as a sovereign, independent country in the comity of nations was a social, political and economic debacle for Pakistan. Since the birth of Pakistan in 1947 the educated Bengalis were afraid that the Pakistani ruling group wanted to destroy the Bengali language and culture. The West Pakistani leaders and bureaucrats were under the impression that the Bengali language and culture were Hindu in origin and character, and therefore a Bengali; unless he disowned his own language and culture, should be considered a Hindu and not a true Muslim. Several efforts were made by the Pakistan's ruling group to denigrade Rabindranath Tagore and stressed the desire to accept Nazrul Islam as the most important poet of Bengal. Anti-Tagore move of Pakistani ruling clique was vehemently opposed by students, intellectuals and other sections of Bengali society. The more the Pakistani ruling group attacked the Bengali culture, the more conscious the East Bengalis became of the rich heritage of their language and culture (*Hashan*). The first revolt of the East Bengal broke out in 1952 on language issue when its Western Wing tried to impose Urdu as their national language.

Pakistan, its Western Wing in particular, had brought on itself the war of 1971 by its rejection of democracy, an adherence to which would have made Sheikh Mujibur Rahman the country's Prime Minister because of his Party's electoral victory. The election of December 1970 was the first national poll in the history of Pakistan based on universal suffrage. But the creation of Bangladesh falsified not only Jinnah's two-nation theory but the themes of Islam as well. Pakistan seemed to have failed all those who had invested their dreams and aspirations in it. Its founder, Quaid-e-Azam Mohammad Ali Jinnah, had dreamt of a secular Pakistan where 'Muslims will not be Muslims and Hindus will not be Hindus, not in a religious sense, but in a political sense, as citizens of a secular, democratic Pakistan'(*Shahin,1999*). On the basis of the collectivist sentiment of Islam, which believes that the community is bigger than the individual, Jinnah, too, had hoped, as a secular individual, that the country he had helped create would evolve into a nation. With it, some of the fundamental postulates that had justified Pakistan's existence as an independent state were torn to shreds. For instance, it had been held that Islam provided a cementing force for uniting diverse peoples and nationalities transcending the pulls of subnationalism, language, and culture and chauvinism. The separation of Bangladesh after a bloody civil war destroyed the validity of some of the ideological props on which Pakistan had been supported.

When Bhutto took the reigns of administration in Pakistan in December 1971, he was faced with the almost insurmountable problem of resurrecting the country virtually from the ashes, as he himself put it, 'He had to define a new ideological basis for the existence of the "rump" Pakistan. Apart from dealing with certain immediate problems such as securing the release of the prisoners of war, recognising Bangladesh, and, above all, putting the national economy back on the rails, Bhutto had to formulate a new equation with India more in consonance with Pakistan's position on the subcontinent' (*Bahadur,1978*). By 16 December 1971 the Pakistani army of 90,000 in East Pakistan had surrendered to the Indian commander in Dacca. In the West, too, it was India which wrested the initiative and ended the war with 2750 square miles of Pakistan's territory in Indian hands as compared with 50 square miles of Indian territory in Pakistani hands. Severe casualties were inflicted by India on the much smaller Pakistani Navy, which lost its only submarine off Visakhapatnam. Though the war was so brief, its impact on Indo-Pak relations was most momentous. The war left a truncated Pakistan, smarting under a humiliating defeat. It left Pakistan with the military demoralised and its organisation weakened. Bhutto's visit to Simla in 1972 was a step-in right direction.

The end of Bangladesh war was followed by an agreement between the two countries at Simla. The ground for such a summit was prepared for the talks between the special emissaries of the Prime Minister of India, Sri D.P. Dhar and the President of Pakistan, Sri Aziz Ahmed at Murree and Rawalpindi from April 26 to 29, 1972. In the talks, the Prime Minister of India insisted on a simultaneous settlement of all Indo-Pakistan disputes, including Kashmir. Bhutto suggested that Indo-Pakistan disputes should be settled step by step and not in one stroke. He further suggested that the Kashmir dispute should be considered after the other disputes and differences had been resolved(*Bhutto,1978*). After due deliberation between the two parties on the 3rd of July 1972 the historic Simla Agreement was finally signed. The first clause of the Agreement states that "the principles of the Charter of the United Nations shall govern the relationship between the two countries', and then goes on to say in the next clause that both countries will settle their differences by peaceful means through bilateral negotiations. Both sides were calculating their loss and gain from the agreement. But perhaps the most concrete achievement from Pakistan's point of view was India's agreement to withdraw its troops from West Pakistan territory. This was vital as refugees from border areas were posing serious internal problems for Pakistan. By persuading India to accept a step by step settlement, Bhutto gained an important victory, for he needed time to win over the internal opposition in Pakistan, specially on the vexed issue of recognising the independence of Bangladesh. The Indians had all along persisted for 'a package of settlement' or, to use the phrase of D.P. Dhar at the Murree talks in March 1972, 'a bouquet of roses' – to which Bhutto had smartly replied, 'No, no, not a bouquet of roses, one rose at a time (*Taseer,1980*).

In nutshell, the Simla Agreement of 1972 was more in favour of Pakistan than of India. However, following it the Indo-Pak relations became generally less acerbic than before. Once the parameters of the new relationship were staked out, inconspicuous efforts were undertaken to reduce frictions: India reassured Pakistan that it was not encouraging disruptive activities in Baluchistan and the North West Frontier Province; and Pakistan appeared almost ready to abandon its hopes regarding Kashmir (*Ziring,1982*). According to Ayub, a significant and substantive change in the Pakistani attitude was the Bhutto Government's acknowledgement that the Kashmiris' right to self-determination was no longer a 'sacred duty' of Pakistan, but a right to be won by the Kashmiris themselves (*Ayub,1976*).

But, above all, the agreement had enhanced Bhutto's stature as class one tactful politician. He was assigned to work between his own people's exaggerated expectations and the Indian position – a tightrope walks.For the benefit of his countrymen he maintained his militant posture, but on the other he became increasingly conciliatory as the date of the summit approached. He adopted a perfect manner and succeeded in bringing about the Simla Agreement. Cunningly he revealed his hand, carefully playing each card so as to gain the very maximum. He talked sadly of the deterioration in relation between the two countries, regretted the tragedy in human suffering that the war had brought about, and expressed hope of a bright future for both countries if there was a lasting peace in the subcontinent. The very first argument of Bhutto was that it was the first democratically elected government in Pakistan's history, and unlike the dictators of the past, was directly answerable to the people of Pakistan. He made it a point that if an agreement failed to arrive at, or if he was forced to accept a humiliating settlement, he was at risk of being overthrown by the army. The Indian side including Prime Minister, was feared that if we fail to agree, we would have to deal with a military dictator. This struck a chord with Indira Gandhi who, above all, showed herself a political realist. It became clearer when in her speech in the Rajya Sabha after the Simla Agreement she said, 'Whether we like him or not, he has also got elected with a fairly big majority'. The agreement was a achievement not only for Bhutto but also for Pakistan. Pakistan had gone to Simla a defeated country, and yet came away with an agreement that involved no further compromise.

Despite the gains at Simla, Pakistan was a great loser in the subcontinent. The 1971 conflict radically changed the regional structure created in 1947. It cut Pakistan to size and doomed its efforts to claim and attain parity with India forever. Pakistan lost a big part of its territory which it can never hope to regain. There emerged on the scene not two but three independent states on the subcontinent. India not only came out of the conflict a victor but also acquired a position proportionate to its size, population and resources. In post-war phase the changed situation called for a radical rethinking and reformulation of policies by Pakistan.This readjustment was much more painful and difficult for Pakistan's leadership as the change over involved basic patterns of its foreign policy. In the circumstances, its disappointment with the United States alliance, which had become deep-rooted, added fuel to the fire. The American image was tarnished in Pakistan because of the failure of the former to provide any tangible support in her hour of need. Even Pakistan's connection with SEATO, as described by Howard Wriggins, was a joke. The Strategic Survey commented in 1971', the choice is now either resignation to life as a relatively small Muslim State, almost as much Middle Eastern as Asian, or alternatively a forlorn struggle to retrieve the Eastern territories by diplomacy, perhaps with the aid of China. However, the region remained a centre of super power rivalry and it shaped the course of Indo-Pak relation in coming years. From the Bangladesh war of 1971 till the Iranian Revolution of 1979 and the Soviet intervention in Afghanistan either helped or hindered the evolution of a regional détente in South Asia.

Now, under Bhutto, Pakistan turned its face totally to the States of the Gulf and Middle East. He also associated his country with the Non-Aligned nations and the Group of 77 at the UN. The people of Pakistan had a lot of common to their Indian counterpart but under the changed policy they began to search common grounds or culture between them and the oil-rich Arab countries. Though Pakistan had always a pan-Islamic component in its foreign policy, its full realistation under the new leadership had transformed the secondary theme to a principal instrument in the making of country's external relationships.The successful rebellion and secession of Bangladesh from Pakistan in 1971 not only cut off half the country, but shocked many Pakistanis into a greater awareness of those aspects of their culture which they had in common with the Arab states. Norman Palmer noted in 1974, 'Deprived of its eastern wing and more than half of its population .... Pakistan is bound to look more and more to Southwest Asia and the world of Islam. Some Pakistani spokesmen go so far as to assert that Pakistan should consider itself a Southwest

Asian as much as a South Asian state.

In 1972 Pakistan hosted the Islamic Conference in Lahore and provided specialised assistance to various Gulf States, and by adopting pro-Arab positions on Arab-Israeli issues Bhutto utilised the opportunity to demonstrate Pakistan's utility to the Arab states. Apart from maintaining close relations with the Shah of Iran, he obtained from Teheran an explicit commitment of security assistance in case of need, as well as price concessions on Iranian oil(*Khalilzad,1979*). In the early years of Pakistan's inception when Arab nationalism was still in its infancy and oil had not as yet become a factor of power in itself, Pakistan was projected for some sort of leadership role in the Islamic world. But such a role for Pakistan was not possible because of the emergence of Arab nationalism and Pakistan's commitment to the Bagdad Pact (*Bahadur,1978*). Later on, when its zeal for developing nuclear capability alienated Washington, the downgrading of his connections with the US enhanced his status among the Non-aligned.

The period after the war of Bangladesh till the Soviet intervention in Afghanistan, in particular, Pakistan became an important partner of the Arab states. By 1973, Pakistani training missions had become conspicuous in front-line Arab states like Syria, Egypt, Jordon and Saudi Arabia, and Pakistani civilian and military personnel were becoming prominent in military air operations in Libya, Kuwait and in several Persian Gulf Emirates. During the Arab-Israeli war of 1973, Pakistan supported the Arab cause diplomatically as well as materially. As a result of Pakistan's understanding with the Arab states, Islamabad got the venue of Islamic summit conference held in February 1974; this, in turn, had paved the way for increased Arab economic assistance to Pakistan (*Weinbaum and Sen,1978*).

The new horizon of Pakistan's foreign policy provided the country capital for specific industrial projects. Direct financial assistance to Pakistan from Islamic countries before 1973-74 was almost non-existent. But by mid-1976, five Arab countries and Iran had together given Pakistan loans and credits worth $993 million or almost one-third of all foreign financial aid received over the previous three years. In this period loans were funded to Pakistan on easy terms by Abu Dhaby, Iran, Kuwait, Libya, Saudi Arabia and Qatar. In the seventies Arab states and Iran were also absorbing more than one-fourth of Pakistan's agricultural and industrial export, Saudi Arabia being the largest single market. Theodore P. Wright Jr., in a paper for the Asia Society, New york, had reported that 'by 1977, Pakistan had about 600,000 workers in the Middle East remitting to their families some $ 700 million of savings'. He added that Middle Eastern countries like Iran, Libya and Saudi Arabia had been transferring capital to Pakistan for the growth of industries, in general. By 1979, emigrant remittances accounted for almost half of their country's foreign exchange earnings (*Wright,1980*). Bhutto, the man from Larkana changed the course of his country's foreign policy. He changed the destiny of his country's foreign policy from that of a client to that of a champion. He gave Pakistan a place of honour in the chambers of power. Without a doubt he put the stamp of respect and dignity on the face of Pakistan's foreign policy (*Bhutto,1978*).

Bhutto found at hand an army not only badly defeated but to a large extent demoralised. The war of Bangladesh left India with more than 90,000 Pakistani prisoners of war and almost 6,000 square miles of Pakistani territory. Pakistan for its part, had taken only 600 Indian prisoners and a few enclaves of Indian territory. Fighting in Kashmir had also enabled India significantly to redraw the ceasefire line to its advantage. The event had radically changed the balance of power in the subcontinent and also at the level of Indo-Pak relations. The new post-Bangladesh Pakistani leadership, symbolized by Zulfikar Ali Bhutto was pre-occupied with a series of intricate balancing acts in Pakistan, the first being morale of the army and defence establishment. With East Pakistan no longer a security liability, the Pakistani army had a much more compact area to defend, and, what is more, can be counted upon to be a highly motivated force defending its home territory, if it ever undertook a defensive operation against India. In addition to this, the army is not just an instrument of the government of Pakistan to counter internal and external threats to its territorial and internal security. The armed forces have indeed designated themselves as the protectors of the ideology of Pakistan and as the final repository of the responsibility of protecting and consolidating its nationhood. It has claimed for itself a responsibility higher than that of any civilian government regardless of the process by which such governments come to power (*Dixit,1999*). The Pakistani army claims to be the shadow of God responsible for exercising state sovereignty for the welfare of the Pakistani people of which they claim to be the most competent judge (*Dixit,1999*).

The new incumbent took several steps to reorganise the army with a view to seek defence parity in comparison with India. There had been a considerable quantitative increase both in terms of manpower and equipment of the Pakistani armed forces. For example, the army had increased from 278,000 to 420,000 and there had been a corresponding increase in armour and fire power. Air and naval capabilities have also increased and friendly, conservative Arab regimes, particularly Saudi Arabia, had made substantial financial contribution to the expansion of the Pakistani armed forces (*Ayoob,1982*). After 1971, Pakistan also diversified the sources of her arms supplies, China and France still remained important sources of supply but Iran and Sweden, besides Saudi Arabia, Jordon and Libya, figured as important new sources of supply. The Pakistan navy acquired 5 Midget SX-404 submarines, 3 Daphne class submarines from France, all since 1971, and had built up a fleet of 19 Patrol boats, in addition to the light cruiser and 4 destroyers, which had all been operational in 1971. The combat strength of the

Pakistani air force was put at 247 aircraft in 1978, but these included the advanced Mirage V and F 86s from France and the MIG-19 from China in addition to the existing Canberra bombers acquired from the United States (*Kodikara,1983*). Though successful explosion of a nuclear device by India in May 1974, followed by the annexation of Sikkim to the Indian federation in 1975 was also a point.

However, these all failed to ensure Pakistani ruler and the press as well that Islamabad's claim for its parity with New Delhi stood somewhere. India's total victory in 1971 war reflected the Indian army's new image since its reorganisation, begun in 1962, and the effects of the Government's new arms production and procurement policies. In the aftermath of the war statements in Pakistan indicated that the government of Bhutto had come to terms with the reality of Indian power and that the quest for a military balance with India was a thing of the past. The Dawn stated, 'For Pakistan the achievement of parity in military might with India was not a practical proposition even before 1965. It is even less so in today's condition. Therefore, Pakistan cannot enter into an arms race. In the same vein, The Pakistan Times declared that 'we on our part have to rid ourselves of the fiction of equality of status with India' (*Kodikara,1983*). But as the dividends of Pakistan's Arab states' connection began to reach Islamabad, Bhutto seemed to belie this intention.In July 1973, he expressed his intention to seek resumption of US military aid 'to attain military parity with India'. He visualised a qualitative change' in Pakistan's policy from one of confrontation to consultation and negotiations with India. Bhutto also felt the need of Pakistan's nuclear development, of which, he was the real founder. He immediately sought nuclear guarantee failing which it would move to acquire its own nuclear bomb.

Even before his assumption of power, Bhutto was anxious to break the chain between military and the bureaucracy in Pakistan. Thirteen years of military rule left the Pakistan army an unpredictable political force. Senior officers had grown accustomed to participating in and influencing events that had nothing to do with their job. The Yahya Khan Junta, in particular, had exceeded all previous norms by predicting election results; negotiating with political parties; manoeuvring and playing off one political group against the other; and so on. Under the new dispensation, structural changes were organised in the armed forces so that the Chief of Staff's tour of duty would be fixed, with no extensions allowed. Various para-military forces under independent command were set up in order to balance the army's power. It was the defeat of 1971 that led to the restructuring of a whole process within the army. It included several appointments, removals and institution of inquiry. He justified his action to the nation by declaring: The People of Pakistan and the armed forces themselves are equally determined to wipe out Bonapartic influence in the armed forces. Bonapartism is an expression which means professional soldiers turning into professional politicians.Ido not use the word "Bonapartism", I use the word "Bonapartic" .... Bonapartic influences must be rooted out in the interests of the armed forces (*Taseer,1980*). But his attempts were opposed by some senior army officials with an unslaked thirst for power.

However, the other side of the coin was not so pleasant. Bhutto gave Pakistan a new constitution in 1973. It was passed by the National Assembly of Pakistan on 10 April 1973 and was authenticated by the President of the National Assembly on 12 April 1973. The Constitution had a preamble in which emphasis was put on the principles of democracy, freedom, equality, tolerance and social justice as enunciated by Islam. According to it the Muslims of Pakistan were to be enabled to order their lives in the individual and collective spheres as set out in the Holy Quran and Sunnah. Though the new constitution was the result of a consensus among all the political parties, it was for the first time that the functions of the military were defined within the constitution. The notion of High Treason was also defined comprehensively. Under Article 6 of the 1973 Constitution, it was enacted that 'Attempts of conspiracy to abrogate or subvert the Constitution by use of force or by other unconstitutional means, or aiding and abetting for the same shall be an offence constituting high treason. As to the normal functions of the military Article 245 of the Constitution stated that the military, under the direction of the Federal Government, was required to 'defend Pakistan against external aggression or threat of war and, subject to law, act in aid of civil power when called upon to do so.' Apart from constitutional provisions Bhutto warned, while addressing the Pakistan Military Academy passing-out parade at Kakul, that Pakistan would not allow under any circumstances, its soldiers and citizens to become tools for political exploitation by any other power.

But from 'taking lessons' point of view the 1971 war was for Pakistan what the war of 1962 was for India. In pre-war phase though the large part of time was dominated by the martial law, the military as an institution did not get directly involved in the civil administration, but exerted control through a military-bureaucratic alliance. Now, under the new scheme, especial emphasis was given on the education of army officers, including sending them to foreign universities. The war experience also shifted the military's politicisation within a more ideologically motivated framework which extended beyond the military's traditional focus on the national interest and its own corporate identity. The officer corps, after 1971, was indoctrinated by the Jamaat-e-Islami, the party of the religious right on the onehand and by the left wing of the PPP on the other. With the prevalence of politicisation by both, the army had lost its neutrality and thereby its ability to act independently of any particular political group. By the time there was a growing number of officers who were the products of the indigenous educational system and were known to the Jamaat-e-Islami which dominated most of the campuses. The Bhutto government, in course of remodelling the army limited its powers in the Constitution but allocated more resources to the military than any previous government. During the period of 1971-72 and 1975-76 the defence expenditure showed a rise of about 89 per cent. At the sametime there was also an increase of salary and other allowances of the army.

Despite Bhutto's efforts to tame the army, he, in the initial years of his rule, was forced to take help of the army when an ethnic conflict was erupted in Sind and the non-PPP governments of Baluchistan the North-West Frontier Province began to remit troubles for the central government. In both these smaller provinces a National Awami Party and Jamiat-e-Ulema Islam coalition commanded a majority in the legislature as a result of the 1970 General Election. The ethnic tension of Sind was between the Urdu-speaking settlers and indigenous Sindhis on the one hand and the Punjabi settlers and Sindhis on the other. It often took a violent turn and the central government not only felt the need of interference, but stern action with the help of the army was the only solution. Gradually the use of army became a regular feature of the Bhutto government and it was called out to deal with the language riots in Sindh Province in July 1972, anti-Ahmadiya riots in 1974 and the conflict between the civil administration and tribesmen of Dir, in Frontier Province in October 1976.

Since its inception the society of Pakistan had been deprived of democracy and its allied developments. Militarism along with international level, had also expanded in the developing states. In a state like Pakistan where military profession had developed massive defence budgets, it has established greater autonomy and assumed a privileged position in society. In such a situation, the military evolves its own doctrines of state and government which drive it to seek to influence state formation. This sense of purpose, along with the desire to increase its power and privilege within the state, leads the military to abuse its legitimate function and make inroads to the political structure of the state (Mazari,1996). The term 'militarisation' is closely linked to the concept of militarism – reflecting it at the behavioural level of state and civil society.

Lack of democratic infrastructure in Pakistan for such a long time had created a society civil and militarized, with intra-provincial and ethnic conflicts. It was a result of the new thinking that had emerged following the growing discontent with the existing state of affairs. The beginning of the idea of civil society can be traced to this period after World War II when, while the main focus of attention was on the creation of new states and politics, there was also a carryover of the concern with citizen-based, 'constructive work'-oriented activist politics. This aimed at creating another set of institutions and thinking that were self-generating and autonomous of the State-centered framework of the polity (Kothari,2003). In this context, we begin with three points. First, 'civil society' has emerged as a process of moving away from domination by the state and its institutions. Second, civil society is a concept used to highlight the role of associational life which is beyond the full control of the State apparatus. Third, therefore, civil society emphasises 'self-organising' and 'autonomous' quality of life, providing a ground for opposition to the state or operating from sites, other than the institutions of the state, and enhancing a basis for mobilising plural agencies and alternative sites within the framework of the democratic society (*Kothari,2003*). Unfortunately, these qualities are absent in Pakistan's society. Failure of democratic politics paves the way for domination by either the state or some other authoritarian framework. During the six years rule of Bhutto the people had grasped the failure of the regime to build a state structure in which power could actually go to citizens at the grass roots; a political system within which the ruling People's Party could generate new leadership at several levels of society.

Viewing the society of Pakistan as hard pressed, Bhutto, through his constitution of 1973 tried his level best to give it a socialistic look. The state was to eliminate exploitation and enable each individual to fulfil the fundamental principles, from each according to his ability, to each according to his work. Under the socialistic plan in January 1973 he nationalised some basic industries. The objectives of nationalisation were three-fold: to fulfil his manifesto undertakings, to rationalise the country's economic structure and, perhaps for Bhutto the most vital, to destroy the industrialists as an anti-Bhutto power bloc. The Nationalisation Order covered thirty-two companies and ten categories of basic industry, including steel, chemicals, heavy engineering and cement. A series of similar moves followed: banks, insurance companies, shipping, vegetable oils, rice husking, cotton ginning and flour mills, all came under government control. Earlier, Bhutto had taken the taste of socialistic approach during general elections in December 1970, when this powerful slogan of 'bread, clothing and shelter' had pushed aside the Islamist parties.

These proved an easy prey for Bhutto. Disorganised as a group and demoralised by his apparent unassailability, they barely resisted. There were no press campaigns or political protests. Their long history of rapacity and lack of social commitment left them without support at the ground level. But, Bhutto, even if knowing that the balance of power has rested with land-owning families, and the business community, he went on to warn the same, 'I have two CID's. One is the government CID; the other is People's CID. You will not be able to play hide and seek with me'. At another occasion, while addressing a group of industrialists at Karachi airport, he gave them a lecture on how to behave in the new

Pakistan. Regime's hatred for private enterprise certainly succeeded in wrecking the existing framework but it failed to replace it with anything better and it backfired. Despite the tall claims, economic growth during the period had slowed down markedly. Industrial growth fell from an average of 13 per cent in the 1960s the only 3 per cent in 1972-77. Similarly, agricultural growth declined from an average of 6.65 per cent in the 1960s to a mere 0.45 per cent in the period 1970-76 (*Hussain,1996*).

These steps touched the social set up directly but no detailed or staged plans were ever worked out. The nationalisation of banks and credit expansion for financing loans to capitalist farmers and industrialists led to heavy deficit financing and an associated increase in the money supply. Excess of money resulted in a steep rise in the inflation rate, increasing the wholesale price index from 150 in 1971 to 289 by 1975. Though it enabled the ruling PPP to broad its base in urban petit bourgeoisie by providing jobs, licenses and loans, the funds available were not enough to enrich the entire petit bourgeoisie. Consequently, a large section of the lower middle class that did not gain from the PPP, suffered an absolute decline in their real incomes due to the high inflation rate.

It was from here that a solid ground was provided to the Pakistan National Alliance, an electoral alliance of nine opposition parties. Under the new economic system, no drastic measure was taken to alleviate poverty, unemployment, hunger and disease. The disillusionment ofthe people was expressed by their silence when the PNA led an urban revolt to destabilize the regime. Further Bhutto was made responsible for the rigging of the 1977 election in which the PPP had won 154 seats out of 200 seats in the National Assembly. It was the sole public issue on which the Bhutto government was brought to its knees, and thus determined the foundation of future regimes in Pakistan. As the agitation rose in intensity, Bhutto searched various options, but of no avail. In July 1977, in a military coup, Bhutto was overthrown by General Zia-ul-Haq. The change proved extraordinary because it led to the hanging of the first popularly elected Prime Minister of Pakistan. Bhutto became a legend in Pakistan. His enduring contribution in articulating the aspiration of the poor and in giving a new dignity and pride to the wretched of the earth was acknowledged by the people of Pakistan when his daughter Benazir Bhutto took on the mantle of leadership in the struggle against the dictatorship of General Zia-ul-Haq, the people once again responded with both passion and heroism.

Benazir Bhutto

Since the murder of democracy in 1977 with the hanging of Zulfikar Ali Bhutto rose the sun of the system in 1988. Zia's experiments with limited democracy which started in 1985 was, by no means, a democratic one. The regime of General Zia witnessed not only the emergence of an increasing number of politico-religious parties into the mainstream of the polity, but also the growing tendency for these parties to use violence against each other. Months before his death, Zia, in May 1988, dissolved the National and Provincial Assemblies. One underlying reason for this action as was perceived, was a growing independence of the civilian political elite which threatened to betray the military's corporate interest. The ruling military establishment visualised it with more accuracy when following the dissolution General Zia and several of the military elite were killed in an air crash in August 1988. The psychological trauma of this act of sabotage against the ruling elite itself led the military to agree to the holding of General Elections on a Party basis in which the Pakistan People's Party (PPP) emerged as the single largest party. No single party could gain clear majority in the National Legislature.

In the circumstances, as a result of the compromise

Benazir Bhutto became the first woman Prime Minister of Pakistan and hence she was bound to adjust with the existing structures of power, with the division of powers tilted in favour of the President, who was still in a dominating position. During the cold war, the Pakistani establishment had patronised the religious parties. They promoted them in the world community as the anti-Soviet anti-atheistic force to counter communism. The establishment supported the Muslim brotherhood with dictatorship while democrats were marginalised. But the rays of democracy brought forth the rebirth of the plant of freedom and free market. The democratic order born that year demonstrated that democracy and development can go together. The high growths, high revenues, high investments achieved under democracy remained unmatched under controlled democracy as well as outright dictatorship. The remarkable rise of the democratic polity coincided with the rise of women leaders in the Muslim world (*Bhutto,2002*). This rise demonstrated that Muslim masses wanted to join the rest of the world community in overcoming prejudices and building a society where each individual could prosper on the basis of equality.

However, with the restoration of a civilian democratic government, expectations that militarisation and Islamisation would recede from civil society proved futile. After her election a propaganda war started with mullahs openly declaring a woman Prime Minister as un-Islamic. Benazir could do very little to break the ISI-religious parties' nexus. She was unable to fight them and so she had no option but to join them. As a first step, immediately after her election as Prime Minister, she went straight to General Headquarters to take directions from the then Army Chief General Mirza Aslam Beg. Though the PPP did show an inclination to roll back the Ziaist Islamisation but it was not in a position to make much headway. The strength of the Ziaist legacy was best illustrated by the induction into office of President Ghulam Ishaque, an experienced bureaucrat and one of Zia-ul-Haq's key adviser.

He was quick to indicate his own orientation and preferences, including one for the continuation of Ziaist Islamisation. Another telling feature was the continuation in office of Nawaz Sharif – indebted to the Generals for his elevation and in the vanguard of opposition to PPP. It is also to note that the jehad in Kashmir began during her tenure when she was clearly told by the establishment to stay away from foreign policy and defence matters. Though she did try to establish good relations with India, she was told in no uncertain terms to curb her enthusiasms. As the PPP grew restless within the confines of the prevailing structure of power–a ruling troika composed of the Prime Minister, President and Chief of Army Staff came into being. By the time the military has become increasingly sophisticated in terms of the quality of its professional expertise and the structure of decision making, and had achieved greater insulation from interventions by civilian authority.

In short, during her period the military maintained a decisive authority but under overall civilian supremacy. This civilian government failed to check the ethnic and sectarian conflicts. Even in Sindh, where the provincial government was in the hands of the PPP, kidnapping, dacoity and political violence seemed on the increase. Her government became soft to military power to deal with the near anarchic situation in the province. It shows how violence in civil society can compel the state to take recourse to violence. At last, the same establishment-mullah nexus caused her downfall in August 1990 with dissolution of the National Assembly by the pro-military President Ghulam Ishaque. In previous decades, the concept of security itself has changed. The national security in the 1960s was perceived as the ability of a nation to protect its internal values from external threats. In 1990s the notion of national security has been greatly enlarged to mean the capacity to control those domestic and foreign conditions that the public opinion considered necessary for its autonomy, prosperity and well being. It has been interpreted by some to mean any condition which might degrade the quality of life of the inhabitants of a state.

Benazir's second term as the Prime Minister of Pakistan commenced in October 1993 when the PPP led–alliance formed the government. This time she returned with a new strategy and tactical dressing. With a dupatta and tasbih she tried to win over the fundamentalists and followed the establishment in letter and spirit. She allowed the military establishment and her own cabined colleague Nasirullah Babar to create the Taliban, who unleashed upon the world the worst form of religious fundamentalism. She left ISI to cope with the foreign policy and devoted herself to consolidating her rule at home. However, Pakistan is the second largest Muslim country. Its democratisation impacts on the larger Muslim world where questions are being asked about solutions that can breed an environment conducive to a diverse world united by common goals. Given the larger battle in the Muslim world, a military regime with Generals bedecked in brass simply sends the wrong messages.

The PPP under Benazir Bhutto is generally considered to be more enlightened in its outlook on religion. But her ability became limited in the context of changing an environment of religious intolerance and sectarianism which owed a lot to Zia's years. The democrats stoically faced the theocrats in upholding the banner of freedom and human rights during past decades. The politico-religious parties which got a major setback in the recently held election, were still in a position to help tilt the balance between the two major parties on occasion. She was surrounded by a social milieu comprising well-organised, armed and often well-financed politico-religious parties and groups, insistent on carrying forward many of the changes brought about by Zia, essentially for political ends, left no room for manoeuvring (*Rashid,2002*).

Despite the unfavourable conditions declared in May

1994 two amendments were made in Section 295-C which provided punishments for the use of derogatory remarks, etc., in respect of the Holy Prophet. Earlier a Shariat Court ruling under the Nawaz Sharif government did away with the option of life imprisonment and made capital punishment mandatory for anyone convicted under Section 296-C. For the reasons best known the minorities, especially the Christians were fearful of the large-scale misuse of the law. As the existence of such laws tended to create an environment of hysteria, Benazir's cabinet had given its approval to two amendments in blasphemy law. In the first, the police could only register a case under this law after a competent court had ascertained that there was enough substance to warrant such registration. Secondly, any one making false allegations would be liable to the severe punishment of a ten-year prison term. It meant to discourage the casual registration of such cases as a way of settling scores or getting someone out of the way.

On the other hand, her readiness to project herself as a religious person was misplaced. No one was in a position to accept it, though she made several rounds of mazars she got very little in return from the peers. When she tried to curb ethnic violence in urban Sindh, she was confronted. She succeeded partly but MQM, as the establishment's creation, accused Benazir of extra judicial killings. Her government did not find it simple to alter the institutional setting which reflected a narrow-minded religiosity. A further complication was that the Pakistan Muslim League junejo group, the junior partner of the PPP had more in common with their former colleagues regarding such matters. Her efforts to have an eye on ISI and the army bore no fruit resulting in the dismissal of her government in November 1996 by her very trusted President Farooq Leghari. The Presidential Proclamation promised next elections to be held in February 1997, which knocked the country with the return of Nawaz Sharif.

What cost more Benazir in her second inning was the ever-deteriorating economic condition and India-baiting. J.N. Dixit, former Foreign Secretary and High Commissioner to Pakistan had counted the causes of her downfall and added, 'Benazir Bhutto's credibility and capacity to govern Pakistan had reached saturation point. The overriding factor was the deepening economic crisis. Dipping foreign exchange reserves and a stiff prescription from IBRD and IMF, including cuts in defence spending, further upset the Army, already disenchanted with Benazir (*Indian Recorder,1996*). Almost the same view was expressed by S.K. Singh, another High Commissioner to Pakistan, 'she had messed up the law and order, messed up the economy. Her family was divided, her province Sindh was divided, her party was divided and she had not been getting along with the Army Chief and the President. There was more than adequate reason to get rid of her (*Indian Recorder,1996*).

On being influenced from the ruling nexus Benazir adopted an anti-India propaganda that was rejected by the people of Pakistan. Perhaps, with a view to divert the attention of the public from the bad economic condition of the country she raised again and again the issue of Kashmir at several national and international fora. For instance, hardly, a month before her dismissal she called for an international conference on Kashmir to project it as an international issue. The US State Department in a statement on October 4, 1996, rejected the call by the Prime Minister of Pakistan and held the view that it should be resolved through bilateral talks between India and Pakistan. Bhutto's proposal was aimed to a multilateral dialogue for peace and security in South Asia with the participation of India. Pakistan, the five permanent members of the Security Council and other major powers like Japan and Germany (*Indian Recorder,1996*). Just to continue in office as Prime Minister of Pakistan Benazir tried to appease her nexus and the public opinion as well.

After the massive victory of Nawaz Sharif, Benazir was frank enough to admit in course of a television interview on February 15, 1997, that her "hawkish policy on India" has been rejected by the people in the elections. 'We had more hawkish policy on India but he (Nawaz Sharif) is the one who has come with a three-fourth majority. So obviously people have endorsed his stand to open negotiations with India and they have rejected our stand that unless India moves on the Kashmir dispute there should be no talks' (*The Tribune, 1997*). A survey conducted by Herald, a publication from Karachi, in its annual number, revealed that friendlier ties with India have been favoured by most people across the regional divide in the country. It published a city-wise break up of those in favour of good neighbourly relations with India. Karachi (67.8), Lahore (52.2), Islamabad (50.6), Peshawar (52.2), Quetta (80.0), Multan (61.7) and Sukkur (43.9). In fact, a majority of men in the young, high income group were in favour of more interaction. Poor women, on the other hand, took a diametrically opposite and stemer view of the situation. Men it seemed were far more pro-India (67.0) than women (50.0), overall with affluent and middle-class men the most in favour of breaking down the walls (*Indian Recorder,1997*). Thus, because Benazir had worked in anti-podal direction, with surprise to none, she lost the battle despite democratic background of her family and the Pakistan People's Party.

Nawaz Sharif

Within twenty months after the popularly Prime Minister Benazir Bhutto had come to power, the people once again went to the polls and they expressed their dissatisfaction with the performance of her regime by voting in favour of the Islami Jamhoori Ittehad, the multi-party-political alliance formed against Ms. Bhutto during the 1988 general elections. Nawaz Sharif had a strong backing of the prevailing ruling nexus of the country. During her tenure as, Prime Minister

Nawaz Sharif was the Chief Minister of the Punjab province, actually indebted to the generals for his elevation in the opposition to the Pakistan People's Party. Though Sharif made his own power-nexus in afterwards but his first inning as the Prime Minister of Pakistan was known as working on behalf of the old power-cocktail. And so, it was natural for him to extend wholehearted support to Kashmir cause. Soon after becoming Prime Minister for the first time in 1990 he had given a new diplomatic twist to Pakistan's Kashmir policy asserting that Islamabad would extend 'moral political and diplomatic support to the Kashmiri people on the Indian side on the Line of Control (*Indian Recorder,1997*). At one stage when he was the leader of the opposition, he insisted in Parliament that Pakistan should not shy away from extending 'material support to the Kashmiri people under Indian rule.

Another important step, he took at the time, was in the direction of Islamisation of Pak society. Though Islamisation started with the induction of Prime Minister Junejo into the system in 1985, when a Shariah Bill was introduced in Parliament in 1985 by Senator Samiul-Haq, followed by the ninth Constitutional Amendment Bill on the sameline. It failed to be passed at the time because President Zia dissolved the assemblies in May 1988, however, momentum and contents of the Shariah kept alive through the passage of a Shariat Ordinance. It got partial success during the Premiership of Benazir Bhutto when a modified version of the Bill was passed by the Senate. But it lapsed later as the assemblies were once again dissolved by President Ishaque in 1990.

It was during the Premiership of Nawaz Sharif that Shariah Bill could see the light of the day. The issue of this controversial Bill, which had been in the pipeline since 1985 and sought to ensure the supremacy of the Islamic laws in the country, was taken up when Nawaz Sharif became the Prime Minister of Pakistan. Passage of the Bill was largely due to President Ishque's identification with the Bill and the

Islamisation project generally. In this regard Sharif, in particular, became helpless on account of the amendment made by Zia in Article 58 of the 1973 Constitution which read, 'The Pakistan shall dissolve the National Assembly if so advised by the Prime Minister.......'. An amendment was passed in it that made Article 58 (1) and a Clause 2 added by Presidential Order No. 14 of 1985 which read: 'The President may also dissolve the National Assembly at his discretion, where, in his opinion, an appeal to the electorate is necessary' (*Rashid,2002*). The new Prime Minister continued to remain apprehensive of the use of this power by the President as such powers had already been used twice to dismiss elected Assemblies in an arbitrary manner, once by Zia in 1988 followed by Ishaque in 1990.

The Shariah Bill was passed and made an Act in 1991. As the country was now to govern as per the Islamic laws, the women and minorities opposed its enactment on various grounds. Challenged by women who see within it the seeds of gender discrimination, it has been opposed by progressive women's organisations, the PPP and almost all the left parties. But merely making the Shariah an Act was not enough and it can not take effect without an enabling constitutional amendment. The main import of the Act lies in the direction which it makes out for the legislature and the government with regard to Islamisation, bringing to bear greater pressure to this end. For instance, it commits the state to take steps for Islamisation of the economy (clause 8), take effective steps to Islamic education (Clause 7). On the other hand, clauses 18 and 19 of the Act specifically exempt Pakistan's international financial dealings from the constraints of the Shariah until an alternative economic system is evolved. With a view to save the Family Law Ordinance, the Act protected the rights of women as guaranteed by the Constitution (Clause 20). In spite of protests the Act was notified on June 18, 1991. Along with the minorities, including the smaller Muslim groups like the Shias and Ahmediyas which also face persecution, women are the worst victims of the kind of paranoid orthodoxy that is followed in Muslim countries to keep them in subjugation. If the excessive Western emphasis on individual liberty has led to the break up of the family, the Islamic world has erred on the other side by insisting that women should remain confined within the four walls of the family home with the window panes painted black, as in Afghanistan, so that outsiders can not see them (*Ganguli,1998*).

Again, Nawaz Sharif became the Prime Minister of Pakistan in February 1997, having got three-fourth majority. The circumstances in which Benazir's government was dismissed was an indicative that Indian efforts to bring an element of normalisation into Indo-Pak relations, had received a setback (*Sreedhar,1997*). Though Sharif made this historic victory on pro-India plank and he was the first ever Prime ministerial candidate to announce an intention to make peace with India, and so he had a bigger mandate than what the Muslim League received in 1946. He, on the one hand believed that he can take on Islamabad and strike a new relationship with India, but expressed Pakistan's serious concern about India's nuclear and ballistic programme on the other, while addressing a gathering of the senior military officers of the National Defence College in Islamabad, on April 16, 1997 (*Indian Recorder,1997*). He added that Pakistan could not ignore the 'threat' to its security and 'it must have the capability to deter the aggression, he however, stressed that Islamabad would remain committed to nuclear non-proliferation.

Unfortunately, though Nawaz Sharif returned with an unprecedented majority but with the help of his sponsors he was quick and prompt to yield before the establishment completely. His policies were dictated by establishment right from the beginning. He targeted the opposition and used religion for the purpose. Though democrat he was, he never interfered in the ISI's proxy wars in Afghanistan and

Kashmir. He praised and encouraged the military thinkers to think of highly ambitious plans to 'teach the enemy a lesson'. The donation boxes at shops, Lashkar posters and statements on walls and Osama posters all surfaced for the first time during his premiership.

It is more appropriate to say here that after the death of General Zia in 1988, which followed by the Soviet's withdrawal from Afghanistan, the military leadership relinquished power directly in the hope of ruling indirectly, pinning its hopes on two pillars of its policy. The first was to invest the President with the power to dismiss governments. The second was to create a suitable political puppet to give the façade of democracy to its indirect rule. It led to the destabilisation of governments, who were anti-nexus, but the manipulation of the elections to bring to power the civilian face of the establishment led to quandary. In the situation while the government in power enjoyed an overwhelming Parliamentary majority, it lacked popular support. Again, to substitute the lack of popular support, a two-pronged strategy was prepared. First, to exploit the name of religion to give legitimacy to an otherwise illegitimate regime. The second, to eliminate the democratic choice through judicial abuse (*Bhutto,1999*). However, both the cases gave way to the negligence of governance.

Perhaps with a view to gain popular support, Nawaz Sharif had shown his skills at alliance-building by bringing sub-nationalist elements from Sindh, NWFP and Baluchistan provinces when he came to power in February 1997. The perception of Sharif as promoted by "neutral" observers was one of an alliancemakers who mended fences and avoided confrontation, something that a cruelly divided country in the post-Zia era craved. Nawaz Sharif's policy of normalisation with India was welcomed by all realists as a "practical" step. But the common thread running through these alliances with diverse forces was opposition to the ousted ruling party of Benazir Bhutto, the Pakistan Peoples Party. As a result of these alliances Sharif underlined the fact that his real political base remains in Punjab, his home province. In due course the accusation that Nawaz Sharif had concentrated more and more power around his person and his family had helped in the formation of a new political platform, the 'Oppressed Nations Movement' (ONM). The new group consisted of the nationalists from the three provinces other than Punjab. Despite the alliance spirit of Nawaz Sharif, it was difficult to come by a new compact with the widening fissures between the Punjab and the three other provinces.

Till Nawaz Sharif came to power Pakistan was governed by three as: Allah, Army and America. To this the new Prime Minister added two more: Abbajan (father Mian Mohammad Sharif) and Atomi Taqat (nuclear power). On the jehadi front, being a zealot himself and an obedient child of his father he never interfered in the ISI's proxy wars in Afghanistan and Kashmir. In the last week of May 1998 Pakistan not only evened its nuclear explosion account with India but went a step further by exploding six nuclear devices in place of five by New Delhi on May 11 and 13, 1998. Just after the explosions by New Delhi and Islamabad several world powers, the United States, in particular, imposed economic and defence-related sanctions on India and Pakistan. By exploding nuclear devices Nawaz Sharif had propagated the myth that Pakistan had now become "a nuclear power", equal not only to India but to the other nuclear powers seated in the UN Security Council (*The Friday Times,1999*). The expression of Pak potential in nuclear and defence – related fields showed that Nawaz Sharif remained a minor player in security and foreign policy matters over which the Army has tight grip. It also became clear that after the sweeping electoral victory, the Prime Minister's honeymoon is over.

Among the troika that ruled Pakistan – the Army, the President and the Prime Minister, Nawaz Sharif's office was the weakest. Even though he had during the past year established himself in the country's political system and institutions, he was not able to address the fundamental problem that plagued Pakistani society: the need for social engineering. Power was still vested in the landed classes, the economy was sluggish, the industrial base narrow, agriculture was patchy, and the population was rapidly rising. Sectarian strife was not only intense, but also widespread. However, overwhelmed with a heavy mandate in 1997, he successfully took on the Presidency and had curbed the Head of State's powers by amending Article 58 (2b) of the Pakistani Constitution. He sorted out the judiciary and added insult to injury by physically assaulting its apex court. Gradually he became dictator, weakened the Supreme Court, stripped the President of the power to dismiss him and intimidated the opposition and press. While the Army had clearly demarcated the areas of responsibility the new Prime Minister was to fix the economy, foreign policy and security – and arbitration in Constitutional confrontations – were the Army's job, Sharif tried his level best to establish himself as people's representative.

Further he used religion, took controversial Shariat Bill and tried to Islamise Pakistan. This Bill had sought to empower the Federal Government to decide what laws, measures, policies are in accordance with Islam, irrespective of any existing laws, the constitution or judgements of any court. Critics doubted that this would spell the death knell for constitutional and democratic governance. It roused the ire of a wide array of the opposition political parties, NGO's and human and civil rights advocates. This theocratic agenda was aimed to give pride of place to the Shariat over the more secular constitution was obviously a matter of concern because it was bound to encourage the more militant adherents of the faith. For any of the members of the Assembly it was difficult to say openly that he is against the primacy being given to the Shariat. Of course, they put it in a different way when one member said "what we are opposing is the fact that this amendment is being used to stabilise and prolong the day of the government. It was also criticised as it was against the interests of smaller provinces, and even the conservative Jamaat-e-Islami had charged the government that it merely wanted to divert the attention of the masses from actual problems.

In Post-explosion phase compulsions of Nawaz Sharif was probably more economic than anything else. The economic disasters which had befallen Pakistan during his premiership were unprecedented. As a practical approach he changed his focus from Kashmir to investment, trade, business. The World Bank and IMF adamantly gave prescription after prescription for the sick economy and had also pressurised Pakistan to improve relations with India. With a view to boost-up the Pak economy Nawaz Sharif undertook a visit of the US in December 1998 from where he returned almost empty-handed. There, he could not get sanctions on the conventional military assistance lifted, nor did Washington agreed to mediate on the Kashmir issue (*Singh,2000*). Incidentally, the power structure and their respective political compulsions in both the countries demanded an end of confrontation. It resulted in Atal Bihari Vajpayee's visit to Lahore on the inauguration of Delhi-Lahore bus service. For a clever politician it is a favourite trick to use either religion or the bogey of national security to bolster their position. In case of Pakistan resort to the first option is easier in Muslim countries because of the all-pervasive role of religion.

Army with the President continued to be the most powerful and real ruler of the country. Nawaz Sharif's move to curtail the Presidential power was a signal for the army too. In the first place Sharif had conspired with President Ghulam Ishaq Khan to get rid of COAS General Aslam Beg by nominating his successor far in advance, in November 1997. Sharif's actions sent a firm message down to the military,

and to the country that henceforth this Prime Minister intended to exercise state authority by himself, in a style that should be called monolithic. Though the power of dismissing an elected government and dissolving Parliament was taken away from the President, in effect, it was taken away from the army, too, which hitherto was exercising it through the President. Even the explosion of nuclear devices by Pakistan conducted during Sharif's regime was full of message to the army. With the conventional war having been made less likely, it was only a matter of time before the need to keep a large standing army would come under public scrutiny. In the circumstances the army in Pakistan needed to evolve a new doctrine to justify an enhanced role for itself in the country's internal and external security.

Impatient position of the Army along with shaky fate of Nawaz Sharif prepared the ground for the outbreak of a full-fledged war between the two countries in Kargil sector. Indeed, the event was in pursuance of phase II of operation to pace outlined by General Zia in April 1988 at an ISI gathering. The opening sentence of the scheme says, 'Exert maximum pressure on Siachen, Kargil and Rajouri-Pooch sectors to force the Indian army to deploy serve formations outside the Kashmir valley' (*Rajeswar,1999*). Pakistan fully realises that in the event of a full-scale conventional conflict, India's greater military strength and economic-industrial capability would turn the tide against it. Therefore, Islamabad decided to adopt the strategy to keep strategically important areas of Kashmir, Punjab and Assam in continuous turmoil through 'low-medium intensity warfare' and avoided an all-out conflict.

Months after the visit of Atal Bihari Vajpayee to Pakistan, Kargil occurred. Two factors in the internal structure had caused the aggression. First, the desire of the army to acquire renewed importance in the governance of the country. Second, the salience acquired by Islamic militants in the political system of the country through their successes in Afghanistan and their strong nexus with ISI, the army and the political class. Initially Pakistan went along with the mad misadventure painstakingly cobbled together by the ISI and sections of the Pakistani army but soon Sharif realised that he had bitten off far more than he could comfortably chew. At last, he decided to withdraw primarily because of the decisive and determined counter-offensive undertaken by the Indian armed forces. External criticism of Pakistan and American pressure were only a secondary factor. Of all the four military misadventures mounted by Pakistan, none had been so devastating to it than Kargil. Military humiliation was nothing new to Pakistan. But what stunned Nawaz Sharif this time was the confirmation before the world as a terrorist sponsoring state, exposure of its potential for barbaric savagery, the terrible alienation of the mercenaries that it had nursed for years (*The Times of India,1999*). In the war Pakistan had fully expected the big powers to intervene because of the potential nuclear peril thereby effectively internationalising the Kashmir dispute. When nothing of the sort happened, the entire exercise became dangerously counter-productive.

Yousuf Raza Gillani

On 18 February 2008, the general elections in Pakistan were held for the 272 National Assembly seats and four Provincial assemblies. Among apprehensions it was conducted more or less fairly and international monitors gave the election an overall clean chit which paved the way for real empowerment and democratic sovereignty in Pakistan. The restoration of democracy in the country was welcomed by all and the verdict had made it manifestly clear that the people of Pakistan are quite capable of deciding who would run their country and how? The nation-wide election results and the overwhelming Pattern of voter preferences showed a determined endorsementof parties and players identified with the campaign for democracy on the one hand and, on the other, clear disapproval of the supporters of the retired general and president Pervez Musharraf. Significantly it also sidelined the Islamic extremists whose coalition fared badly in the elections. The victory of democratic forces in Pakistan was expected in view of recent anti-democratic developments in the country and American backing of Musharraf's authoritarian rule since 2001. In the year the General had took a strategic decision to align with the United States in its anti-terror campaign against Islamiccountries and put forward the plea that Pakistan, as a moderate Islamic republic, is a target of terrorists. It helped him to have a constructive effect in certain areas such as country's relations with India but at the same time it strengthened Musharraf's position at home to consolidate as an authoritarian at the expense of Pakistani civil society. The continued efforts of the United States to shore up his position in the face of growing political opposition have created a situation in which the restoration of democracy was considered as a vital element of the quest to regain sovereignty in critical matters such as national security strategy and foreign policy. The changed and charged mood of today thinks the way as said by Asma Jahangir, Chairperson of the Human Rights Commission of Pakistan, 'We believe that if the US wants partnership with us, they should be good partners and help in promoting democratic principles' which will also take care of the religious extremists to a large extent (*The Hindu,2008*).

The making of the present democratic mood did not emerge overnight and it started in March 2007 when Pervez Musharraf suspended Chief Justice Iftikhar Chaudhary but was forced to reinstate in June following a loud outburst of protests from lawyers. Further the declaration of emergency in November 2007 was taken by the public as Musharraf's second coup and the series of actions that followed it directly assaulted the democratic aspirations of ordinary Pakistani, who were becoming increasingly politicized by the chain of events that appeared to rob them of their sovereignty. Adding to this was the attitude of the new Army Chief General Ashfaq Kayani, who made it clear that he wants the military to withdraw from the political arena (*Parthasarathy,2008*). In all fairness the outcome of the election was a mandate to revive Pakistan's institution and empower its Parliamentary democracy. It has the promise of ending decades of military rule and its consequences of perennial servitude to a host of vested interests, internal and external.

The first strong effect of public pressure was the coalition of the major players, the Pakistan People's Party and the Pakistan Muslim League(Nawaz) which set aside their differences and worked together on a platform to advance the key goals of democratic agenda. On March 9, 2008, in an act of unprecedented statesmanship they resolved the differences dogging their power sharing talks and a joint summit declaration signed by them, said that the coalition partners are ready to form the governments at national and provincial levels. The Pakistan Muslim League(N) would join the Pakistan People's Party- led government at the Centre, while the PPP would join a PML(N)-led government in Punjab.

However, the landmark victory in the election and the coalition of PPP and PML(N) to form a government at the Centre and States have pushed the country in a further trouble. It is no secret that from the 1950s, Pakistan was drawn into a trap in the form of the American strategic alliance, enabling a succession of military dictatorships in conjunction with the civil bureaucracy to thwart the emergence of political processes and parties. This time too the US and Musharraf have got a kind of power sharing understanding with the late PPP chairperson Benazir Bhutto ahead of the scheduled election. Earlier they both had hoped that this paradigm would hold the. strategies of containment that had served successive. regimes. Still the United States of America holds a very poor opinion about Pakistan and its

people as revealed by Admiral William Fallon, the US Central Command chief, 'Pakistan is a very immature democracy. Look at the history of the place. It is rough. There is that group of folks that wants nothing more than to start a war with India (*Vardarajan,2008*). His views are important in Pakistan's context because he is America's points man for all military dealings with Islamabad. The US perception is a major hurdle before the policy makers of Washington and consequently it is unwilling to see an elected government exercise control over the country's defence and security policies.

Another significant issue which concerns the all internal and external factions and democratic integrity of Pakistan as well is the restoration of the judges who were dismissed by Pervez Musharraf simply for refusing to endorse his illegal methods. At the Murree meeting apart from forming the coalition government PPP leader Asif Ali Zardari and PML(N) leader Nawaz Sharif also agreed that the superior judges sacked by General Musharraf would be reinstated within a month of government formation through a resolution of Parliament. For both the political parties this is an important matter of principle but in pushing the agenda the coalition needs to think carefully of how it is to be done. More important than this is the task of rebalancing of constitutional amendment made in 2002 in Article 58. (2) (b) which empowers the President to dissolve Parliament (*Vardarajan,2008*). This has become easier as Fazlur Rahman, leader of the Jamiat-Ulama-e-Islam faction, has announced its decision to join the PPP led coalition at the Centre and as a result, the strength of the new dispensation in the National Assembly has risen to the two-thirds required to get rid of the said controversial constitutional amendment.

The last hurdle in forming the government was removed by the Murree meeting of PPP leader Asif Ali Zardari and ML(N) leader Nawaz Sharif. As a further step the PPP having taken al considerations in view nominated Yousuf

Raza Gillani as its candidate for the post of Prime minister on 22 March 2008 and the very next day he was elected country's Premier with a huge majority in the National Assembly. On 24 March 2008 President Musharraf administered him the oath of office. A week later on 31st March in a 24-member cabinet Shah Mahmood Qureshi of PPP became the Foreign Affairs Minister. With this the wheel has turned for both Musharraf and Pakistan. It is the President's weakest moment and one of celebration for democrats.

Yousuf Raza Gillani, the new Prime Minister of Pakistan, has a long political career and joined politics first in 1978 as a member of Pakistan Muslim League and later became a minister in 1985 during the Premiership of Mohammad Khan Junejo. In 1988 he joined the Pakistan People's Party and became vice-president of the party. He served the nation as a speaker of the National Assembly form 1993-1997 when second time Benazir Bhutto became the Prime Minister. Recently he was convicted by a National Accountability Court set by Musharraf regime and jailed for 10 years for handing out jobs illegally during his term as speaker and using more than Rs. 10 million from public funds through the misuse of official transactions. For four long years he remained in jail and was released in 2006 following an order of the Punjab High Court. Throughout the period he remained in PPP as a staunch loyalist of slain leader Benazir Bhutto and also well known for his principles. Newspapers of Pakistan welcomed Gillani as a loyal to his party who is not a "yes-man". A graduate in journalism from Punjab University is seen as a good team player and a steady hand. Although the recent election was fought on nation-based issues, country's relations with the US an India remained a potential factor as earlier.

The assassination of Benazir Bhutto in the midst of election campaign was a jolt for the United States of America particularly on its global war against the ideology of terrorism. Earlier it had succeeded in managing an understanding between Benazir Bhutto and Pervez Musharraf and entire hope was pinned on forming of government by this alliance. The changed situation and result of the general elections have compelled the two democratic political parties—PPP and the ML(N) to come together and agree on forming the government naturally sidelining the President Pervez Musharraf and other extremist factions in Pakistan. In a clearer term the development has aggravated the US interests in ways more than one as this time the people of Pakistan voted against the authoritarian regime of Pervez Musharraf.

On 24 March 2008, the day Gillani took the oath of office, the US officials including Deputy Secretary of State John Negroponte and Assistant Secretary of State Richard Boucher met president Musharraf and leaders of the government with a view to woo the new dispensation and smooth relations between it and Musharraf, amid tears that instability in the nuclear-armed nation would hurt efforts to tackle Islamic militancy (*The Hindustan Times,2008*).They found the new leaders having a different tone. Nawaz Sharif, leader of the ML(N) and a significant coalition partner told the two US envoys that the new government would review President Musharraf's "one man" anti-terror strategy and focus on Pakistani need. Pakistan wants to see peace in every country, including the US. However, to ensure peace in other countries we cannot turn our own country into killing fields (*Baruah,2008*). The same spirit was reiterated by Premier Gillani when George W. Bush, the President of United State, congratulated him and told that he was ready to work with him to fight Islamist extremism.The US President had also cleared the way for giving millions of dollars to Pakistan to fight terrorism. It, however, makes, no meaning for the present as Gillani in a clear message to the US President, emphasised a broader approach to the war on terror including political solutions and development programmes. He told the US President that Pakistan would continue to fight terrorism in all its forms and manifestations since it is in Pakistan's own national interest. He also utilized the opportunity to express country's commitment to maintaining long-term close ties with the USA. Thus, from the US points of view the initial response of the present regime of Pakistan was far from satisfactory and require some more time to analyse the real priorities of Pakistan. Move on several issues in national life including the real position of the president of Pakistan in country's administration, would perhaps, clear the clouds.

Since the inception of Pakistan in 1947 its relations with India has remained number one factor in foreign policy considerations. In long yester years when Pervez Musharraf was at the centerstage, India treated its relations with Pakistan half way consequently not taking any advantage of Musharraf's flexibility. Earlier in the 'Charter of Democracy' both Benazir Bhutto and Nawaz Sharif in 2006 had pledged to resolve the Kashmir in accordance with the United Nations Security Council Resolution that President Musharraf had described as irrelevant. But in election campaigns and thereafter the leaders of both the political parties took a greater lead forward and committed to improve country's relations with India. Asif Ali Zardari, the PPP leader and co-Chairperson, in particular laid stress that both countries should 'agree to disagree' on Kashmir and focus instead on building trade interdependence on the basis of respect and honour (*Subramanian,2008*). He, along with the majority of Pakistanis appear to agree that Kashmir should not be allowed to hijack relations between the two countries any more.

The day Gillani took over as the Prime Minister of Pakistan, his Indian counterpart Dr. Manmohan Singh while greeting on assumption of office, expressed his wish for India-Pakistan ties to become the best ever. This time in particular there is more than one reason to believe that things would improve. First, bilateral relations are clearly better than ever before with more interaction between people

across the border. Intellectuals, academics, think tanks, and artists are increasingly talking to each other. Second the post-poll scenario in Pakistan, it is for the first time that the military is on the backfoot. As an institution the army stands to lose its credibility and hold over the polity with huge Khaki corporate empire it has built up in the last 50 odd years. Last but not the least important is the fact that the present army Chief General Kayani has instructed the commanders to shun politics and focus on professional responsibilities (*The Hindustan Times,2008*). However, in comparison to the earlier regime when Pervez Musharraf was seen as the ideal single-window clearance in his double role as president and the Army chief, now New Delhi would have to navigate the "troika" of Prime Minister, President and Army chief. General Kayani a day after Zardari's statement on Kashmir said that a national consensus exists on the Kashmir issue and that the Pakistan Army was committed to the cause in line with the aspirations of the people.' In the circumstances, it would be certainly harder to move in the positive direction and get something substantial.

In between the position of India and the United States, no less troublesome is the condition of Pakistan itself internally. The new Prime Minister Yousuf Raza Gillani, a day before his oath ceremony, ordered the release of ousted Chief Justice Iftikhar Chaudhary and other senior judges who had been placed under house arrest by President Pervez Musharraf. Now and as agreed by the coalition partners they had to be reinstated within month through a parliamentary resolution failing which Aitzaz Ahsan, President of the Supreme Court Bar Association and prominent PPP functionary, has threatened to take the streets again which in turn would get the sympathy of the civil society and further pressure the dispensation of listen to their demands (*The Times of India,2008*). Reinstation of deposed judges would pave the way for opening President Pervez Musharraf's file and make his position change even removal. And if it happens the common target of coalition partners would vanish from the scene. It might take a course of coalition dissension. Barring the Awami National Party; the Muttahida Quami Movement and the Jamiat-e-Ulema Islami who has e also joined the coalition, the major party Muslim League(N) and its leader Nawaz. Shard may not be satisfied playing the role of a junior partner and the moment Musharraf departs from the scene, this coalition could come apart.

On his part Prime Minister Gillani immediately after easily winning a National Assembly vote, made a call for strengthening Parliament and other institutions including the judiciary. He raised democratic spirit by committing himself and his government to protect the 1973 Constitution, strengthen democratic institutions, ensure the independence of judiciary and the media and work to make parliament a sovereign body (*The Hindu,2008*). He took terrorism and extremism on top of his challenges and offered talks with militants willing to give up arms and as a gesture of goodwill revoked a special colonial era law Frontier Crimes Regulation(1901) to remove backwardness and alienation of the frontier tribal region. Military men serving elsewhere for the civil purposes have also began to return to their original posts of Pakistan's defense (*The Hindu,2008*). Despite Pervez Musharraf's conciliatory statements that he will work with any elected government the Gillani-led coalition will have to work with Army Chief Ashfaq Kayani who will be conscious of the role of the military as an institution in Pakistan's future. At best the political leadership and the army brass as well will have to display an unprecedented appetite to work together to tackle the rising problems of Pakistan in the coming years. There will be plenty more situations when their democratic credentials and capabilities will be tested. At the moment the common people of Pakistan can only hope that these changes are for the long-term and that public statements will be backed by action.

Imran Ahmad Khan Niazi

As a result of general election held in Pakistan for 342 members of National Assembly on 25 July 2018, the present Prime Minister, popularly known as Imran Khan, secured total 176 seats with 8 other allies who helped him in forming the government at the Centre, aithough all Opposition Parties including the Pakistan Muslim League (N), alleged a large scale rigging charges, the other agencies and European Union Election Observation Mission to Pakistan termed the overall situation of the general election as satisfactory. In apost-election development Imran Khan took the oath of office of Pakistan' Premiership on 18 August 2018, becoming the 22nd Prime Minister in country's history and apart from making a full-fleged ministry, in major bureaucratic reshuffling appointed Lieutenant General Asim Munir as the Director-General of Inter-Services Intelligence (ISI).In more than three yearsImran has largely experimented with his policies in spheres of economy, society, domestic and in Pakistan's relations with regional countries along with super power, the United States of America as well as Beijing, the top well wisher of Islamabad in today's context. Recently, he became famous due to his preferential/growing friendship with the People's Republic of China and simultaneous deteriorating understandings with the US in manner more than one and openly supporting Taliban in capturing power in Afghanistan with Chinese help and Russian silent consent at the its relationship with Washington aon other democratic nations of the region and the globe as well.

Originally, Imran Khan is an international cricketer-turned politician who was born on 5 October 1952, in a Pashtun family in Lahore, graduated in 1975, from Keble College, Oxford and also remained Chancellor of the University of Bradford in the United Kingdom from 2005to 2014. He started his career as a cricketer at the age of 18 in a test series against England and played the game till 1992 where he served as the team's captain internationally between 1982 – 1992 and under his captainship, Pakistan also won the Cricket World Cup, nation's only and first victory in the sphere. After career in cricket Imran turned to politics and founded a political party named, Pakistan Tehreek-e-Insaf (PTI) on 25 April 1996, began serving the party as its chairman, won a seat in the National Assembly in the year 2002 and represented Mianwali as opposition leader until 2007. Although, his party, the PTI, boycotted the general election held in 2008 after the end of Pervez Musharraf's regime but in subsequent general election held in 2013 his party participated and emerged as the second largest party with forming the government in Khyber Pakhtunkhwa province with coalition partners of the time.

From the beginning of his career Imran Khan was a popular figure and always remained in public eye as a cricketer, a philanthropist and a wider believer in the ideas of poet-philosopher Muhammad Iqbal and the Iranian writer-sociologist Ali Shariati in his youth time and generally described as a nationalist and a populist. His early proclaimed political leanings include: Islamic values to which he rededicated himself in 1990s; liberal economics, with the promise of deregulating the economy and creating a welfare state; decrease bureaucracy and the implementation of anti-corruption laws, to create and ensure a clean government; the establishment of an independent judiciary; overhauling of country's police system and an anti-militant vision for a democratic Pakistan. Now, after entering in politics he experienced a religious awakening, embracing Sufi Mysticism by shedding his earlier playboy image at national level and remained a critic of continuing corruption and economic inequality in Pakistan and opposed the Pakistani Government's decision to co-operate with the United States of America in fighting militants near Pak-Afghan border. In the context, throughout his career, Imran Khan remained soft and supportive of Taliban active in Federally Administered Tribal

Area (FATA), and strongly believed in negotiation with Taliban. Attached to it was the issue of US drone attacks and Imran was dead against of these events. Being conscious on Pakistan's cultural and religious norms he criticized political and economic elites who, accordinh to him had become Westernised and out of touch of country's traditional heritage. On other sensitive issues like 'forced conversion'and 'problem of Jammu and Kashmir' between India and Pakistan he was then very clear of his views. He described the forced conversion of anyone including the Hindu girls in Pakistan as un-Islamic and considered the issue of Jammu and Kashmir as humanitarian rather than territorial

Gradually, the socio-political and religious ideas of Imran Khan began gaining ground in the public domain of Pakistan and in an opinion, poll conducted in the year 2012, he was found to be the most popular political figure in the country. His continued efforts and different types of movements launched by Imran Khan proved him a successful leader of Pakistan and as a result, he won just less than half of total seats for which general elections were held in May 2013. In this election, although he failed to form a government, he was assigned by the people to discharge the functions of an accountable Opposition Party in country's politics in days to come. In post-election phase the leak of Panama Papers on Sharif's corruption and Supreme Court's 2017 verdict disqualifying Nawaz Sharif for holding public post, substantiated Imran Khan's way to the throne of Pakistan an easy one, leading his oath as the 22nd Prime Minister of the country on 18 August 2018.Around the time Imran Khan delivered his victory speech in which he promised to make Pakistan a humanitarian state based on first Islamic State of Madina, mainly focused on needs of the poor and commoners of the country and expressed his dedication towards them to uplift their standard of living. On the occasion he declared his intention not to victimize the opponents and maintain country's unity at any cost. He expressed his wish to make the Prime Minister's house an educational institute and use the governor house for the welfare of the general public. In sphere of foreign policy, he hoped to have abetter relation with Afghanistan, United States and India and maintaining a balanced relationship with Saudi Arabia and Iran.

After taking the oath of office, Imran Khan, first faced the domestic financial challenge which he inherited as legacy of the previous government. It was a twin balance of payment and debt crisis with a large current account deficit as well as fiscal deficit. To address the issue Khan's government, on the one hand sought a bailout package from the International Monetary Fund (IMF), and slashed government's subsidies spanding in the energy sector along with unveiling an austerity budget to check the fiscal deficit and controlling government borrowing in the global market. In addition, Pakistan, in collaboration and consultation with the IMF, stepped-up several steps to improve the overall conditions of country's economy and gained significant stabilization by raising tarrifs to collect higher tax revenue and devaluating the currency and imposing heavy import duty which helped curtail the current account deficits. These improving steps registered a hopeful situation for the balance of payment and debt crisis in the year 2020, by narrowing down the deficit to less than 1% of Gross Domestic Product (GDP), and stabilizing the Central Bank's foreign exchange reserves in the same year.

Pakistan, apart from implementing IMF-guided reforms achieved concrete gains on business operating climate and introduced several policies to improve the continuing situation. In the year 2019, Pakistan earned a record revenue from domestic taxes without raising any tax in import taxes, resulting in improvement of world ranking and achieving primary surplus, although the economists of the country gave its credit to an increase in non-tax revenues rather than an increase in tax revenues, yet this growth in tax collection continued in the first quarter of the fiscal year 2021. In respect to economic policy, the government introduced from January 2020 the second phase of the China-Pakistan Free Trade Agreement and as a result of renegotiation with Beijing Islamabad began to receive many concessions on Pakistani exports of godds and services which ultimately reduced the burden of tariff on Pakistan. The agreement with China was termed as a significant milestone in country's foreign policy as it expanded Pakistan'strade with a country, earlier known for co-operation in defence and security fields.

At the time Imran Khan assumed office in Pakistan he found the country economically poor and weak with multiple problems such as flawed energy policies, spiraling fiscal deficit, grossly inadequate tax to Gross Domestic Product ratio, multiple bailouts by international agencies and under investment in education, health and skills sector which have marred the sustainable growth of the nation. In particular, Imran's party, the Pakistan Tehreek-i-Insaf (PTI), also identified antiquated governance and all-pervasive corruption and lack of political leadership as the reasons for the long -term decline in the economy. With the coming of Imran Khan as the Prime Minister of Pakistan he set a reform programme for various sectors of economy and creation of a fiscal space of 9% of Gross Domestic Products along with a 5% increase in tax collection 2% reduction in wasteful expenditure and 2% reduction in public sector in losses of PSEs. For further,it projected a target of a growth rate of 6%, inflation to be brought down to 7%, fiscal deficit to be brought down to 4.5 percent, tax revenue to be raised by 15 percent and a four-fold increase in welfare spending.

The ongoing welfare schemes required a financial help from outside the country and to whom it shouls be procured, was a dilemma before the new government. One such option was to look to the IMF, but due to pressure of the United

Stated of America, it felt some limitations and imposing tough conditions were imminent in the context. The next option was to move towards the People's Republic of China whose 62$ billion dream projects were already in progress and called China-Pakistan Economic Corridor (CPEC). Although, initially and in afterwards, the Government of Pakistan has continuously supported the Belt and Road Initiatives (BRI) scheme, the other recipients of BRI loans have expressed anxieties in paying Chinese debt and its high interest rates. In reference to Pakistani CPEC, the NGO Centre for Global Development has also warned that Chinese development schemes may add Pakistan's risk of debt distress. In the circumstances, Islamabad could either return to the IMF or further increase its volume of Chinese debt. As the Trump Administration of US is very hard on Pakistan due to its failure to tackle Islamic extremism, the former might put pressure on IMF to ensure that its loans given to Islamabad, are not used to repay the Chinese loan, taken in context of BRI. Pakistan is also reluctant in receiving IMF loans because it would compel Islamabad to disclose the terms attached to China-Pakistan Economic Corridor. In the situation, non-availability of funds for Imran Khan will cap Imran's election commitment of an Islamic welfare state along with removing inequalities in Pakistan.

Initially for months, the Government of Pakistan avoided IMF loan due to strict conditions attached with it and arranged the same from Saudi Arabia, the United Arab Emirates and China but as they all were insufficient to meet the needs of Islamabad and the economy of Pakistan worsened further, it went to the IMF in 2019 for the 22nd time in the history of Pakistan and demanded a loan of SDR $1 billion. The International Monetary Fund, although sanctioned the said loan with conditions as hike in energy tariff, removal of energy subsidy, increase in taxation, privatization of public entities and fiscal adjustment to the budget. In addition, Pakistan also gave concrete assurance that it would not divert the IMF loan to service its Chinese debt. In fact, Beijing is the biggest donor to Pakistan after the IMF which is around $19-20 billion of total $ 90 billion of total debt and libbilities of Pakistan and has increased fastly from 2015. According to an estimate, by 2024, Pakistan will have to pay back to China $100 billion on the total investment of $ 18.5 billion which China has invested in bank loans and 19 early harvest projects under the China-Pakistan Economic Corridor (CPEC).

Not only economically but socially and culturally too, the coming of the government of Pakistan's PTI under the Premiership of Imran Khan signified the end of one and beginning of a different era in the history of Pakistan. Earlier, the dramatic arrest of Pakistan's ex-Prime Minister Nawaz Sharif and his daughter in corruption chargesafter the Panama paper leak signaled the charged and changed political environment in the country. It ultimately paved the way for PTI and its leader Imran Khan who, apart from launching a 'movement for Justice' also emerged as a hope for corruption-free Pakistan, the long cherished will of the common people of the country. For more than two decades, Imran Khan had been piloting several anti-corruption movements and in last five years, since 2013 his party's performance in Khyber-Pakhtunkhwa (KP). A large number of people, especially, women who formed 44% of the electorate and rarely come out for voting as well as others who were self-exclude from election process due to societal and cultural constraints turned out to use their franchise in block, many of whom for the first time.In addition, the two slogans of PTI-running a clean government and transforming hospitals and schools attracted a large number of technocrats and educated Pakistani, who openly joined Imran Khan's election campaigns and it all led the victory of Pakistan Tehreek-e-Insaf to form a government in the country. All appeared avowed to relace ond Pakistan through a new one where there was no place for 3Ps of the old Pakistan-power, privilege and patronage.

Now, gone are the days when two main parties of Pakistan-Pakistan Peoples Party led by Asif Ali Zardari and Pakistan Muslim League-Nawaz (PML-N) whose leader was Nawaz Sharif dominated the politics of Pakistan for decades. Never before the election of 2018, corruption remained an issue in central or provincial elections in past while this time the word 'corruption-free Pakistan' became the main theme of whole election campaign and the leaders of PTI including its leader Imran Khan, repeatedly urged the people get rid of the corrupt elite of country. With the change of guard and coming of Imran Khan in lead role, new social and cultural dimensions are likely to emerge on the scene.The overall impression of Pakistan's new regime under the Premiership of Imran Khan was the result of his agenda of *Naya Pakistan* which promised an Islamic welfare state free of all types of corruption with an increased sense of pride for the nation to move it forward. The new prime minister had been a critic of previous governments on many counts which ignored national security and interests of the country. In sphere of foreign policy Imran has been a critic of China-Pakistan Economic Corridor and frequent drone strike. In last three years amd more Imran government has faced more challenges in its foreign relations with three regional countries-India, the United States of America, China and Afghanistan. Islamabad's relations with all these countries have been in fous in pre-Imran phase and the theme/legacy of past continued in present dispensation with new turns and twists.

At the time Imran Khan took the oath of office, he found a tense relation with India in which India has been blaming Pakistan for its engagement in terrorist activities in Indian State of Jammu and Kashmir along with other parts of India while Pakistan regularly blame India for supporting rebellious elements in Baluchistan, however, the most contentious issue between them still remains the problem of Jammu and Kashmir, and recently some reservations on China-Pakistan Economic Corridor (CPEC), which has passed through the territory of Pak-occupied Kashmir (PoK). Although with his coming Imran urged India to take one step to improve relations, and in response, Islamabad would take two steps, in the present circumstances, it appeared difficult because Pakistan faces a number of vexing regional and international challenges. His major challenges in foreign policy include the deteriorating US-Pakistan relations, managing nuclear tension with India, growing peace challenges in Afghanistan, increasing volume of foreign debt, especially of China, but above all, Imran's own and his party's relations with Pakistan' powerful army, which is, in practice, all powerful in country's foreign policy/relations.

India alike, Pakistan's relations with the United States of America has been under stress particularly since US President Donald Trump charged Islamabad for adopting double standard- taking American help in the name of combating terrorism, but helping terrorists in Afghanistan in fighting against the US and NATO forces. The perception of common Pakistani is also against the US and according to an estimate about 52% people of the country believed that America was responsible for 9/11 attacks and Imran himself initiated his political career by criticizing US drone attacks along with his agenda of freeing Pakistan from a relation of patron-client. He was of the view that Pakistan should continue to maintain with the US a mutual relationship rather than of using Pakistan as a "hired gun" that has proved fatal for Islamabad in past. Even the initial efforts of Pakistan to satisfy Washington failed to deliver any desired results and in a further step America cancelled Pakistan's coalition support fund worth $300 million and also suspended other such helps provided in previous decades and years to the needy nation, Pakistan. Imran regime's freely anti-US batting and increasing nearness with the Peoples Republic of China proved costly for Islamabad, however, the two again appeared coming closer in context of ongoing peace negotiations in reference to early US exit from Afghanistan. They both viewed the occasion significant for their own specific purposes.

Earlier, the independent Pakistan found a golden opportunity to enter in Afghan politics and society openly when in December 1979 the Soviet Army intervened in Afghanistan and installed a pro-Soviet Government to curb the anti-Communist forces in the country, perhaps, forgetting the fact that it was the phase of Cold War in international politics and the United States of America will respond instantly to check/control the increasing influence of USSR in the country and the region as well. As expected by all, apart from criticizing the acts of Soviet Union by the nations of the world, the United States, in particular come forward and with the active help and support of Pakistan prepared a group of youths of surrounding countries, including Afghanistan, Pakistan and others to give a potential fight to the Afghan Army backed by the Soviet forces. They were taught, trained and fully prepared with full arms and ammunitions supplied by the US and ultimately after one decade of intense fighting, the Soviet forces withdrew from Afghan being defeated by Mujahideen, the private militia army, nurtured and controlled by Pakistan. Taking benefits from the Soviet exit and prevailing situation of civil war, anarchy, and rampant violence, Taliban- a group of Afghan students who are totally committed to form an Islamic State in the country, formed in 1994, assumed power in 1996 and rule at the close of 2001, when they were dethroned by the US in response to its launch of war against the terror groups, mainly in search of Al-Qaeda chief Osama bin Laden, the mastermind of fatal disaster that took place in the US on 9/11, an unforgettable blot on superpower's face forever. The twice beginning of war in Afghanistan left no option before the US but to seek Pakistan's active co-operation, without which nothing was possible.

From the day of its creation the whole policy of Pakistan- national and international has been India-centric and this universal truth too applies in case of Afghanistan where the entire sum of Islamabad's activities focused on harming India in ways more than one and, thus, Pakistan has got, in the form of Taliban, a source of terrorizing and frightening India apart from making foil Indian investment and efforts in reconstruction of torn Afghanistan during the phase of violence and thereafter. In today's context and for the days to come its objectives include; a. to undermine New Delhi's influence in Afghanistan while promoting its own, b.to maximise Taliban's influence in a weak Kabul government, c. to maintains strategic depth against an Indian invasion, d. to facilitate training and operations by Pakistani-backed extremist group, e. to marginalise historical Afghan claims on Pakistani territory, f. to develop trade relations with Central Asian Republics, and h. to curb other state's influence in Afghanistan. Of the all objectives, Pakistan has got some measure of success in keeping the Kabul government weak and off-balance and supporting the Taliban a safe haven to the group's leadership as well as continuing insurgency and preventing Afghan government from asserting more authority. But on the other side, its meagre investment of $1.3 billion stands nowhere while comparing $300 million development assistance provided by India and as a result Pakistani works are invisible in the whole of Afghanistan. It is also lagging far behind India in in terms of economic links and export markets in Central Asian Republics (CARs).

While viewing Pakistan's objectives in Afghanistan in detail, it appears that Islamabad wants to make Kabul its colony in traditional sense to use, misuse and abuse it for the benefits of Pakistan with the active support and co-operation of Taliban. By training, funding, munitions, supplies and safe haven to Taliban and Haqqani network, in one stroke it targets India, Afghan government, and the US as well. In the matter of peace negotiations, from the beginning Pakistan has made itself essential by preventing moderate forces of the Taliban from participating in talks as Islamabad had always become a barrier in peace progress of which Pakistan was not a part in order to give three clear messages: a. it controls who participates in reconciliation, b. it must play a central role in any discussions on ending violence in Afghanistan, and c. it will obstruct negotiations that do not advance its own interests. The aid and assistance that Pakistan has provided to Afghanistan also aimed to expand its trade and export in Central Asian Republics in addition to Afghanistan on the one hand and erect an obstruction in India's excess to these countries by blocking its route. However, despite all efforts Pakistan has not succeeded in preventing regional integration in Afghanistan, expand its own reach into CARs or undermine Indian economic or political influence. The main reason for Pakistani failure in its mission owes largely to its internal rivalry between civilian leadership and the security institutions and Pakistan's continuing support for Jihadists, the Haqqani network in particular, have isolated Pakistan with its potential partners in the region and beyond.

The decades of understanding on terrorism between Pakistan and the US took a U turn on August 2017 when American President Donald Trump announcing his new strategy for Afghan war accused Pakistan for playing a double game by providing safe heavens to extremists. He expressed his soft corner for the people of Pakistan who suffered the most but criticized the establishment for sheltering the organisation whose people are killing US armies and NATO forces every day mercilessly, although, it resulted in an increase of anti-American sentiments in Pakistan across the country, but Trump was well convinced about his perception and again reiterated on. 1 January 2018 when criticizing Pakistan said that it has given US nothing except lies and deceit and charged the government in its failure in taking any effective actionahainst the Afghan Taliban militants who have taken shelter in different parts of the countryand controlling their activities in Afghanistan. However, the US mood towards Pakistan changed somewhat when Imran met Donald Trump at the Oval Office in July 2019 where some compromising points were sought to normalize further relations between the two countries. In particular, the case of Afghanistan is a delicate one as Islamabad has several geostrategic significances for both India and China and among them all Pakistan continues to be an important player in US efforts to get the situation normalized in Kabul and elsewhere in the country. As such, they both maintained working/productive relationships at high level keeping in view the respective interests in Afghanistan. In other words, at the one end it is , as always, supportive of Pakistan but on the other has allowed Islamabad to continue with its negative regional policies and involve in promoting terrorism with no any memorable punishment. For the present, the US feels the need to get Pakistani help and support to ensure peace, security and development in Afghanistan, despite the fact that US-China rivalry has begun and Islamabad is moving closer to Beijing than to Washington.

In the background of strong China-Pakistan understanding on regional and global issues the relations between the two strengthened further with the coming of Imran Khan as the Prime Minister of Pakistan. In recent decades and years, they both developed an all-weather strategic cooperative partnership with each other which generally considered a fruitful diplomatic tie established for the promotion of mutual benefit. The central pillar of Imran's vision of "Naya Pakistan" is geo-economics that seeks to transform Pakistan into an economically vibrant country through development partnerships, connectivity, and regional peace. It aims to leverage its geo-economic location and burgeoning population of 220 million - as a melting pot and economic hub for positive global interests.Under this vision, the government of Pakistan started implementing decisive and far-reaching reforms in every sector of the economy. As a result, the country is moving progressively in a higher, inclusive, and sustainable growth path. Despite the challenge posed by COVID-19, our GDP was projected to grow by 3.94 percent with major contributions from the agricultural, services, and industrial sectors during fiscal year 2020-21. In the context, the Chinese Belt and Road Initiative became very popular all over the world and about 140 countries gave their consent for the scheme, while many of them reached on the verge of bankruptcy and became defaulter before Beijing, especially after the world -wide spread of pandemic COVID-19. The new situation also posed several hurdles in further implementation of CPEC projects in Pakistan, also causing a lot of harassment and accusations.

The China-Pakistan Economic Corridor is one of the biggest and largest infrastructural development schemes of independent Pakistan, intended to rapidly upgrade its required structural basics and strengthen its economy by the construction of modern transportation networks, numerous energy projects and special economic zones. This renovation plan for Pakistani economy includes at large: a. projects in Gwadar Port and City, b. roadway projects, c. railway projects, d. energy sector projects, e. other areas of co-operation-agriculture and aquaculture, science and technology. The plan being a landmark project in the history of Pakistan, is the largest investment Pakistan has ever attracted since independence and also largest by China in any foreign country, and therefore both Pakistani government and media as well have called the investment a 'game and fate changer' for the region that will ultimately make country a regional economic hub further strengthening and cementing ties between the two countries. The first impact of Chinese investment was visible in energy sector which the country was facing since long and was in shortfall of over 4500 MW on a regular basis but in December 2017, Pakistan succeeded in producing surplus electricity.

In addition to the schemes and detail of projects, there

was a separate arrangement for the finance of the works which would come in the form of concessional loans, interest-free loans, private consortia, and assistance from Asian Development Bank. Of the total approximately $11 billion will be dispersed by the Exim Bank of China, China Development Bank and the ICBC at an interest rate of 1.6% while as per an announcement made by the government of China in August 2015 concessionary loans for several projects in Gwadar totaling $757 million would be converted in 0% interest loans. In a further development in September 2015 China announced that the $230 million Gwadar International Airport project will be considered grants which the government of Pakistan will not be required to repay. For energy purpose $15.5 billion are to be constructed by joint Chinese-Pakistani firms, rather than by the governments of either China or Pakistan. The Exim Bank of China will finance those investments at 5-6 % interest rates. The other about a dozen projects are to be financed by the Asian Development Bank.

From all counts number one beneficiary of the China-Pakistan Economic Corridor is Beijing and if all things remain normal it is in the interest of Islamabad. It will provide China with an alternative route for energy supplies, as well as new route by which Western China can conduct its trade, however, in context of Straits of Malacca dominated by the US, in particular, the CPEC provides China an alternative route in case of any negative action by the United States of America. In addition, China is heavily dependent upon sea routes which pass through the South China Sea near the disputed area, Spratly Islands and Paracel Islands, currently a source of tension between China, Taiwan, Vietnam, the Philippines and the United States of America and in the circumstances, the alternative route provided by CPEC would decrease the possibility of confrontation between Beijing and Washington. The CPEC alignments will improve connectivity to Xinjiang province of China increasing the region's potential to attract public and private investment. As a result of the CPEC, Chinese imports and exports to the Middle East, Africa, and Europe would require much shorter shipment times and distances and also alternative route to Afghanistan and Central Asia.

As the people's Republic of China is the most resourceful country of the region, there is no doubt in its funding capability but the repayment capacity of Pakistan has remained always in doubt keeping in consideration the already torn economic condition of Islamabad which was pushed further on decline due to slowing down of global economy in context of pandemic COVID-19 began at the close of the year 2019 from Wuhan, China, and spread over two hundred countries of the world. Thus, in the situation, political fragility, increased interference of security agencies and the army establishment in matters of civilian administration, have put additional pressure on Chinese ambitious CPEC projects currently ongoing in Pakistan. The hurdles faced by China in the implementation of its projects related to Belt and Road Initiatives (BRI) have disappointed Beijing and deferment of the crucial10thmeeting of China-Pakistan Economic Corridor's Joint Co-operation Committee (JCC) testify their differences on the issue. Since the commencement of the projects the Opposition parties of Pakistan have also abused it as a political tool not suitable for the country like Pakistan.

In addition, Pakistan endeavors to promote trade, transit, and energy flows as well as people-to-people exchanges between Middle East, Central Asia, South Asia, and China. Our geo-strategic location offers the shortest route to international seas to all Central Asian republics and China through Karachi and Gwadar ports. Pakistan will strive to serve as the gateway to Central Asia, Afghanistan, and China. Pakistan's earnest desire for peace in Afghanistan is also an effort to share the dividends of peace and prosperity for the region and beyond.

Earlier, the independent Pakistan found a golden

opportunity to enter in Afghan politics and society openly when in December 1979 the Soviet Army intervened in Afghanistan and installed a pro-Soviet Government to curb the anti-Communist forces in the country, perhaps, forgetting the fact that it was the phase of Cold War in international politics and the United States of America will respond instantly to check/control the increasing influence of USSR in the country and the region as well. As expected by all, apart from criticizing the acts of Soviet Union by the nations of the world, the United States, in particular come forward and with the active help and support of Pakistan prepared a group of youths of surrounding countries, including Afghanistan, Pakistan and others to give a potential fight to the Afghan Army backed by the Soviet forces. They were taught, trained and fully prepared with full arms and ammunitions supplied by the US and ultimately after one decade of intense fighting, the Soviet forces withdrew from Afghan being defeated by Mujahideen, the private militia army, nurtured and controlled by Pakistan. Taking benefits from the Soviet exit and prevailing situation of civil war, anarchy, and rampant violence, Taliban-a group of Afghan students who are totally committed to form an Islamic State in the country, formed in 1994, assumed power in 1996 and rule at the close of 2001, when they were dethroned by the US in response to its launch of war against the terror groups, mainly in search of Al-Qaeda chief Osama bin Laden, the mastermind of fatal disaster that took place in the US on 9/11, an unforgettable blot on superpower's face forever. The twice beginning of war in Afghanistan left no option before the US but to seek Pakistan's active co-operation, without which nothing was possible.

From the day of its creation the whole policy of Pakistan-national and international has been India-centric and this universal truth too applies in case of Afghanistan where the entire sum of Islamabad's activities focused on harming India in ways more than one and, thus, Pakistan has got, in the form of Taliban, a source of terrorizing and frightening India apart from making foil Indian investment and efforts in reconstruction of torn Afghanistan during the phase of violence and thereafter. In today's context and for the days to come its objectives include; a. to undermine New Delhi's influence in Afghanistan while promoting its own, b.to maximise Taliban's influence in a weak Kabul government, c. to maintains strategic depth against an Indian invasion, d. to facilitate training and operations by Pakistani-backed extremist group, e. to marginalise historical Afghan claims on Pakistani territory, f. to develop trade relations with Central Asian Republics, and h. to curb other state's influence in Afghanistan. Of the all objectives, Pakistan has got some measure of success in keeping the Kabul government weak and off-balance and supporting the Taliban a safe haven to the group's leadership as well as continuing insurgency and preventing Afghan government from asserting more authority. But on the other side, its meagre investment of $1.3 billion stands nowhere while comparing $300 million development assistance provided by India and as a result Pakistani works are invisible in the whole of Afghanistan. It is also lagging far behind India in in terms of economic links and export markets in Central Asian Republics (CARs).

While viewing Pakistan's objectives in Afghanistan in detail, it appears that Islamabad wants to make Kabul its colony in traditional sense to use, misuse and abuse it for the benefits of Pakistan with the active support and co-operation of Taliban. By training, funding, munitions, supplies and safe haven to Taliban and Haqqani network, in one stroke it targets India, Afghan government, and the US as well. In the matter of peace negotiations, from the beginning Pakistan has made itself essential by preventing moderate forces of the Taliban from participating in talks as Islamabad had always become a barrier in peace progress of which Pakistan was not a part in order to give three clear messages: a. it controls who participates in reconciliation, b. it must play a central role in any discussions on ending violence in Afghanistan, and c. it will obstruct negotiations that do not advance its own interests. The aid and assistance that Pakistan has provided to Afghanistan also aimed to expand its trade and export in Central Asian Republics in addition to Afghanistan on the one hand and erect an obstruction in India's excess to these countries by blocking its route. However, despite all efforts Pakistan has not succeeded in preventing regional integration in Afghanistan, expand its own reach into CARs or undermine Indian economic or political influence. The main reason for Pakistani failure in its mission owes largely to its internal rivalry between civilian leadership and the security institutions and Pakistan's continuing support for Jihadists, the Haqqani network in particular, have isolated Pakistan with its potential partners in the region and beyond. However, for the present, Taliban's occupation of Afghanistan by force finally on 15th August 2021, is being considered a temporary diplomatic victory of Pakistan over Washington and New Delhi.

References

Ayoob, Mohammed (1996). 'India and Pakistan: Prospects for Détente,' *Pacific Community*, October, p.165.

Bahadur, Kalim (1978). 'India and Pakistan,' *International Studies*, Vol.17. July-December, New Delhi, pp.518-19.

Baruah, Amit (2008). 'All in it Together,' *The Hindustan Times*, 17 March.

Bhutto, Benazir (1978). Foreign Policy in Perspective, Lahore, pp.40-43.

Bhutto, Benazir (1999). Ordinary Pakistanis Need and Trust Politicians,' *The Hindustan Times*, 6 December.

Bhutto, Benazir (2002). 'War Paint Against Terrorism,' *The Hindustan Times*, 26 January.

Dixit, J. N. (1999). 'A Difficult Neighbour,' *The Hindustan Times*, 30 October.

Ganguly,Amulya (1998). 'Bigots as Neighbours,' *The Hindustan Times*, 21 September.

Hashan, Murshid, *The Cultural Background of the Struggle for Independence in Bangladesh*, Calcutta, pp.39-43.

Hussain, Akmal (1996). 'The Dynamics of Power: Military, Bureaucracy and the People,' Kumar Rupesinghe and Khawar Mumtaz, eds. *Internal Conflicts in South Asia*, London, pp.40-41.

Indian Recorder (1996). Vol.3, No.48, November 25-December 1, New Delhi, p.2418.

Indian Recorder (1996). Vol.3. No.52, 23-31 December, New Delhi, p.2487.

Indian Recorder (1997). Vol.4, No.13, March 26-April 1, New Delhi, pp.2690-91.

Indian Recorder (1997). Vol.4, No.16, May 28- June 3, New Delhi, p.1695.

Khalilzad, Zalmay (1979-80). 'The Superpowers and the Northern Tier,' *International Security*, Vol.4, No.3, Winter, pp.6-30.

Kodikara, Shelton (1983). 'Strategic Factors in Inter-state Relations in South Asia, *Canberra Papers on Strategy and Defence*, No.9, New Delhi, pp.11-12.

Kothari, Rajni (2003). 'Counter-evolution, *The Hindustan Times*, 12 July.

Mazari, Shireen M. (1996). 'Militarism and the Militarisation of Pakistan's Civil Society: 1977-90, Kumar Rupesinghe and Khawar Mumtaz, eds., *Internal Conflicts in South Asia*, London, pp.40-41.

Parthasarathy, Malini (2008). 'Pakistan: A Chance as Never Before,' *The Hindu*, 26 February.

Rajeswar, T. V. (1999). 'Pakistan's Misadventure,' *The Hindustan Times*, 13 June.

Rashid, Abbas (1996). 'The Politics of Fundamentalism,' London, pp.74-77.

Shahin, Sultan (1999). 'Bigotry in Pakistan,' *The Hindustan Times*, 14 December.

Singh, Rajkumar (1999). *India-South Asia Minus Congress Regimes*, Patna, pp.83-84.

Sreedhar (1997). 'Indo-Pak Relations in Post-Benazir Period,' *Strategic Analysis*, Vol.19, No.12, March, New Delhi, p.1695.

Subramanian, Nirupama (2008). 'Pakistan's Democracy and Peace Process,' *The Hindu*, 22 March.

Taseer, Salmaan (1980). *Bhutto: A Political Biography*, New Delhi, pp. 141-43.

The Friday Times (1999). 6 October.

The Hindu (2008). 25 March.

The Hindu (2008). 30 March.

The Hindustan Times (2008). Editorial, 27 March.

The Times of India (1999). 5 August.

The Times of India (2008). Editorial, 27 March.

The Tribune (1997). Chandigarh, 15 February.

Varadarajan, Siddharth (2008). 'The Glimmer that Elusive Dawn,' *The Hindu*, 11 March.

Weinbaum, M. G. and Sen, Gautam (1978). 'Pakistan Enters the Middle East,' *Orbis*, Fall, pp.596-604.

Wright, Theodore P. (1980). 'Where Does Pakistan Belong, South Asia or Muslim West Asia,' *The Times of India*, 20 August.

Ziring, Lawrence, ed. (1982). *The Sub-continent in World Politics*, New York, p.43.

Select Bibliography

Documents

Annual Report to Congress: Military Power of the People's Republic of China, Office of the Secretary of Defence, 2007.

Bangladesh and India's Security (Palit & Dutt, Dehradun, 1972).

Blackett, P.M.S., *Scientific Problem of Defence in Relation to the Indian Armed Forces: A Report to the Honourable Defence Minister*, (Government of India, New Delhi, 1948).

Buzan, B. and Rizvi, *South Asian Insecurity and the Great Powers* (Macmillan, London, 1986).

DavidAlbright and Tom Zamora,'*India's and Pakistan's Nuclear Weapons*', Bulletin of the Atomic Scientists, June 1989.

Government of Pakistan, *The Constitution of Islamic Republic of Pakistan* (1973).

International Atomic Energy Agency, Nuclear Power Status Around the Word Bulletin,1998.

India, Kashmir and the United Nations(External Publicity Division, New Delhi, 1948).

India, Muslims in India (Ministry of Information and Broadcasting, New Delhi, 1966).

Pakistan-China Agreement on Nuclear Cooperation,1986.

Pakistani President Pervez Musharraf's Address at the Woodrow Wilson International Centre for Scholars, 12th February 2002, (Washington, 2002).

*Pakistani Foreign Minister Abdul Sattar's Address to the Carnegic International Non-Proliferation Conference,*15th June 2001, (Washington, 2001).

Resolution,Ministry of External Affairs (New Delhi, 1970). Suhrawardy H.S., *Statement on Foreign Relations and Defence* (Government of Pakistan, Karachi, 1957).

United States Department of State,Patterns of Global Terrorism: 1987, Department of State Publication, August 1988.

US Central Intelligence Agency, *Report on Heroin in Pakistan: Sowing the Wind* (September 1992).

US Government, Department of State, 'Security Decision-making in Pakistan', Report Prepared for the Office of External Research, Department of State, September 1980.

World Armament and Disarmaments SIPRI,Year Book (Oxford 1974-2000).

Books

Ahmed, Akbar S., *Pakistan Society: Islam Ethnicity and Leadership in South Asia* (Oxford University Press,New Delhi, 1988).

Ahmed, Ishtiaq, *The Concept of an Islamic State in Pakistan* (Vanguard, Lahore, 1991).

Ahmed, Aziz, *Islamic Modernism in India and Pakistan 1957-1964* (Oxford University Press, London, 1967).

Allen, Douglas (ed.) *Religion and Political Conflict in South Asia* (Oxford UniversityPress, New Delhi, 1993).

Ali Tariq, *Can Pakistan Survive: The Death of a State* (Penguin, Harmondsworth, 1983).

Ali Tariq, *Pakistan: Military Rule or People's Power* (Jonathan Cape, London, 1970).

Ahmed, Kamruddin, *The Social History of East Pakistan* (Crescent Book Store, Dacca, 1967).

Amin, Tahir, *Ethno-National Movements of Pakistan* (Institute of Policy Studies, Islamabad, 1988).

Ayub Khan, Mohammed, *Friends Not Masters: A Political Biography* (Oxford University Press, London,1967).

Azar, Edward E., and Chung In Moon (eds.), *National Security in the Third World: The Management of Internal and External Threats* (Edward Elgar Publishing, Aldershot, 1988).

Bahadur, Kalim, *Democracy in Pakistan: Crises and Conflict* (Har Anand Private, New Delhi, 1998).

Bhuiyan, Abdul Wadud, *Emergence of Bangladesh and Role of Awami League* (Vikas Publishing House, New Delhi, 1982).

Banuazizi, Ali and Weiner, Myron (eds.), *The State Religion and Ethnic Politics: Pakistan Iran and Afghanistan* (Anguard Publishers, Lahore, 1987).

Basrur, R.M., *South Asia's Cold War: Nuclear Weapon* (1979).

Bose, Sugata and Jalal, Ayesha, *Modern South Asia: History, Culture and Political Economy* (Oxford University Press, New Delhi, 2004).

Bose, Sumantra, *Kashmir-Roots of Conflict and Paths to Peace* (Vistaar Publications, New Delhi, 2003).

Brecher, Michael, *The Struggle for Kashmir* (Oxford University Press, New York, 1953).

Chakravarty, S. K., *The Evolution of Politics in Bangladesh 1947-1978* (Associate Publishing House, New Delhi, 1978).

Chaudhri, Muhammad Ali, *The Emergence of Pakistan* (Columbia University Press, New York, 1967).

Chari, P.R., Cheema, P.I., and Cohen, S.P., *Perception, Politics and Security in South Asia: The Compound Crisis of 1990* (Routledge Curzon, London,1990).

Cheema, P. I., *Pakistan's Defence Policy, 1947-58* (Macmillan, London, 1990).

Chisti, General Faiz Ali, *Betrayal of Another Kind: Islam, Democracy and the Army in Pakistan* (Asia Publishing House, Cincinnati, 1990).

Cohen, Stephen P., *The Pakistan Army* (Himalayan Books, New Delhi, 1984).

Davis, Kingsely, *The Population of India and Pakistan* (Princeton University Press, Princeton, 1951).

Dixit, J.N., *India-Pakistan in War and Peace* (Routledge, London, 2002).

Dixit, Aabha, *Ethno-Nationalism in Pakistan* (Institute for Defence Studies and Analysis, Delhi, 1996).

Esposito, John L. (ed.), *Islam in Asia: Religion Politics and Society* (Oxford University Press, Oxford, 1987).

Feldman, Herbert, *Revolution in Pakistan* (Oxford University Press, 1967).

Gardezi, Hassan and Rashid Jamil (eds.), *Pakistan: The Roots of Dictatorship: The Political Economy of a Praetorian State* (Oxford University Press, Delhi, 1984).

Gupta, R.C., *US Policy Towards India and Pakistan* (B.R. Publications, Delhi, 1977).

Haq, Iqramul, *Pakistan: From Hash to Heroin* (Anoor Publisher, Lahore,1991).

Harrison, Selig S., *In Afghanistan's Shadow: Baluch Nationalism and Soviet Temptation* (Washington,1981).

Jackon, Robert, *South Asian Crisis: India, Pakistan and Bangladesh* (Chatto and Windus, London, 1975).

Jahan, Rounaq, *Pakistan: Failure in National Integration* (Columbia University Press, New York, 1972).

Jalal, Ayesha, *Democracy and Authoritarianism in South Asia: A Comparative and Political Perspective* (Cambridge University Press, Cambridge,1995).

-------------, *The State of Martial Law: The Origins of Pakistan's Political Economy of Defence* (Cambridge University Press, Cambridge, 1990).

Kodikara, Shelton U.(ed.), *External Compulsions of South Asian Politics* (Sage Publications, New Delhi, 1993).

Kukreja,Veena,*Contemporary Pakistan-Political Process, Conflict and Crises* (Sage Publications, New Delhi, 2003).

------------- *Civil-Military Relations in South Asia: Pakistan, Bangladesh and India* (Sage Publications, New Delhi, 1991).

------------- *Military Intervention in Politics: A Case Study of Pakistan* (NBO, New Delhi, 1985).

Kumar,Satish,*The New Pakistan* (Vikas Publishing House, New Delhi, 1978).

Malik, Iftikhar H., *State and Civil Society in Pakistan: Politics of Authority, Ideology and Ethnicity* (St. Martin's Press Inc., New York, 1997).

Michael Krepon and Chris Gagneeds., *The Stability-Instability Paradox: Nuclear Weapons and Brinkmanship in South Asia* (Washington, 2001).

Mishra,Pramod K., *South Asia in International Politics* (Udh Publishers, Delhi, 1984).

Moore,R.J.,*Tradition and Politics in South Asia* (Vikas Publishing House, New Delhi, 1979).

Naik, J.A., *Pak Bomb and Rajiv's India* (National Publishing House, New Delhi, 1986).

Nayak,Pandav(ed.), *Pakistan: Society and Politics* (South Asia Publishers, New Delhi, 1984).

Nehru, Jawaharlal, *Glimpses of World History* (L. Drummond, New York, 1949).

Pye, Lucian W., *Asian Power and Politics: The Cultural Dimensions of Authority* (Harvard University, Cambridge, 1985).

Roy, Asim, *Islam in South Asia: Regional Perspectives* (South Asia Publishers, New Delhi, 1996).

Roy, J.K., *Security in the MissileAge* (Allied Publishers, Delhi,1967).

Singh, Jasjit(ed.), *Kargil 1999: Pakistan's Fourth War for Kashmir* (Knowledge World, New Delhi, 1999).

Singh, Mahavir(ed.), *International Terrorism and Religious Extremism-Challenges to Central and South Asia* (Anamica Publishers,New Delhi, 2004).

Singh, Rajkumar *Indo-Pak Nuclear Tension 1974-1998* (Samiksha Prakashan, New Delhi, 2001).

------------- *Past,Present and Future of Kashmir*(Gyan Publishing House, New Delhi, 2008).

------------- *India and Pakistan-Social, Political and Military Perspectives* (Regal Publications, New Delhi, 2009).

------------- *Relations of NDA and UPA with Neighbours* (Gyan Publishing House, New Delhi, 2010).

------------- , *Contemporary India with Controversial Neighbours* (Gyan Publishing House, New Delhi, 2011).

------------- , *Myth and Reality of Terrorism in South Asia* (Kalpaz Publications, New Delhi, 2013).

Syed, Anwar Hussain, *Pakistan: Islam, Politics and National Solidarity* (Praeger, New York, 1982).

Smith,Chris,*The Diffusion of Small Arms and Light Weapons in Pakistan and Northern India*(Brossey's, London,1993).

Spear,Percival, *India, Pakistan and the West* (Oxford University Press, London,1958).

Tahir-Kheli, Shirin,*The United States and Pakistan: The Evolution of an Influence Relationship* (Praeger Studies, New York, 1982).

Taseer, Salman, *Bhutto: A Political Biography* (Vikas Publishing House,New Delhi, 1980).

Tellis, A.J., Fair C.C.and Medby, J.J., *Limited Conflicts Under the Nuclear Umbrella: Indian and Pakistani Lessons from the Kargil Crisis* (Santa Monica, C.A.RAND, 2001).

Varma, S. P. and Narain, V. (eds.), *Pakistan Political System in Crisis: Emergence of Bangladesh* (University of Rajasthan, Jaipur, 1972).

Waseem, Mohammad, *Politics and State in Pakistan* (National Institute of Historical and Cultural Research, Islamabad, 1994).

Weiner ,Myron, *Political Change in South Asia* (Firma K.L.M. Calcutta,1968).

White, Lawrence J., *Industrial Concentration and Economic Power in Pakistan* (Princeton University Press, Princeton, 1974).

Zaidi, Akbar S.(ed.), *Regional Tribalance and Regional Questions in Pakistan*(Vanguard Books, Lahore,1992).

Zingel, Wolfgang Peter and Zingel, Stephinie Lallemant (eds.), *Pakistan in the 1980s: Ideology Regionalism, Economy, Foreign Policy* (Vanguard Books, Lahore, 1985).

Articles in Books, Periodicals and Newspapers

Adhikary, Prakash Chandra and Pranab Karamakar,'State of Afghan Economy during Taliban Period and the Aftermath,' *South Asia Politics*, Vol. 9, No. 1, May 2010 (New Delhi, 2010).

Ahmad, Emajuddin, 'Current Trends in Islam in Bangladesh,' *Economic and Political Weekly*, Vol. 18, No. 25, 18 June 1983).

Ahmar, Moonis, 'Ethnicity and State Power in Pakistan: The Karachi Crisis,' *Asian Survey*, Vol. 36, No. 10, (October 1996).

Ahmed, Eqbal, 'Islam and Politics,' in Mohammad Asghar Khan (ed.), *Islam, Politics and the State* (Zed Press, London, 1985).

Ahmed, Feroz, 'Ethnicity and Politics: The Rise of Muhajir Separatism,' *South Asia Bulletin*, Vol. 8 (1988).

Ahmed, Samina, 'The United States and Terrorism in South Asia: The Lesson of History,' *International Security* (2002).

Alam, Dr. Aftab, 'Pakistan's Nuclear Development and Capability', *Third Concept,* April-May1998 (New Delhi), pp.16-17.

Anand, Som,'Islamism and Pakistan's Social Realities,' *Man and Development,* Vol. 2, No. 1 (March 1980).

Ayoob, Mohammed, 'Two Faces of Islam,' *Asian Survey,* Vol. 19, No. 6, June 1979.

Bahadur, Kalim, 'Ethnic Problems in Pakistan,' *World Focus,* Vol. 15, Nos. 4-5, (April-May 1994).

Bhadrakumar, M.K., 'Taliban's Return and India's Concerns,' *The Hindu,* 28 June 2011.

Baudrillard, Jean, 'The Spirit of Terrorism,' 2 November, 2001.

Beg, General Mirza Aslam, 'Pakistan's Nuclear Programme: A National Security Perspective,' (London, 1996).

Beri, H. N., 'Pakistan and CENTO,' *Strategic Analysis,* (New Delhi), Vol. 1, No. 3, January, 1977.

Bidwai, Praful, 'Nuclear Policy in a Mess-NWFZ The Realistic Way Out; *The Times of India,* 28th November 1991.

------------- , 'Lahore Verdict Opens New Phase in Pakistan,' *The Times of India,* 14 January, 1999.

Bindra, S.S.,'Chinese Strategy in South Asia', *The Indian Journal of Political Science,*Vol.LXX,No.4,October- December 2009 (Meerut,2009), p.1171.

Chakravarty, Sukh Ranjan, 'The Pakistan National Movement,' *Foreign Affairs Report,* Vol. 25, No. 1, (1976).

Cheema, Iqbal Pervez, 'Impact of the Afghan War on Pakistan,' *Pakistan Horizon,* Vol. 31, (1988).

Cheema,Iqbal Pervaiz,'Security in South Asia: An Approach', in Shelton U.Kodikara (ed.), *External Compulsions of South Asian Politics* (Sage Publications, New Delhi, 1993), pp.46-47.

Cheema, Iqbal Zafar, 'The Role of Nuclear Weapons in Pakistan's Defence Strategy', *Islamabad Policy Research Institute Journal* (Islamabad), Summer, 2004.

Chellaney, Brahma, 'Jehad on Jehadi,' *The Hindustan Times*, 20 September 2001.

------------- , 'Fighting Terrorism in South Asia: The Lessons of History', *International Security* (2002).

Chopra, Surendra, 'Islamic Fundamentalism and Pakistan's Foreign Policy', *India Quarterly*, Vol. 49, No. 1-2, (January-June 1993).

Cohen, Stephen Philip 'Indo-Pak Track II Diplomacy: Building Peace or Wasting Time?' in P.R. Kumaraswamy, *Security Beyond Survival*(Sage Publications, New Delhi, 2004), pp.199-200.

Dar, A. N., 'Need for Cautious Approach in Kashmir', *The Hindustan Times*, 27 August, 1997.

Das, P. L., 'Afghanistan: The Epicentre of Terror', in Mahavir Singh (ed), *International Terrorism and Religious Extremism-Challenges to Central and South Asia*, (Anamica Publishers, New Delhi, 2004).

Dieter, Bram, 'Changes in South Asia Intra-regional and External Relationship', *The World Today*, Vol. 34 (London, October 1978).

Dixit, J. N., 'In the General's Own Words', *The Hindustan Times*, 2 February, 2000.

Diwan, Vivek M., 'Perspectives on India-China Relations', *Third Concept*, Vol.24, No.288, February 2011(New Delhi), p.9.

Doval, Ajit, *'Islamic Terrorism in South Asia and India's Strategic Response'* (Oxford University Press, New Delhi, 2007).

------------- , Outsourcing Terror', *The Times of India*, 18 July, 2011.

Dworkin, Anthony, 'Beyond the War on Terror: Towards a New Transatlantic Framework for Counterterrorism, 13, *European Countries on Foreign Relations* 1 (2009).

Girardet, Edward, 'Corrupt Officials Reap Spoils of Afghan War,' *The Christian Science Monitor*, 7 September, 1988.

Engineer, Asghar Ali, 'Pakistan's Policy and its Viability', *The Hindu*, 14 October 2000.

Hersh, Seymour, 'Watching the Warheads: The Risks to Pakistan's Nuclear Arsenal', *The NewYorker*, 5th November 2001.

Hoodboy, Pervez, 'Pakistan and the Deep Cut Regime', in Harold A. Feiveson(ed.), *The Nuclear Turning Point: A Blueprint for Deep Cuts and Declarating of Nuclear Weapons* (Brookings Institution, Washington,1999)p.227.

Huria, Sonali, 'War on Terrorism in South Asia-Af-Pak and Beyond', *Institute of Peace and Conflict Studies*, No. 108 (New Delhi, 2009).

Iqbal, Anwar, 'Is the Tide Turning Against the MQM?', *The Muslim* (Islamabad), 17 May, 1989.

Iqbal, Javed, 'Islamization in Pakistan', *Journal of South Asian and Middle Eastern Studies*, Vol. 8, No. 5 (Spring, 1985).

Jain,Girilal, 'US Arms for Pakistan', *The Times of India*, 6th January1980.

Janik, Anton I, Jr., 'Prosecuting Al-Qaeda: America's Foreign Policy Interests Are Best Served by Trying Terrorists Under International Tribunals', *Denver Journal of International Law and Policy*, September 2002.

Jha, Prem Shankar, 'Where Next with Pakistan,' *The Hindustan Times*, 12 February, 2000.

Kalkat, A.S., 'Ensuring Security in the Age of Global Terror,' *The Hindu*, 13 September, 2006.

Kamal, A. Nazir, 'Karakoram Highway- A Nation Building Effort,' *Strategic Studies*, Vol. 11, No. 3 (Islamabad, 1979).

Kanwal, Gurmeet, China's War Concepts', *Air Power Journal*, Vol.3, No.3, July-September 2006, pp.68-69.

Khan, Firoz Hassan, 'Challenges to Nuclear Stability in South Asia', *The Non-Proliferation Review,* Spring 2003, p.60.

Kumar, Dilip, 'Resurgence of the Taliban-Lessons Learned,' *South Asia Politics,* Vol. 6, No. 1 (New Delhi, 2007).

Kumar, Satish, 'Militant Islam: The Nemesis of Pakistan,' *Strategic Digest,* Vol. 30, No. 8 (August, 2000).

Kumar, Sumit, 'Pakistan's Jehadi Apparatus: Goals and Methods,' *Strategic Analysis,'* Vol. 29, No. 12 (March, 2001).

Kurup, V.S.P., 'America's Double Standards: Politics of Nuclear Fuel' *The Times of India,* 25th April, 1978.

Lancaster, John and Kamran Khan, Musharraf Named in Nuclear Probe', *Washington Post,* 3rd February 2004.

Laport, Jr. Robert, 'Pakistan in 1995: The Continuing Crisis,' *Asian Survey,* Vol. 36, No. 2 (February, 1996).

Leventhal, Paul and Brahma Chellaney, 'Nuclear Terrorism: Threat, Perception and Response in South Asia', *Institute for Defence Studies and Analyses,* 10th October 1988 (New Delhi), pp.1-2.

Malkani, K. R., 'Inside the Muslim Mind,' *The Hindustan Times,* 13 October, 2001.

Masood, Salman and David Rohde, 'Musharraf's Disclosures a Factor in North Korea Talks', *International Herald Tribune,* 26th August 2005.

Masud, Anwarul Kazi, 'Terrorism in South Asia and US Foreign Policy,' Paper No. 3292, 5 July, 2009, *South Asia Analysis Group* (New Delhi, 2009).

Mazari, Shireen M., 'The Militarization of Pakistan's Civil Society,' in Kumar Rupesinghe and Khawar Mumtaz (eds.), *Internal Conflicts in South Asia* (Sage Publications, New Delhi, 1996).

Mir, Amir,'Where Terror and the Bomb Could Meet', *AsiaTimes,* 7th July 2005.

Mohan, Raja C., 'Musharraf to Press China for Second Reactors', *The Indian Express,*12th June 2006.

Mukherjee, Uddipan, 'Jinnah's Tottering Pakistan,' *South Asia Politics*, Vol. 8, No. 10, February (New Delhi, 2010).

Narain, Virendra, 'Bangladesh and Changing International Context: An Analysis of Perceptions,' in S.P. Verma and Virendra Narain (eds.), *Pakistan Political System in Crisis: Emergence of Bangladesh* (South Asia Publishers, New Delhi).

Nelson,Dean, 'Pakistan Upgrades Nuclear Arsenal', *The Sunday Times*, 30th July 2006.

Padgaonkar, Dileep, 'Pak Crisis and India's Choices,' *The Times of India*, 19 August, 1990.

Pathak, Sukumar, 'Obstacles to Afghan War on Terror-Pak's Hesitancy and Karzai's Apostasy,' *South Asia Politics*, Vol. 9, No. 10, February 2011 (New Delhi, 2011).

Pattanaike, Smruti S., Islam and the Ideology of Pakistan,' *Strategic Analysis*, Vol. 22, No. 9 (December, 1998).

Quinlan, Michael, 'How Robust is India-Pakistan Deterrence?', *Survival*, Winter 2000-01,p.148.

Qureshi, S. M.M., 'Pakhtunistan: The Frontier Dispute Between Afghanistan and Pakistan,' *Pacific Affairs*, Vol. 39, No. 1-2, (Spring-Summer, 1996).

Radyuhin, 'Russia's Tempered Response to Abbottabad,' *The Hindu*, 13 May, 2011.

Rahman, M. Anisur. 'East Pakistan: The Roots of Estrangement,' *South Asian Review*, vol. 3, No. 3 (April, 1970).

Ramesh, Randeep and Julian Borger, 'Pakistan Launches Huge Nuclear Arms Drive', *The Guardian*, 25th July 2006.

Rashid, Abbas, 'Pakistan: The Ideological Dimensions in Mohammad Asghar Khan (ed.), *Islam, Politics and The State: The Pakistan Experience* (Zed Press, London, 1985).

Rashid, Ahmed, 'Taliban, Islam, Oil and the New Great Game in Central Asia (London, 2000).

------------- , 'The Taliban Exporting Extremism,' *Foreign Affairs*, Vol. 58, No. 6 (November-December, 1999).

Rauf, Tariq, Learning to Live with Bomb in South Asia: Accommodation not Confrontation', *Centre for Non-Proliferation Studies,* 30th December 1998.

Rex, Hudson A., 'The Sociology and Psychology of Terrorism: Who Becomes a Terrorist and Why?' *Federal Research Division, Library of Congress,* September, 1999.

Rimington, Stella, 'Terrorism Did Not Begin on 9/11,' *The Hindustan Times,* 8 September, 2002.

Roy, Oliver, 'Why the War is Going on in Afghanistan: The Afghan Crisis in Perspectives,' *Journal of International Affairs,* Vol. 5, No. 4, December 2000-February 2001.

Saighal, Vinod, 'USA-PAK Potentially More Menacing Than AF-PAK,' *South Asia Politics,* Vol. 9, No. 1, May 2010 (New Delhi, 2010).

Sanghvi, Vir, 'US Since 9/11-Lessons and Conundrums,' *The Hindustan Times,* 15 September, 2002.

Salik, Ahmad Naeem, 'Pakistan and the Future of Non-Proliferation', *International Peace Research Institute Journal,* Vol.VI, No.1, Winter 2006, pp.21-45.

Saran, Shyam, 'Weapon That has More Than Symbolic Value', *The Hindu*, 4th May 2013.

Sengupta, Bhabani, 'A Deeply Divided Nation,' in Pran Chopra (ed.), *Contemporary Pakistan-New Aims and Images* (Vikas Publishing House, New Delhi, 1979).

------------- , 'Global Change Cripples Pakistan,' *The National Herald*, 22 February, 1990.

Shane, Scott, 'CIA to Expand Use of Drones in Pakistan,' *The New York Times*, 4 December, 2009.

Sharma, Madan Lal, 'World After 9/11 *Third Concept,* September 2007 (New Delhi, 2007).

Shu, Yang, 'Afghanistan-Buffer State and Centre for Terrorism,' in Mahavir Singh (ed.), *International Terrorism and Religious*

Extremism-Challenges to Central and South Asia (Anamika Publishers, New Delhi, 2004).

Singh,Dr. Rajkumar,'Nuclear Deterrence: More Real Than Myth', *Third Concept*, Vol.19, No. 217, March 2005 (New Delhi), p.17.

Steele, Jonathan, 'The Taliban's Wish List, '*The Hindu*, 22 January 2011.

Swami, Praveen, 'Osama's Death a Gift to Resurgent Al-Qaeda,' *The Hindu*, 3 May 2011.

Subramanian, Nirupama, 'Pakistan and China: Great Expectations', *The Hindu*, 23 November, 2006.

Thomas, K.T., 'The Economic Roots of US Intervention in Afghanistan,' *Proceedings of the Indian History Congress*, 68th Session, Delhi, 2007 (Delhi, 2007).

Thornton, Thomas P., 'Between the Stools, US Policy Towards Pakistan during Carter Administration', *Asian Survey*, Vol.22, No.10, October 1982 (New Delhi), p. 969.

Verma, A. K., 'Radical Islam and Terror,' *South Asia Politics*, Vol. 7, No. 8, December, 2008 (New Delhi, 2008).

Verma, Jagdish Prasad, 'If You Wish for Peace, Understand Terrorism,' *South Asia Politics*, Vol. 9, No. 7, November 2010 (New Delhi, 2010).

Victor, Cecil, 'Busting Terrorist Bases no Solution,' *The Patriot*, 18 May, 1990.

Warwick, Joby, 'Pakistan Expanding Nuclear Programme', *The Washington Post*, 24 July 2006.

Waxman, Mathew C., 'The Structure of Terrorism Threats the Laws of War,' *Duke Journal of Comparative and International Law*, Vol. 20, May 2010.

Wriggins, Howard W., 'Pakistan's Search for a Foreign Policy After the Invasion of Afghanistan,' *Pacific Affairs*, Vol. 57, No. 2 (The University of British Columbia, 1984).

Zaidi, Mubashir, 'Jehadi in Retreat,' *The Hindustan Times*, 20 January, 2002.

Zaman, Uz Rashid, 'WMD Terrorism in South Asia: Trends and Implications' (University of Bangladesh, Dhaka).

Newspapers

Asia Times

The Asian Age

The Dawn (Karachi)

The Financial Times (London)

The Guardian

The Hindu (Madras)

The Hindustan Times (New Delhi)

The Indian Express(Delhi)

The International Herald Tribune

The Khaleej Times

The Kyodo News International

National Herald (New Delhi)

The Nation (Islamabad)

The New York Times(NewYork)

The NewYorker

The New Republic

The Open Source Center

The Opinion (Weekly)

The Pakistan Times(Lahore)

The Patriot (NewDelhi)

The Statesman (Delhi)

The Sunday Standard(NewDelhi)

The Sunday Times

The Times (London)

The Times of India (New Delhi)

The Tribune (Chandigarh)

The USA Today

The Washington Post (Washington)

Periodicals

American Political Science Review(NewYork)

Asian Affairs

Asian Survey (NewDelhi)

Eastern Economists(Bombay)

Economic and Political Weekly (Bombay)

Forbes Magazine

Foreign Affairs (NewYork)

Foreign Policy Report (NewDelhi)

Frontline (Chennai)

India Quarterly (New Delhi)

International Security

International Peace Research Institute Journal

India Today (New Delhi)

International Studies (New Delhi)

Pacific Affairs (NewYork)

Political Science Quarterly (NewYork)

Strategic Analysis

Strategic Insights (California)

South Asia Politics (New Delhi)

Third Concept (New Delhi)

Washington Quarterly (Washington)

World Today (London).

Index